MUSIC IN AMERICAN LIFE

A list of books in the series appears
at the end of this book.

Dixie Dewdrop

THE
UNCLE
DAVE MACON
STORY

MICHAEL D. DOUBLER

UNIVERSITY OF
ILLINOIS PRESS
Urbana, Chicago, and Springfield

Publication of this book is supported by the Dragan
Plamenac Endowment of the American Musicological
Society, funded in part by the National Endowment for the
Humanities and the Andrew W. Mellon Foundation; and
by the Judith McCulloh Endowment for American Music.

Library of Congress Cataloging-in-Publication Data
Names: Doubler, Michael D. (Michael Dale), 1955– author.
Title: Dixie Dewdrop: the Uncle Dave Macon story /
    Michael D. Doubler.
Description: Urbana: University of Illinois Press, [2018] |
    Series: Music in American life | Includes bibliographical
    references and index.
Identifiers: LCCN 2017060727 | ISBN 9780252083655
    (pbk. : alk. paper)
Subjects: LCSH: Macon, Uncle Dave, 1870–1952. | Country
    musicians—United States—Biography. | Banjoists—
    United States—Biography.
Classification: LCC ML420.M13858 D68 2018 |
    DDC 787.8/81642092 [B] —dc23
LC record available at https://lccn.loc.gov/2017060727

Ebook ISBN 978-0-252-05069-5

To my Mother,
Mary Victoria Macon Doubler
The guardian angel of our family and
the granddaughter of Uncle Dave Macon

We hope that the WSM Grand Ole Opry will last at least one hundred years. Regardless of how long a life it may have, the name of Uncle Dave Macon should always be remembered with gratitude by all the members of the cast and by the managers and officials of WSM. . . . Our hats are off to this grand Tennessee farmer who has done and is doing good wherever he goes with his three banjos, his plug hat, gates-ajar collar, gold teeth and his great big, Tennessee smile!

—GEORGE D. HAY, "The Solemn Old Judge" of the
   Grand Ole Opry

Contents

Illustrations follow page 62

Preface

"IT WOULD TAKE A GOOD SIZED BOOK to tell the story of Dave Macon." So states the promotional publication, *Song Favorites of WSM and the Grand Ole Opry* from 1942. It turns out they were right. In the nearly seventy years since his death in 1952, no major biography of Uncle Dave Macon has ever appeared, despite the fact that the popularity of the "Dixie Dewdrop" and his music remain strong. In many circles, especially among old-time and country musicians and dedicated fans in Tennessee and elsewhere, Uncle Dave Macon has emerged as a bigger-than-life figure, the stuff of folklore and legend. Truth be told, there is so much to support those claims.

Uncle Dave Macon was the first major superstar of the Grand Ole Opry and thus stands at the very headwaters of the country music industry. After performing locally in Tennessee for two decades, he first recorded in New York City in the summer of 1924, more than a year before WSM went on the air and more than three years before Jimmie Rodgers and the original Carter Family were discovered. He was the very top performer among the roster of twenty-five musicians who comprised the original Grand Ole Opry cast in 1926, and he maintained a strong presence on the Opry for twenty-six years. His unique appearance and sound, combined with a quick wit, love for laughter, and unabashed willingness to opine on nearly any subject, endeared him to millions and still attracts legions of fans.

Today's top country music stars can trace their music and performance heritages directly back to Uncle Dave. He was the first entertainer to achieve an important trifecta: member of the Grand Ole Opry, popular recording artist, and successful on tour. He was not only talented but energetic and prolific; in fourteen commercial recording sessions, the Dixie Dewdrop cut over two hundred songs. The topics were nearly infinite, as he sang of love, life, romance, politics, religion, money, food, cars, animals, and a host of other topics of interest to the common working man and his family. Those seeking solace during the severities of the Great Depression and World War II found refuge in his music. A member of the Country Music Hall of Fame, the most telling tribute to Uncle Dave's life and career is that nearly a century after cutting his first records, his music still inspires and entertains so many worldwide while enjoying respectable sales.

The present work seeks to achieve a number of objectives. Foremost, it aims to fill a huge gap in the historiography of country music by presenting the very first cradle-to-grave account of Uncle Dave Macon's life. The writings on him are generally short and scattered, and *Dixie Dewdrop* attempts to pull all of this together into a larger, comprehensive whole, all enlarged and buttressed by new and previously unexploited, primary source materials. By necessity, it too serves as a needed corrective to the plethora of factual and conflicting errors in print regarding Uncle Dave's life, especially during his early years and at the start of his career. He had a powerful influence on others wherever he went, and for the first time, the great, hidden forces on Dave Macon's personal life and career are exposed, including a musically inspired mother, a loving and patient wife, seven sons, an enthusiastic and supportive sister, other local musicians and Grand Ole Opry stars, and the powerful message of the Christian Gospel. All the while, it seeks to place Uncle Dave's long career within the context of the evolving broadcast and recording industries.

The Dixie Dewdrop had a long, active life, and readers should prepare themselves for a journey that takes them far and wide. It begins in the pinelands of North Carolina and then moves to the hills of Tennessee and the streets of downtown Nashville. You will visit one-room schoolhouses, country stores, and small churches where Uncle Dave sang, played, joked, and philosophized before heading to recording studios in New York City, Chicago, New Orleans, and elsewhere. All about you will appear the sights, sounds, and personalities of the entertainment, broadcast, and recording industries, especially at WSM and on the Grand Ole Opry. Much time will be spent in the South, where you will encounter the graces and peculiarities of its people and their way of life. Brace yourself for the deep pain of sudden, personal loss and the shocks of the Great Depression and World War II. Get ready to bump along in wagons drawn by mules, jostle along in Model T automobiles, rumble down railroads in coach cars, and even go flying. The longest legs of the trip will carry you from Tennessee to California and back by train and car. The last journey will take you to Uncle Dave Macon's final resting place. Most of all, prepare to laugh a lot and even cry a little.

Much more than a geographic trek, the journey of Uncle Dave Macon's life is an exploration of the common human condition, with all of its forces and foibles, triumphs and tragedies. *Dixie Dewdrop* seeks to go beyond the recounting of a human chronology by exploring the actions, ideas, and emotions that reveal the strength and resilience of Dave Macon's character. It wasn't all fun and hype. The glitz and glamor of performing, broadcasting, recording, and moviemaking were all mixed together with the drudgeries of travel and deal making and the darkness of mental disease and alcoholism. Some might view the inconsistencies between Dave Macon's drinking and revelries and the profession of his religious beliefs as the height of hypocrisy, but in reality, he was trying to apply the latter to overcome the former, and he did so with demonstrated success. In so many ways, Dave Macon's life is a very human story, reflecting the basic needs of most people; the craving for love and attention, the motivation to develop special talents, resilience in the face of adversity, struggles against tragedy and loss, and a desire to draw closer to God.

A work of such length, depth, and complexity by necessity requires the efforts of more than one single person. One of the most gratifying aspects of the project was that no matter who was approached—whether individuals or institutions—I was greeted with great enthusiasm and interest in the Dixie Dewdrop's life and career. As a great-grandson of Uncle Dave Macon, those genuine reactions were not only personally gratifying, but informed me over and over of the great appeal and interest that still exists for Uncle Dave's reputation and music. On so many occasions, people told me how much they enjoyed my great-grandfather's music, even while freely admitting that they knew little or nothing about his actual life. Those remarks motivated me even more to complete this biography.

At the very top of the list of thanks stands Mary Dean Wolfe, the widow of the late Dr. Charles K. Wolfe, a prolific collector, researcher, author, teacher, and music historian. Her unqualified support for the project greatly eased my mind and imparted the confidence to move forward. This biography would not have been possible without the full use of Dr. Wolfe's previous research on Uncle Dave, especially numerous audio tapes, which contain rich and detailed interviews from the 1970s with members of the Macon family and those musicians who performed with the Dixie Dewdrop, most notably Sid Harkreader, Sam and Kirk McGee, and Roy Acuff. In a very real sense, I stood on Charles Wolfe's broad shoulders, and from that vantage point, aided by new sources of information, was able to see and hear much more of Uncle Dave's life and music than anyone previously.

A most sincere thanks goes to the staff of the Center for Popular Music at Middle Tennessee State University in Murfreesboro, Tennessee. Their knowledge, expertise, and welcoming spirit is second to none, as is their fantastic research facility. Any serious student or researcher of country music can no longer afford to miss this growing treasure trove of archival and audio wealth dedicated to American popular music. The expansive Charles K. Wolfe Collection is among the center's richest holdings. I want to thank Dr. Dale Cockrell, the first Center for Popular Music director I encountered, as well as his wife, Lucinda Cockrell, who was the head archivist and coordinator at the time. The current director and head archivist and coordinator, Dr. Gregory N. Reish and Rachel Morris, respectively, were especially generous with their time. If Dale and Lucinda helped me to get started, Greg and Rachel helped me to cross the finish line. My deeply felt thanks extends to the entire staff: Yvonne Elliott, Martin Fisher, John Fabke, Lindsay Million, and Olivia Beaudry.

Very special recognition must go to the extended Macon-Doubler family. My mother, Mary Macon Doubler, deserves special accolades for sharing her clear, insightful recollections of her grandfather, reading the draft manuscript, sitting for interviews, and answering so many questions. The day we spent touring the historic Uncle Dave sites in Readyville and Kittrell will never be forgotten. The same goes for my uncle, David Ramsey Macon, who provided his recollections of the Dixie Dewdrop as well as documenting his role in the start of one of the South's most popular summer music festivals, Uncle Dave Macon Days. Ramsey's wife, Edna Shewcraft Macon, did yeoman's service in preserving family genealogy and important artifacts. A lengthy, incredible interview with Vesta Blair Kinney convinced me more than anything else that Uncle Dave's story had to be told, as did conversations with Bill Knowlton, family friend and living legend in the radio and bluegrass world. My brothers and sister—Bernard, Paul, John, and Katie—all read the manuscript and made comments while providing constant love and support, even as I bombarded them with tales of Uncle Dave and other "Maconisms." A special salute goes to brother John, a recognized musician in his own right, for keeping me straight on the technical aspects of old time music and the banjo, because as Uncle Dave himself famously declared, "when it comes to the scientifical parts of music, I know nothing about it." My cousin, Dave Macon III, also read the manuscript and provided feedback. A special thanks goes to my Richardson cousins, John and Rosetta Donnell, for welcoming me into their home, sharing key family history and making it possible for me to see and hold one of Uncle Dave's original banjos.

A number of fellow music historians and archivists assisted in various capacities. Brenda Colladay, a true expert on the history of country music and the Grand Ole Opry, gave generously of her time and expertise, providing photos, articles, access to artifacts in the Roy Acuff Collection, and an insider's tour of Ryman Auditorium. John Rumble, the senior historian at the Country Music Hall of Fame and Museum, was so helpful in answering questions and providing materials. Jim Costa, an independent folklorist and musician, aided me in better understanding Uncle Dave's early playing and singing. The staff at the Rutherford County Archives in Murfreesboro, Tennessee, members of Haynes Chapel Methodist Church, and administrators at cemeteries in Nashville and Murfreesboro assisted in locating information on Uncle Dave that had been hidden for more than a century. A number of historians were so generous with their knowledge, interest, and support: Stephen Wade, Tony Russell, James Akenson, Don Cusic, and Ted Olson.

A number of personalities in entertainment lent their assistance. Popular old-time musician Leroy Troy gave freely of his time and knowledge, providing me an extensive tour of his awesome, personal music archive and a close-up banjo twirling demonstration. Ricky Skaggs sat with me for two hours talking about Uncle Dave, further firing my own lines of inquiry regarding my great-grandfather. The great Mac Wiseman was so kind and gracious as he shared his personal recollections of touring with Uncle Dave in the late 1940s. Eddie Stubbs and Bill Cody of WSM shared their interest and enthusiasm while keeping their listeners informed as to the progress of my work. A special thanks goes to the director of the University of Illinois Press, Laurie Matheson, who from the start, understood the importance and great need for this biography and was such a delight with whom to work.

More than anything else, I want to express publicly my thanks to Almighty God for supplying the graces and talents necessary to complete this project, especially the great blessing of November 6–7, 2014. My final aspiration is that Uncle Dave himself would approve and delight in this biography. On the day we finally meet, I'm sure Uncle Dave will be proud to show me "How Beautiful Heaven Must Be."

Dixie Dewdrop

"Rock of Ages"

ARCHIE MACON STEPPED OUT onto the back porch of his family's large farmhouse, drawing the kitchen door closed behind him. With an empty milk pail dangling from his left hand, he ambled down the porch steps and across the backyard in the early morning light, making his way toward the barn where a milk cow awaited. Archie pulled his fedora work hat down low across his face and gathered his jacket around him against the morning chill. The prospect of once again returning to a familiar routine of daily farm chores and hammering at his blacksmith's anvil brought a welcome sense of relief, because Archie Macon was a man who needed a break.

For the last sixteen days, Archie had endured a grinding and stressful death watch at Rutherford Hospital in Murfreesboro, Tennessee. His father, Uncle Dave Macon, was dying. Uncle Dave had been hospitalized on Sunday morning, March 3, 1952, with symptoms of fatigue, nausea, and a possible obstruction in his throat. The night before, Uncle Dave had made his last appearance on the Grand Ole Opry, and at the end of the performance, the country music superstar had been too exhausted to arise from the chair in which he always sat and played. Assisted by other musicians and stage hands at Ryman Auditorium, Uncle Dave's son Dorris had somehow managed to lift his father, chair and all, and carry the old man backstage. Dorris and his father had then made the forty-mile drive back to the Macon homestead in Kittrell, Tennessee. When Uncle Dave was no better the next morning, Archie had driven to Kittrell, and the decision was made to take Uncle Dave to the hospital.

A battery of medical tests and examinations revealed an obstruction in the upper abdominal cavity, and exploratory surgery was performed a few days later. Midway through the lengthy procedure, the surgeon had emerged from the operating room with dire news for the assembled family. Archie was the eldest of Uncle Dave's seven sons and the family's senior representative that day. The surgeon informed him that a large, advanced tumor had developed near the stomach and attached itself to surrounding tissue. The viable alternatives were limited: either remove the tumor with radical surgery, which Uncle Dave might not survive, or sew him back up and let nature take its course. A realist, Archie had been prepared for the grim diagnosis. He told the surgeon to close his father's surgical wound and to let God's will be done.

Since the operation, members of Uncle Dave's family had been beside him constantly, seeing to the patriarch's needs and ensuring that he was comfortable. On the Opry, Roy Acuff encouraged WSM's listeners to send their get well wishes to Uncle Dave, and cards and letters from across the entire nation flooded the hospital's mail room at the rate of 200 per day, all wishing him a speedy recovery. Still, the grind of acting as the primary caregiver, while consulting with doctors, nurses, and staff, and making necessary decisions, had taken a toll on Archie. Dorris had agreed to take over his older brother's duties for a few days so Archie could get some rest.

Reaching his somewhat dilapidated log barn, Archie made his way into a side stall where his milk cow stood waiting. He placed the milk pail in the proper position, turned on a small radio which stood on a nearby shelf, and sat down on a low stool. The radio had two knobs, one for power and volume and the other for tuning. In reality, it needed only one knob because it was always tuned to the same station: WSM at clear channel 6:50 a.m. Whenever he worked in the barn, Archie always listened to the "Air Castle of the South."

As he milked and listened to WSM's programming that morning, Archie's mind probably dwelled on his father. For the last thirty years, Uncle Dave Macon had been one of America's most recognized and popular music performers. A unique aspect of his career is that he did not become a professional entertainer until age fifty. The delayed debut gave him distinct advantages in his abilities to play, sing, and perform at the top of his game and the maturity to manage his own business affairs. He was the first superstar of the Grand Ole Opry and had been among the very first to cut a commercial country music record. The "Dixie Dewdrop" had gone on to make over two hundred recordings and to appear at venues nationwide. In his personal appearance, musical abilities, and business acumen, Uncle Dave Macon was simply a cut above the rest. With his plug hat, gates-ajar collar, gold teeth, big Tennessee smile, and a banjo on his knee, Uncle Dave sang of the people and country that he loved. He had been vital to the development and maturation of both the country music industry and the Grand Ole Opry. Because of his popularity, longevity, and expanded musical repertoire, he had well earned the nickname, "The Grand Ole Man of the Grand Ole Opry." Though he loved his father very much, Archie had remained strangely detached from Uncle Dave's music career.

The morning news came on WSM at 8:00 a.m. A breaking news item topped that morning's announcements: Uncle Dave Macon had died in Murfreesboro at 6:25 a.m. that very morning at age eighty-one. Funeral arrangements were still pending. Even though Archie had been expecting the sad news, hearing the first word of his father's death over WSM hit him hard. He reached up, turned the radio off, and sitting on his milk stool, buried his face in his hands. Alone in the dim, dank barn stall, Archie tried to absorb the news of the tremendous loss he had just suffered while coping with the sudden, sharp sting which the finality of death imparts.

Minutes later, Archie exited the barn with his full milk pail in hand. When he reached the house, his wife Melissa met him at the back door. She told him that just moments after he had left for the barn that Dorris had called with news of Uncle Dave's death. Dorris and another older brother, Harry Macon, had been with their father when the last breath had come. Archie immediately phoned the hospital and was soon talking with Dorris. Uncle Dave's body had already been removed to the Moore Funeral Home in downtown Murfreesboro and was being prepared for the visitation and burial. Because Uncle Dave had been such a prominent public figure for so long, it was important that the final arrangements be made public as soon as possible to allow mourners, from prominent people in the entertainment industry to the common working man, to alter their schedules and attend the funeral. Archie and Dorris decided that all family members would meet at the funeral home at 1:00 p.m. to finalize the memorial plans.

Meanwhile, news of the death of the Dixie Dewdrop flashed across the nation. Ironically, the very same medium—commercial radio—which had helped to propel Uncle Dave to national stardom, now transmitted the news of his death across America. In Houston, Texas, Alton Delmore, the eldest sibling of the famous duo the Delmore Brothers, sat down before the radio in the front parlor of his home to listen to the noon news. The unexpected announcement of Uncle Dave's death floored Alton. The Grand Ole Man of the Grand Ole Opry had been a friend and mentor to the Delmore Brothers. The previous twelve months had been extremely devastating for Alton; he had endured the loss of his father and even a young daughter. The news of Uncle Dave's death was just too much; Alton Delmore broke down and began weeping uncontrollably. Another daughter, Norma, suddenly came into the room and was alarmed at seeing her father's distraught condition. Tormented by the news of Uncle Dave's death, Alton was further distressed that a lack of money and time would prevent him from attending the funeral in Tennessee. Sadly, he would experience another loss nine months later with the death of his younger brother and performing partner, Rabon. Alton Delmore would never recover from the string of sudden deaths in his life. From December 1952 until his own passing twelve years later, the prolific musical genius remained a broken, distracted man.

In faraway Yuma, Arizona, Vesta Blair Kinney was hard at work at her job in the meat department of a local grocery store when the news reached her of Uncle Dave's passing. Vesta paused a moment to recall the opportunity and acts of kindness the Macon family had extended to her at a very difficult juncture in her young life. She had last seen Uncle Dave in October 1943 during the war and held cherished memories of the seven years she had worked for the Macons. At the same time, Vesta recalled a single night of sudden shock and sadness that she had shared with Uncle Dave.

Back in Murfreesboro, the extended Macon family met at Moore Funeral Home to draw up plans for the memorial service and burial. One important decision was already settled: Uncle Dave would be buried in the historic Coleman Cemetery some five miles east of Murfreesboro alongside his beloved wife, Miss Tildy, who had died thirteen years earlier. Haynes Chapel, the small, country Methodist church where Uncle Dave had worshipped for most of his adult life, was clearly inadequate to accommodate a large funeral service and the expected throng of mourners. First Methodist Church, one of the largest Christian cathedrals in downtown Murfreesboro, was suitable and available. Archie wanted the funeral held two days hence, on a Monday afternoon, to allow more time to plan for such a sizable event. Dorris disagreed and pushed for the memorial to occur the very next day. Many members of the Grand Ole Opry would certainly want to attend, Dorris argued, and it would be much easier for them to do so on Sunday rather than on Monday, when most would have to depart Nashville for previously scheduled appearances. After a short discussion, the family decided that the funeral would occur the next afternoon, Sunday, March 23.

News of Uncle Dave's death and pending funeral initiated planning elsewhere. In Nashville, George D. Hay, the "Solemn Old Judge" of the Grand Ole Opry, stoically received the news of his dear friend's death. Nearly twenty-seven years earlier, when the Grand Ole Opry had just started on WSM, Hay had looked for an established music star to boost the program's appeal and popularity. Uncle Dave Macon had come on the scene, more than exceeding the expectations of Judge Hay and the management at WSM. Over time, Uncle Dave and Judge Hay had become recognized as the Grand Ole Opry's principal founders. Hay made the decision to alter the Opry's already established program for that evening in favor of a musical tribute to his dear, departed friend. The Solemn Old Judge quickly threw himself into a task in which he excelled: to pull the necessary strings to make Opry stars, the management at WSM, and the support staff and musicians at the Ryman Auditorium all head in the same direction at the same time.

The visitation for Uncle Dave occurred on Saturday evening at Moore Funeral Home in downtown Murfreesboro. For the most part, it was a crowded but routine affair. Having resided in Rutherford County since 1900, Uncle Dave was well known and beloved by scores of neighbors, friends, and admirers. The funeral home guest book for that night recorded nearly 500 visitors, and surely many more were present. One Grand Ole Opry great in particular attended the solemn event. Sam McGee was perhaps the most innovative and gifted acoustic guitar player of all time and had performed intermittently with Uncle Dave for nearly twenty-five years. Sam and his wife drove over to Murfreesboro from their home near Franklin, Tennessee, to pay their respects to the Macon family. The McGees came early so they could extend their condolences and still allow time to make it to downtown Nashville for the start of the live Grand Ole Opry broadcast at 8:00 p.m.

The Grand Ole Opry program that night became a singular salute to the memory of Uncle Dave Macon. Roy Acuff acted as the master of ceremonies as performers and bandleaders stepped to the microphone in turn to impart their stories and tributes regarding the Dixie Dewdrop. All throughout, only the kindest words expressed the entertainers' sentiments. Sam McGee told the audience, "No better friend did I have than Uncle Dave," and Stringbean declared that everything he knew about performing had come from Uncle Dave. The most memorable, spoken tribute came from a true Opry old-timer. "Fiddlin' Sid" Harkreader, who had started out with Dave Macon in the early 1920s, delivered a stirring testimony about his musical talents and human kindness. Uncle Dave had been a pioneering vocalist years before Jimmie Rodgers and the Carter Family had cut their first records and was especially remembered for his down-to-earth style of music and entertaining. He had been friend to all and mentor to many, and his passing created an empty spot in the hearts of musicians and music lovers nationwide.

The program's close was monumental. For the first time in many years, all the Opry's cast members and their bands were present, an estimated 200 entertainers in all. At Judge Hay's direction, all of them crowded onto the stage at the Ryman and led by Roy Acuff, the entire Opry cast sang "Rock of Ages." Fans wept openly as Ryman Auditorium swooned and swayed with the lilting strains of that most sacred composition. The meaning of the final tribute was clear. It was not only a solemn salute to Uncle Dave's personal profession of faith, but public recognition that the reputation and fame of one of the foundational stones upon which the Grand Ole Opry and the country music industry had been built would stand strong and undiminished in the ages to come.

On Sunday afternoon, March 23, Uncle Dave Macon proved that he still could pack the house, even in death. Mourners converged on Murfreesboro from all over Tennessee, especially from Nashville. By noon, downtown Murfreesboro was a veritable sea of onlookers. The Murfreesboro Police Department had tried to plan for crowd and traffic control, but try as it might, managing the tremendous onslaught of traffic and mourners proved challenging. The police estimated that a throng of over 5,000 had crowded into the city's center. Some had come to pay their last respects, others to catch a glimpse of the many Grand Ole Opry stars sure to be present, and others just to be a part of one of the largest pageants in Tennessee history. With so many mourners present, Tennesseans had perhaps not witnessed such a grand funeral since the interment of President Andrew Jackson at the Hermitage in 1845.

All the streets were jammed with parked and stalled cars as invited groups tried to make their way to First Methodist Church while other drivers just hoped to get closer to the festivities. The presiding minister for the funeral, Reverend Vernon Bradley of Haynes Chapel Methodist Church, had a particularly trying experience with traffic congestion. Reverend Bradley drove in from his home near Woodbury and was taken aback by the horrendous traffic jam in Murfreesboro. Stalled in traffic far from First Methodist Church, Bradley finally gained the attention of a busy police officer by shouting who he was and that he had to get to the church. The harried officer called back, advising him to abandon his car where it sat in the middle of the street, to leave the key in the ignition, and to make his way to the church on foot.

At 1:00 p.m., Uncle Dave's body was taken from Moore Funeral Home and transferred across the street to First Methodist Church. Once the coffin was in place at the head of the sanctuary, the church filled rapidly. A packed bus arrived from Nashville carrying the official delegation from WSM and the Grand Ole Opry. Minnie Pearl was the group's designated head. She had first met Uncle Dave in 1940, and their shared penchant for comedy and a good laugh resulted in them becoming fast friends. The entertainers and radio executives occupied reserved pews, filling a significant portion of the church.

Uncle Dave's pallbearers occupied their own pew up front. The men designated to carry Uncle Dave to his final resting place included an unparalleled pantheon of country music greats. Judge Hay was the head pallbearer. Next to him sat Ernest Tubb, Bill Monroe, Roy Acuff, and Sam and Kirk McGee of the famous Dixieliners. Claude Lampley was next, a dear, personal friend of Uncle Dave and an original member of the old-time band, the Fruit Jar Drinkers. At the end of the pew sat Nashville Police Officer Pat Mulloy who moonlighted as a security guard at Ryman Auditorium. Mulloy and the Dixie Dewdrop had struck up a long friendship, and his inclusion in the roster of pallbearers was vintage Uncle Dave. Mulloy was selected to represent the common working man, the very person who Uncle Dave had so often honored in his songs and entertained at his shows. Other honorary pallbearers included executives and staff members from WSM.

Before the service started, the extended Macon family entered and took their reserved seats at the front of the sanctuary. Archie Macon and his wife Melissa led the group, followed by his brothers and Uncle Dave's grandchildren. Anyone familiar with the Macon family probably noticed some irregularities. John Macon, the second of Uncle Dave's seven sons, and Paul Macon, the youngest of the siblings, had both plied themselves with whiskey in an attempt to cope with the day's difficulties. Another son was completely absent. Glen Macon, the middle child, was an introvert who could not bring himself to attend his own father's funeral, preferring to sequester himself in the refuge of his own small house in nearby Kittrell.

By 2:30 p.m., the choir and presiding ministers were in position, and the memorial service began. It was a joint ceremony hosted by Reverend Bradley and Elder Charlie Taylor, minister of the North Maple Street Church of Christ in Murfreesboro. The two men of the cloth represented a unique, key aspect of Uncle Dave's life. He had been a dedicated Methodist and his wife a devout member of the Church of Christ and, instead of reconciling their religious differences, they had instead supported one another as best they could as members of their own respective congregations. Otherwise, the memorial service was straightforward. In addition to the main eulogies, the First Methodist Church choir performed three of Uncle Dave's favorite hymns: "How Beautiful Heaven Must Be," "Shall We Gather at the River," and "Rock of Ages."

In many ways, the service was emblematic of Uncle Dave's life. Most of all, he was still positioned at front and center, the focus of everyone's undivided attention, just as he had been during countless live performances over his long career. On the right side of the sanctuary sat performers and entertainment executives; on the left sat family and friends. Throughout his life, Dave Macon had spent considerable time and effort attempting to knit those same two groups into a single, homogenous whole in ways that best supported his public career and private life. The two disparate factions were finally joined together in one place under the same roof to pay heartfelt homage to his memory.

Meanwhile, mourners outside crowded close together on surrounding sidewalks waiting for the service to end. One bystander in particular stood out. A tall, lanky figure in a western-style suit and matching cowboy hat had taken a place on a corner sidewalk directly across the street from the church's main entrance. Hank Williams, one of the greatest country crooners of all time, had come to pay his respects to the Grand Ole Opry's first vocalist performer. Hank had driven himself to Murfreesboro that day and, losing his way, had stopped at a gas station to ask for directions. He had arrived downtown late, and not a single, open seat remained inside the church. Folks close by stared in shocked disbelief when they realized they stood so near to the great Hank Williams, who appeared thin and very pale. One young, local musician screwed up the courage to approach Hank to say how much he loved his music. Hank smiled, thanked the teenager, and then commented: "Looks like there's not enough room in there for us, hoss. We'll just stand here and see what's going on." Little did the admirers know that the funeral of another country music great was just months away; Hank Williams himself would die at year's end.

The memorial service lasted about an hour, and when it was all over, the assembly of the funeral motorcade commenced. Mourners poured from First

Methodist Church, making for their own vehicles. The Macon family vacated the sanctuary to do likewise. Archie Macon's old sedan was positioned just behind the funeral hearse, and he slipped into the back seat beside his wife and Mary Macon Doubler, his only daughter. The family looked on as the pallbearers carefully carried Uncle Dave's coffin from the church down a set of concrete stairs and then made ready to slide it gently into the hearse.

As Archie watched the pallbearers, a single figure strode past the gathered crowds and toward the hearse, using the guttered shoulder of East College Street as an open pathway. Archie recognized the person as an elderly black man from Kittrell who had been one of Uncle Dave's friends and neighbors nearly all his life. The mourner suddenly stopped short of the hearse, removed his hat and assumed a dignified posture. Denied access to the funeral service because of the color of his skin, the black man stood in silent salute as Uncle Dave's coffin was placed in the hearse. For Archie, the man's appearance perhaps brought back precious, golden memories of Uncle Dave's complete life, including the earlier decades when he had farmed and operated a freight hauling business before embarking upon his entertainment career. The silent tribute was unambiguous testimony to the fact that even while living in the segregated South, Dave Macon had treated every person he knew with dignity and respect, regardless of their race. Along with those memories came the stark realization that his father, who had been such a big part of Archie's life, was now gone for good.

Suddenly, Archie Macon snapped. For the last three weeks he had stoically soldiered on, suffering in silence as he had supervised all the details and made most of the decisions regarding his father's hospitalization and care. But he just couldn't take it anymore. He began sobbing and then wept and wailed in a frenzy of grief while seated in the back of his own car. Perhaps it was the outpouring of sentiments from the memorial service or the sudden appearance of a lifelong neighbor paying silent tribute to his father that triggered such a strong, sudden reaction. Ecclesiastes declares that there is a time for all things, including a time to laugh and dance and a time to weep and mourn, and for Archie Macon the moment had finally come to weep and mourn for his father.

The funeral motorcade was soon underway. By a great dint of effort, the Murfreesboro police had managed to clear the route of stalled traffic. The procession departed First Methodist Church on East College Street, crossed to East Main Street, and proceeded east out of town on the Woodbury Road. Mourners covered both shoulders of the route, all the way from downtown

Murfreesboro to the destination at Coleman Cemetery. Yet the mood was not all glum. Everyone in attendance that day had an Uncle Dave Macon story. Whether in the funeral motorcade or standing at roadside, people exchanged the tales and jokes the Dixie Dewdrop had used to entertain his fans. Even during his own funeral procession, Uncle Dave managed to put a smile on people's faces and make them forget about their own cares for awhile.

At Coleman Cemetery, memorial flower arrangements blanketed much of the eastern portion of the grounds. The most prominent floral display was in the form of a large, upright banjo that had been sent by Hank Williams's former wife, Audrey. Mourners filled much of the cemetery, including the few vehicle paths that crisscrossed the property. By the time the head of the motorcade reached Coleman Cemetery, Archie Macon had regained his composure and was prepared to resume his role as the family's new patriarch. As the pallbearers carried the casket to the burial site, the Macon family and selected guests took their place at graveside.

A short graveside service was soon concluded, but the crush of mourners prompted a sudden change of plans. The funeral director realized that so many people had been unable to attend the memorial service and suggested that the casket be opened once more to afford mourners an opportunity to file past and pay their last respects before interment. With the Macon family's approval, the casket was opened. A long line soon formed, and mourners began to file past for a final viewing. At last, the members of the Macon family stepped toward the casket for a final farewell.

The last person to approach was John Macon. As he gripped the casket's open edge, John began weeping and crying out for his father and then fell to his knees in an emotional heap. Like his father, John Macon had struggled with alcoholism most of his life and, with two children to support, he had grown increasingly dependent on his father for sustenance and shelter. While he surely wept for his father's loss, John was also acknowledging the near certainty that his own life was about to come apart at the seams. Furthermore, the emotional public display was evidence of things that few people knew about. While everyone loved Uncle Dave's musical and comedic talents, most were unaware that the twin demons of depression and alcoholism had taken deep root at the Macon home in Kittrell, creating anguish for all who fell under their damaging influence and for their loved ones.

When all was said and done, Uncle Dave Macon's massive funeral was a fitting tribute to one of the nation's most beloved entertainers. Those present may have paused to ask an important question: how was it possible that one man had risen from humble beginnings to start a stellar entertainment career at age fifty and ultimately attain national prominence? With almost no formal music training, but with a great, innate talent for singing and playing the banjo and a compulsive desire to please and entertain, Uncle Dave Macon had been a prolific performer, songwriter, and recording artist. Furthermore, he had kept up that pace successfully for over three decades. In the end, he had not only endured but prevailed over depression and alcoholism. How on earth was Uncle Dave able to achieve all of this? It is to the first, full account of this remarkable life's story that we now turn.

CHAPTER 1

"Rock About My Sara Jane"

A YOUNG JOHN MACON stood with his mother, brothers, and sisters in the midst of the vast Appalachian wilderness at daybreak, anticipating another difficult day's journey. Around them towered the high, humped peaks of distant mountains, all blanketed in lush, undulating green forests. The threat from Native Americans had passed, but marauders, thieves, bears, and mountain lions still posed real dangers. A single, rough and rutted track pointed the way westward. The ten members of the Macon family had left their home in Warrenton, North Carolina, weeks earlier, traveling west with a small group of wagons and livestock. The ascent into the Great Smoky Mountains had been most punishing, but now there was cause for optimism. The new day's journey would carry them across the state line from North Carolina into Tennessee, where a new home awaited them in Warren County. John's father, Harrison Macon, had finally sent word in the summer of 1840 for his wife and children to make the hazardous trek to join him near McMinnville, Tennessee.

The Macons left behind them a colorful and distinguished legacy in North Carolina. The family traced its earliest known roots to central France in the fourteenth century. The Macons had become Huguenots under the new, spiritual teachings of John Calvin, and due to religious persecution, many had fled France to seek refuge in England. The first to immigrate to America was apparently Gideon Macon, who by 1674 was established in Kent County, Virginia, just east of Richmond. A man of some ambition and education, Gideon served in the Virginia House of Burgesses and as the sub-sheriff of

New Kent. He earned a law degree and worked at various times as an attorney, secretary to the governor of Virginia, and commanding officer of the Kent County militia. A brass tablet memorial still on display in the Bruton Parish Church in Williamsburg, Virginia, identifies Gideon Macon as one of the church's first vestrymen. Gideon's life demonstrated that he was a man unafraid to meet head-on the often controversial topics of politics and religion, and many of his descendants would do likewise.

By the time of the American Revolution, some of the Macons had migrated south from Virginia to north-central North Carolina. The most renowned of these was Nathaniel Macon who rose to national and political prominence. Born in Warren County in 1758, he was enrolled in the North Carolina militia at the outbreak of the American Revolution. In the early days of the Revolution, Nathaniel and three of his brothers were patriots who served either in the militia or in the Continental Army.

Nathaniel's first elected office in 1780 was as a state senator. A firm believer in individual responsibility and rights, he opposed North Carolina's ratification of the U.S. Constitution. Starting in 1791, Nathaniel Macon served continuously in the U.S. Congress for twenty-four years, a period that covered the administrations of the first seven U.S. presidents. His congressional tenure included eighteen years in the House of Representatives and six years in the Senate. During 1801–1807 he served as Speaker of the U.S. House of Representatives, and during the last half of his six-year Senate term, he served as President Pro Tem of America's greatest deliberative body. Because of his great, national prominence, a number of counties and towns throughout the eastern half of the United States were named in his honor, including Macon, Georgia.

The Macons who were bound for Tennessee were the direct descendants of Nathaniel's brother, John Macon, whose life was both exceptional and troubled. A young patriot, he had accepted an officer's commission in the North Carolina regiment of the Continental Army. John rose to the rank of captain while fighting in a number of battles against the British and enduring the bitter winter encampment at Valley Forge. In 1780, he took leave from the Continental Army to serve in the North Carolina Commons and then in the state senate until 1795. The new nation was already broke and, unable to provide pensions for Revolutionary War veterans, the U.S. Congress compensated them with land grants in the nation's expanding, western regions. In 1787, John Macon received rights to 1,097 acres of land in Warren County, Tennessee, for his war service. John apparently made an impression wherever he went; a contemporary referred to him as "yet unmarried and something of a drinking, dashing blade."

John Macon eventually married and had seven children with his first wife, Johanna. Her death in 1795 at age thirty began a downward spiral in John's life, which became marred by family feuds, legal battles, and chronic alcoholism. A second wife stayed with him for little more than a year. John made plans to move to Tennessee for a fresh start. Meanwhile, afraid that their father might squander all of his money and possessions, some of his children took John to court in an effort to obtain early inheritance payments. He finally moved to Maury County, Tennessee, and died there in 1829. It would not be the last time a Macon was adversely affected by alcoholism.

Put off by family turmoil, John's son, Harrison Macon, devised a plan to steer clear of family conflicts while gaining a valuable asset. Instead of going to court to fight for an inheritance, Harrison decided to leave the family's ancestral home in Warrenton, North Carolina, and to lay claim to his father's land grant near McMinnville, Tennessee. He apparently told his own family to stay in North Carolina until he sent word for them to come to Middle Tennessee. He managed to carve out a new homestead in the Tennessee wilderness and sent for his family in 1840.

Not willing to waste precious hours of daylight, the Macons were soon packed up and plodding their way westward. A few more days of travel would carry them beyond the Great Smoky Mountains and into the lower foothills of East Tennessee. Only eleven years old at the time, young John Macon would one day return to his native North Carolina for one of the saddest and most humiliating events of his entire life.

Harrison Macon and his family settled a large spread centered on the small community of Smartt Station, just a few miles west of McMinnville. Imbued with an entrepreneurial spirit and not afraid to work hard, the Macons soon established a number of new businesses and purchased existing ones. When Harrison Macon died in 1851, public records indicate that the family owned and operated activities as diverse as a grist mill, cotton gin, sawmill, dry goods store, and even a small distillery. In addition, the land holdings supported orchards, farming, and livestock. An undetermined number of slaves provided much of the labor necessary to keep all the enterprises moving.

The details of John Macon's early life are few, but he was certainly very central to the operating of the family's businesses. The Macons put an emphasis on receiving a good education, and John attended and graduated from Irving College in McMinnville. Upon Harrison Macon's death in 1851, John was appointed executor of his father's estate over his older brother—testimony to John's administrative abilities and trustworthiness.

A few short years following his father's death, a young, local girl caught John's fancy. Martha Ann Ramsey was nine years his junior and originally from Viola, Tennessee, a few miles south of McMinnville. When John asked for Martha's hand in marriage, it was one of the best decisions he ever made. They were wed on December 9, 1855, and soon built a new home together. A large house was constructed near Smartt Station and dubbed "Macon Manor" in honor of an ancestral home by the same name back in North Carolina. Their first child, Eugene LaVanderbilt Macon, was born in 1857, followed by daughters Lou and Bettie in 1859 and 1861, respectively. (For a complete listing of the members of the John and Martha Macon family see Appendix A.)

The onset of the American Civil War brought dramatic and devastating change to the South and the Macon family. Four Macon brothers had fought together previously in the American Revolution, and now four brothers from a new generation of Macons joined to fight for the Confederacy. In their eyes, the brothers were participants in a second revolution of sorts to retain their lands and property and to preserve the Southern way of life. While two of his brothers enlisted in Confederate cavalry units, John decided to recruit his own infantry company. He formed Company D, 35th Tennessee Infantry and was elected as its captain. John's younger brother, Romulus, served as a private in Company D. Over the next fifteen months, John Macon and his company saw action at the battles of Shiloh, Perryville, and Murfreesboro. Confederate war records indicate that he was still in command of Company D as late as July 1863. However, the specific nature of his duties for the remainder of the conflict remains unknown.

Throughout the war, Martha spent as much time as she could with her husband. Leaving her three children in the care of relatives and family servants, Martha joined her husband at faraway Confederate winter encampments in Mississippi, Tennessee, Alabama, and Georgia. As a result, the Macons had two more children born during the Civil War.

The Yankee invader finally made it to Macon Manor in June 1863. Only a day or so earlier, Martha had given birth to her fourth child, a boy named Emory John Macon. Martha's mother, Polly Stroud Ramsey, had come to Macon Manor to act as midwife for the delivery and to run the household and care for her grandchildren until Martha was back on her feet. A sudden disturbance outdoors caught Polly's attention, and upon looking outside, she was terrified to see a group of northern soldiers with rifles and bayonets rummaging through the barn and other outbuildings. The Union army was advancing southward from Murfreesboro to Chattanooga, and an infantry squad had paused at Smartt Station to search for food or anything else of value. At first not sure what to do, Polly Ramsey decided to confront the invaders. She went to the kitchen, found the longest, sharpest paring knife available, and gripping the handle tightly, thrust the knife into the front pocket of her apron.

Polly squared her shoulders, stepped out onto the front porch and called to the soldiers, all the while keeping a clenched fist around the handle of her concealed weapon. Surprised by the sudden interruption, the bluecoats stopped their rummaging to focus their attention on the lady of the house. Polly announced that her daughter had just given birth and that mother and child needed calm and rest, not the distress of an unexpected intrusion. With all the courtesy she could muster, Polly asked the soldiers to please leave her family alone and to move along. To her great relief, the sergeant in charge tipped his hat, apologized for the disturbance, wished her well and ordered his men from the farm. Polly Stroud stayed on the porch until the soldiers were out of sight, all the while keeping her paring knife concealed and at the ready.

The end of the war found John Macon back in his native North Carolina in the spring of 1865. Having given their all for the Confederate cause, John and the surviving members of the 35th Tennessee decided to call it quits, surrendering to Union forces at Greensboro, North Carolina, on May 1, 1865. Shortly thereafter, John made the long trek home back over the mountains to Warren County. By the early summer of 1865, he was reunited with his wife and children at Macon Manor. In honor of his war service, the Macon family referred to their father as "Captain John" for the rest of his life.

Reconstruction was an especially trying time for Southerners as they grappled with social dislocation, political upheaval, and economic hardships. The Macons were no exception. Macon Manor was in disrepair, with all the slaves freed, livestock gone, no crops planted, and the family's businesses in shambles. Undaunted and clinging to optimism, Captain John managed to reopen a store at Smartt Station and to place the grist mill and distillery back into operation. By 1868, John and Martha Macon shared seven children, three boys and four girls. The couple worked hard to provide for their growing family, but life was a constant struggle.

Apparently, Martha had a great love for music, and she managed to purchase an ornate, square piano for the household. It was a time when the parlor piano had become a desired status symbol of middle-class propriety. Martha believed that a woman needed "a song in her heart" to make her more attractive to a suitor. All of her daughters received piano lessons, and two of them, Lou and Annie, would become piano teachers, part of the growing social practice of families making their own music in the home. Martha's love for music suggests that the innate, musical genius that would one day propel her son Dave to national fame came from the Ramseys, rather than from the Macons.

The grinding poverty that afflicted the South following the Civil War eventually took its toll on the Macons. With little cash available, Southerners struggled to buy and sell even the most basic needs, and money was necessary to feed and clothe families, maintain property, and pay taxes. The economic recovery that people hoped and prayed for never really materialized. Captain John had no choice but to take on more and more debt to keep his family afloat.

It was into this deteriorating financial situation that John and Martha welcomed their eighth child. David Harrison Macon was born at Smartt Station on October 7, 1870, named in honor of his paternal grandfather. Little is known of Dave's early childhood. The earliest known photograph, taken of him at around age five, portrays a robust youngster dressed in a round hat and knee britches standing before Macon Manor. Dave exhibited musical talent at an early age, likely playing on the family's square piano alongside his sisters. The first musical instrument he learned to play was the guitar, not the banjo. The first song he learned was a comic tune named "Greenback," and he soon mastered a growing repertoire of other songs.

The first of a string of family tragedies struck the Macons in 1875. Two years earlier, Martha had given birth to another son, George M. Macon. The Macons organized a large family social at Macon Manor, and at one point, the children and younger relatives played enthusiastically in the front yard. Some of them chased after little George, and in his excitement, the two-year-old dashed toward the front steps hoping to elude his pursuers. The youngster suddenly tripped at the base of the steps and fell forward hard, cracking his head violently on one of the higher, stone steps. The blow knocked George unconscious, and he fell into a coma, dying later that night. The accident cast a pall over Macon Manor, and large family gatherings were never held there again.

Meanwhile, the Macons' financial situation had only worsened. Captain John made the difficult decision to sell portions of the family's hard assets in order to raise required cash. Beginning in 1877, he started selling portions of the family's lands and businesses. While the temporary tactic did raise cash and buy additional time, it did not alter their fundamental economic condition.

Compounding the stressful situation was a running feud with J. C. Fowler, a U.S. Internal Revenue collector, who was responsible for the inspection of distilleries in Warren County. At the time, revenue agents concerned themselves not only with financials but with quality control in bottling and packaging operations. Captain John's two sons, John and Sam, had reopened the family's distillery. Fowler found several irregularities during one visit, imposing a considerable fine, which placed another financial burden on the family. Subsequent inspections only engendered further acrimony. Captain John finally petitioned a local judge who imposed a restraining order forbidding Fowler to conduct further examinations.

A few years later, the Macons finally hit rock bottom. With all the family businesses already closed, Captain John and Martha made the difficult decision to sell their home and the last of their land. In December 1883, Macon Manor and a last 600-acre tract of land were sold. The Macons packed their belongings and headed north for Nashville, hoping for a better future.

John and Martha's oldest son, Eugene LaVanderbilt Macon, who everyone knew as "Van," had moved to Nashville in advance of his parents and siblings. Economic conditions were indeed better in the state capital, and Van made a good living as a livery stable operator in the heart of downtown Nashville. No doubt Van acted as a type of scout for the family's move. Captain John wanted to own and operate his own business once more, and Van soon located a good opportunity near the Nashville riverfront.

The Broadway House hotel was up for sale. Using the last of their savings and the proceeds from the sale of their home and land in McMinnville, the Macons purchased the Broadway House. In order to avoid any possible liens or tax issues from past financial circumstances, the property was deeded in Martha Macon's name under the business designation "M. A. Macon & Co." To minimize living expenses and to ease their management burdens, the family took up residence in the hotel. Located at 166 Broadway, the structure stood near the present-day site of the Hard Rock Café in downtown Nashville.

Nashville of the 1880s reflected the varied musical tastes of the Gilded Age. A new generation of wealthy industrialists and entrepreneurs had turned to classical music and opera for entertainment in a direct mimicry of European aristocracy. Nashville's upper classes naturally followed the lead of the nation's robber barons. Affluent Nashvillians living in the city's western environs favored and promoted classical music venues. Eventually, the city's lawyers, doctors, university heads, book publishers, and captains of railroads and shipping would advance Nashville's culture by branding it the "Athens of the South," even constructing a full-sized replica of the Greek Parthenon along West End Avenue.

Broadway and downtown Nashville stood at the opposite end of West End Avenue and there the Gilded Age's other musical forms were on full display. The saloon was the predominant entertainment venue, where patrons could swill whiskey while enjoying comedy, musical skits, and burlesque. Nashville's saloon scene was a cause of concern, and to outsiders, the entire downtown area seemed awash in whiskey. A city of nearly 45,000 inhabitants in 1880, Nashville had eighty-one wholesale liquor dealers and ninety saloons.

The most respected form of entertainment in downtown occurred in city theaters. The nation's improved and expanded railroad network following the Civil War and the rise of talent management firms had altered the face of entertainment. Improved transportation and management resulted in traveling musical and theatrical troupes that performed in city theaters on established, advertised schedules. The rise of Tin Pan Alley promoted popular music both at home and in public with its ability to write, publish, and distribute sheet music in a systematic, organized manner. More so than in previous eras, the musical venues of the Gilded Age were organized, commercial enterprises.

Vaudeville style variety shows were in vogue, and entertainers not only played instruments but told jokes, philosophized, and lampooned the major political and social issues of the day. In direct response to the sordid saloon shows, the vaudeville movement was specifically designed to present wholesome, variety entertainment to diverse crowds of men, women, and even children. The typical vaudeville show featured in downtown Nashville and elsewhere started with an opening musician followed by acts as varied as comedians, acrobats, musicians, singers, dancers, and even live animal acts. All of this was to build excitement and anticipation toward a final, feature performer. By the 1880s, theaters nationwide hosted vaudeville shows, a format that would endure for fifty years.

Traveling carnivals and minstrel and medicine shows were other popular entertainment forms. Just as railroads allowed traveling musical and theatrical groups, carnival trains rolled across the country eagerly seeking audiences. With their musical acts, high-wire acrobatics, animal shows, and freakish exhibits, circuses were like open-air vaudeville shows on steroids. The most dynamic and sensational circus company operator of the late 1880s was P. T. Barnum, who essentially invented modern mass marketing for entertainment. Minstrel shows had been popular even before the Civil War and continued in the Gilded Age. Blackface minstrelsy, which had first started in the 1830s, grew ever popular after the Civil War. Despite the overtly racist and often derogatory tone of their performances, blackface entertainers introduced segregated, white audiences to the gift of African American music. Black plantation songs and dance routines decidedly influenced popular music with their syncopated beats and ragtime rhythms. Medicine shows were a curious blend of circus and vaudeville, though on a micro scale. Self-proclaimed doctors and alleged healers made music while peddling their elixirs wherever they could park their wagons. Before our current era of omnipresent pharmaceuticals, people suffering with chronic conditions and severe injuries were easily conned into purchasing medicine show tonics in an effort to ease their pain. Even for the healthy, medicine-show hucksterism and music had a unique, engaging appeal.

John and Martha Macon's Broadway House was a favorite stopover for theatrical and musical troupes and individual troubadours converging on Nashville by train and steamboat. During the warm months, carnivals and acting groups put on shows at the riverfront and in the other open spaces scattered throughout downtown. The Broadway House stood within one block of the Nashville wharf, which was always abuzz with some sort of entertainment. Captain John welcomed these groups to his hotel for extended stays, and as partial payment for their lodging, the entertainers provided the Macons with free show tickets. The excitement and hustle and bustle of downtown Nashville stood in stark contrast to the relentless, repetitive grind of farm life in Warren County and, whenever possible, the younger Macon children roamed the streets, fascinated by all the varied sights and sounds. Dave and his younger brother, Bob, took advantage of the free tickets to attend all sorts of entertainment; the two would go on to share several important ventures in adulthood.

More than anyone else, Dave was enthralled with the musicians and entertainers who lodged and rehearsed at the Broadway House and performed at the waterfront and other nearby locales. An unfinished basement at the hotel offered an ideal, spacious venue for bands and single musicians to rehearse. Dave Macon listened to and observed all the visiting musicians. The many traveling performers who frequented the hotel fired his imagination, engendering a love of music and an appreciation for the craft of entertaining.

When young Dave was not busy roaming the streets or working at the hotel—Nashville city directories from 1884–1887 list Dave H. Macon as a clerk at the Broadway House—he attended classes at nearby Hume-Fogg High School. While the teen was good with numbers and enjoyed reading and writing, he shied away from the hard sciences. One teacher especially impressed him, Miss Julia Burton, who taught Dave the merits of maintaining a neat personal appearance, completing his homework assignments, and good penmanship. Even in his sixties, Uncle Dave Macon had fond memories of Miss Burton: "I never write a letter but what her dear face filled with tender instructions comes up before me urging me to do my best." In an age of handwritten communications, Dave took pride in his penmanship. Friends, family and business associates alike enjoyed reading his large script embellished with flowing loops and flared turns, which resembled quality, printed calligraphy more than normal, cursive handwriting.

In the early spring of 1885, a renowned carnival group known as Sam McFlynn's Circus came to Nashville, pitching camp in an open field at the corner of 8th Avenue and Broadway. (The Estes Kefauver Federal Building and Courthouse Annex now stands on the site.) Dave and his siblings were soon exploring the carnival's shows, booths, and animal acts. One of the entertaining minstrels was Joel Davidson, himself a Nashvillian, who was a gifted comedian and musician. Davidson favored the five-string banjo, and he was able to twirl, spin, and flip the instrument as he played and performed. Dave learned a fundamental lesson as he watched Davidson in action; style was just as important as substance when performing before a live audience. Even more important, Davidson's performance imparted to the youngster an abiding love and fascination for the banjo that would endure for nearly seventy years.

Dave Macon was not the first person to be enthralled by the banjo's sound, appearance, or stage presentation. The instrument traced its earliest origins to West Africa where inhabitants attached a long wooden neck to a rounded pot usually fashioned from a gourd. The first banjo strings were either hair from the tails of elephants or long fiber strands taken from palm leaves. The banjo's most distinguishing characteristic was the use of an animal skin spread tight over the gourd resonator, a characteristic that set the banjo apart from the all-wooden instruments, which emerged from Europe. By plucking and strumming the strings, the animal skin and resonator combined to produce the humming and droning sounds which remain the banjo's distinct aural characteristics.

When African slaves were forcibly moved to the New World, the banjo came with them. The instrument took root in the large slave colonies of Jamaica, Guadeloupe, and Martinique, where legions of slaves worked expansive sugar plantations. The banjo fulfilled an important cultural and social role by providing music that reminded slaves of their past freedom, current predicament, and hopes for a better future. In so doing, the banjo gained a reputation as the instrument of choice for the oppressed, wanderers, or anyone seeking to escape hard times. The banjo's versatility allowed it to serve as an instrument of religious worship as well, whether celebrating feast days or mourning the dead.

By the middle of the eighteenth century, the banjo had debuted in America, first taking root in New Orleans and the Carolinas, centers of the cotton plantation slave trade. Having emerged from the wilds of Africa, the banjo seemed equally at home on the untamed, uncivilized American frontier. Musician and entertainer Joel Sweeney is credited with first bringing the banjo to mainstream America. Starting in 1839, Sweeney entertained audiences with his banjo playing, convincing listeners that the instrument had a place on the American stage and was no longer entirely restricted to plantations and slaves. Sweeney has been credited with adding a high, fifth string to the banjo with a separate tuning peg halfway up the neck, but more recent scholarship challenges that assertion. Minstrel show composers such as Stephen Foster—"Oh! Susanna"—and Dan Emmett—"Old Dan Tucker" and "Jimmy Crack Corn"—wrote wildly popular songs best suited for the banjo. Blackface minstrelsy, theater groups, and carnival shows all introduced the instrument to audiences across the nation. By the time of the Civil War, the rap and hum of the banjo could be heard in the encampments of both the Union and Confederate armies. Postbellum industrialization transformed the nation as never before; even the banjo was affected. Banjo-making passed from the skilled hands of individual luthiers to factory mass production, with metal rather than wooden fittings becoming standard. Mass production made the banjo affordable for the working class, and it became as popular as the fiddle, finding its way into homes across the nation.

Joel Davidson's music and minstrel antics in downtown Nashville in 1885 convinced Dave Macon that he wanted a banjo of his very own to play. Martha Macon had already purchased a piano for the benefit of her daughters—the square parlor piano she had acquired in McMinnville years earlier had moved with the family to Nashville—and it was natural then for Dave to approach his mother to ask her to buy him his first banjo. Neither the details of that conversation nor the specifics of the actual purchase are known, but Dave was soon learning to play his new instrument. In 1928, Uncle Dave Macon fondly recalled his mother's patience and love as she endured his early, awkward practice sessions: "For many days and months she listened to the many discords of many hours of practice."

Dave Macon's first banjo was a rather modest affair, a five-string John B. Buckbee standard production model usually sold in jewelry stores. It had a walnut neck with seventeen frets, black ebony tuning pegs, a wooden tail piece, gut strings, and a calfskin head. Thirty-eight metal brackets circled the instrument's pot, which itself had a wooden rim covered with decorative, nickel-plated brass sheet metal. Lacking a resonator, the banjo's open back revealed a round, wooden dowling that gave the instrument rigidity and durability. A formal studio portrait from 1886 shows a dapper, teenage Dave Macon in suit and hat sitting in a wooden chair while clasping his banjo and projecting a thin, slightly nervous smile. The Buckbee banjo would be his for nearly four decades, until more reputable Lyon & Healy, Slingerland, and customized Gibson banjos became Uncle Dave Macon's preferred instruments.

The years in Nashville also reveal a youngster who was already developing a more sophisticated and deeper understanding of music. While visiting the Nashville wharf, Dave paid attention to the various songs sung by the ships' crews. Just as their ancestors had done on plantations decades earlier, groups of black stevedores and coal stokers used songs to help them maintain an even rhythm and smooth work flow during burdensome, repetitive tasks. One song in particular caught Dave's attention. Its rolling, cyclic rhythm mimicked the distinctive thumping of a steamship paddlewheel on the water's surface. Forty years later, Uncle Dave Macon would record the song in New York City as "Rock About My Sara Jane."

If so many people enjoyed the social excitement of Nashville, just as many others considered the downtown area a shameful den of iniquity. In addition to the many saloons, gambling, prostitution, and loan sharking were widespread. By 1885, the situation was so bad that local churches felt completely defeated in their efforts to drain Nashville's filthy swamp of immorality. They needed help, and it arrived in March in the form of the bombastic evangelist, Preacher Sam Jones. A native Georgian, Jones was part of a religious revival movement sweeping the nation. He preached tent revivals, and the best open space in downtown was at 8th Avenue and Broadway, the very same spot where Sam McFlynn's Circus had camped.

With the Bible in hand and the driving spirit of conviction in his heart, Sam Jones hit Nashville with everything he had. Gambling, prostitution, profanity, billiards, low-cut dresses, and even baseball were tools of iniquity. Cigarettes were an "effeminate Yankee concoction," apparently because real Southern men only dipped snuff, chewed tobacco, smoked cigars, or puffed on pipes. Of all sins, drinking was the worst—Jones himself was a recovering alcoholic—and a saloon was a "recruiting office for hell." The only hope for Nashville was to repent and humble itself before God's tender mercies. Saved only by God's grace, the sinner could redirect his life and receive salvation and everlasting life.

One night in May 1885, Captain Tom Ryman attended a Sam Jones revival. A prominent Nashville businessman, Ryman was the owner of one of the largest steamship lines on the Cumberland and Ohio Rivers. That night, Sam Jones got him good. By the end of the service, Tom Ryman had decided to turn his life entirely toward good works, civic virtue, and the spread of the gospel. Somehow Ryman managed to collar Preacher Jones that very night, declaring to the evangelist that Nashville needed a "tabernacle for all denominations that would be amply large to accommodate the largest crowd." Due in no small part to Tom Ryman's personal commitment and philanthropy, the Union Gospel Tabernacle was completed in 1892. Decades later, the great hall was renamed Ryman Auditorium in honor of its founder.

The location of Sam Jones's tent revival was just across the street from where Dave Macon went to school, and it is nearly certain he attended some of those meetings. Near the end of his life, Uncle Dave Macon identified "the preacher and evangelist Sam Jones" as one of the two persons he had always most admired. Such high regard surely took root during the 1885 tent revivals. Furthermore, it is fascinating to consider that the driving personalities behind two of Nashville's most historic and enduring institutions—Ryman Auditorium and the Grand Ole Opry—may have been gathered together one night under the same tent at a Sam Jones revival.

By all accounts the first few years in Nashville were happy ones for the Macons. The younger children enjoyed the excitement of city life while the older siblings found new success. Van continued to thrive as a livery operator. Brothers John and Sam had opened a profitable cider and vinegar distillery. To their astonishment, J. C. Fowler, the same revenue officer who had pestered them in McMinnville, had been reassigned to Nashville and was now frequenting their new distillery to inspect their books and bottling operations. The eldest daughters, Lou and Bettie, were approaching their midtwenties and developing their own work and music skills while inviting available suitors. Lou became an established piano instructor and Bettie a school teacher. Bettie soon fell in love and married.

The new life the Macons had built for themselves in Nashville suddenly began to unravel in late 1885. Bettie passed away unexpectedly on Christmas Eve, perhaps of complications from childbirth. Her husband, Charles Eddins, died only two weeks later in early 1886, probably distraught over his young wife's sudden death. The couple had a surviving child who then passed away in early February. Captain John saw that all of the members of his daughter's family were laid to rest at Mt. Olivet Cemetery in East Nashville. John and Martha's grief must have been overwhelming; they had lost a daughter, a son-in-law, and a grandchild in the short space of only six weeks.

But the cruelest blow of all was still to come. In Tennessee, the 1886 election year included one of the most remarkable political oddities in the state's history. Two brothers—Alf and Bob Taylor—ran for governor in what became an exceptionally colorful and bitter gubernatorial contest. The brothers' debates were the stuff of political high theater and lowbrow entertainment. Confederate veterans like Captain John were solidly in the Democratic camp and adamantly opposed to the policies and rule of Unionist Republicans. Election day came on Thursday, October 14, and with the race expected to be close, excitement was high in downtown Nashville as polling stations closed and the vote counting began.

Early that evening, Captain John was on duty at the Broadway House's main desk when he heard a disturbance outside the hotel's main entrance. He hurried to the front door and was shocked to see his sons John and Sam in a heated argument with J. C. Fowler, the revenue agent. Fowler had been walking past the hotel amid all the election-day excitement on the street and whittling on a small stick with a penknife when the Macon boys verbally accosted him. Captain John joined in the verbal assault "using rather violent language" and calling Fowler a "rascal and a scoundrel." The harsh words led to blows as Captain John and Fowler went at each other. Fowler struck at Captain John with his penknife and inflicted two wounds, allowing him to make a getaway.

A cursory inspection revealed that Captain John had incurred a deep gash in his left arm and a severe cut in his right. He was bleeding profusely from his left forearm, and doctors were summoned. Two physicians soon arrived, and their initial diagnosis was not good. The cut to the left arm had severed an artery and was life threatening; the wound to the right arm was deep but not serious. Captain John soon went into shock, and the Macon boys carried their father to a nearby hospital. Sadly, he did not recover, and the following morning, Captain John passed away. Having survived combat in the Civil War and the rigors of Reconstruction, John Macon died as a result of a street brawl at age fifty-seven. The Macons once again assembled at Mt. Olivet Cemetery on October 16, 1886, to bury their patriarch.

Enraged and horrified by their father's death, the Macons were determined to bring Fowler to justice. The Nashville police soon arrested the revenue officer and pressed charges. A grand jury was seated on October 19 to review the case. At least three of the Macon boys—John, Sam, and Dave—had witnessed the altercation and were willing to testify at trial. After only one day of deliberations, the grand jury indicted Fowler, and the case was turned over for trial.

Both sides quickly lawyered up. Because of Fowler's position as a senior revenue agent with almost twenty years' experience, the federal court district of Middle Tennessee exerted jurisdiction over the case. Robert Vaughn, the acting attorney general for the city of Nashville, headed the prosecutorial team assisted by two lawyers from McMinnville who had knowledge of the long-simmering feud between Fowler and the Macons. Martha Macon assembled her own team of experts, hiring two legal firms and two additional lawyers, all from Murfreesboro.

Martha was surely distraught and dismayed by the unfortunate turn of events that had afflicted her family. In the space of only ten short months, she had suffered the loss of a daughter, a son-in-law, a grandchild, and her husband. But she refused to buckle under the grief. Martha squared her shoulders, clenched her jaw, and determined to move forward. With her husband dead, she sent for her oldest son, Van, who became her closest personal and business confidant, a role he would fulfill for the next two decades. Martha announced to her son that the family would abandon Nashville in an effort to put time and distance between them and bitter memories. She and the younger children would prepare Broadway House for sale and seek a suitable buyer. Van would locate land, and perhaps even a business venture, beyond Nashville where the Macons could begin life anew.

Van Macon fulfilled his assignment in short order, demonstrating a keen eye for prime real estate. His search began along the main road corridor running southeast from Nashville to Murfreesboro, continuing eastward through Rutherford County, and running all the way to Woodbury in Cannon County. An attractive piece of property for sale roughly halfway between Murfreesboro and Woodbury along the main road caught his eye: a large brick plantation-style home with 200 acres of rich farmland. Van closed the deal on his mother's behalf on March 30, 1887, purchasing the house and land for $8,000.

Meanwhile, a series of continuances had delayed Captain John's murder trial, but on May 23, 1887, the proceedings finally commenced. A number of witnesses testified to the events of the killing and the long hostility between J. C. Fowler and the Macons. There was expert, medical testimony on Captain John's wounding and how age and other health issues could have contributed to his death. After three days, the arguments were concluded, and jury deliberations began. The jury reached a decision after only one day. On May 28, the Macons were all present in the courtroom when the verdict was read: not guilty! Fowler was free to go and return to his normal, routine activities; the Macons were finally free to abandon Nashville and somehow get on with their lives.

The Macons' new home east of Murfreesboro was certainly striking. The three-story house had been constructed in 1804, the first brick home to be erected in those parts. Standing near a road intersection, and very close to the boundary line between Rutherford and Cannon Counties, the house and acreage was known as "The Corners." At least three presidents—Andrew Jackson, Martin Van Buren, and James K. Polk—had dined there during their lives, and during the Civil War, the Confederate cavalry wizard, General Nathan Bedford Forrest, had eaten at The Corners while his troopers' horses drank from the Stones River nearby. Over time, The Corners had become a hotel and boarding house, providing livery, lodging, and meals for travelers.

By December 1887, Martha Macon and her younger children were established at their new home. The unsatisfactory trial result only reinforced

Martha's earlier decision to leave Nashville and, using the proceeds from the sale of Broadway House, she had managed to purchase The Corners outright. Martha brought with her most of the family's belongings, including a large china hutch and their square piano. She must have enjoyed hospitality work, because Martha decided to continue running the large house as an inn and boarding house. The Corners was also an overnight stopping point for stagecoach lines, guaranteeing a steady stream of customers.

Martha Macon's children continued to play a large role in her life. If women of the Victorian Era were to appear modest and demur, someone forgot to tell Pearl Macon. The youngest of the Macon siblings, Pearl rolled up her dress sleeves, tied up her long, black hair in a work bandana and over the following years became the undisputed boss at The Corners. Van moved from Nashville to Woodbury to be near his mother, gave up the livery business, and went to raising cattle and hogs, an enterprise which at length made him one of the richest men in Cannon County. Annie Macon eventually settled in Readyville, either living at The Corners or at homes nearby. The distiller brothers, John and Sam, left Nashville and headed west. They moved to Bentonville, Arkansas, and were soon operating the largest brandy distillery west of the Mississippi River and earning international acclaim for the quality of its spirits. The youngest Macon boy, Bob, eventually left Tennessee to join his older brothers in Arkansas. Bob Macon soon settled on a homestead across the state line near Vinita, Oklahoma, and became a successful rancher.

Dave Macon at first followed a different path from that of his brothers and sisters. The years following his father's death were restless. The nature of Captain John's death and the embarrassing trial became a family taboo, a topic better forgotten than spoken about. Dave drifted back and forth between Nashville and Readyville, continuing his education and pursuing his love of music. Few specifics from this period are known, but several developments are all but certain. His interest in music continued to grow, and he might have tried show business for awhile or busking for money throughout downtown Nashville. Still smarting from his father's sudden death and apart from his family, Dave probably turned to the bottle for temporary relief. This also may have been the period when he began to experience irregular but pronounced bouts of melancholy and depression.

One thing is known from this wandering period: Dave Macon fell in love. A surviving letter from February 23, 1890, indicates that he was courting a young woman from Hermitage, Tennessee, and hoped to marry. Dave's appeal to Miss Kittie Bumpous is worth quoting at some length:

If you love me as well as I do you there is no axe can cut our love into [*sic*]. Write me. Worthy of estimation after long consideration of my vocation and the popularity I have in your nation, I would like very much to become your relation.

I am afraid I am not
Yours Truly,
D. H. Macon

The missive reflects the romantic and often sentimental expressions that became a hallmark of Uncle Dave Macon's songwriting and correspondence. Kittie Bumpous must have made a lasting impression because many of the letter's words and phrases Uncle Dave repeated in the 1928 recording of the rapid, frenzied tune, "Worthy of Estimation."

Apparently the relationship was not meant to last, and Dave returned to Readyville to live and work at The Corners on a permanent basis, probably in 1891. He had a love for animals, especially horses and mules, and Dave's younger sister Pearl put him to work as a livery man. With all the stagecoaches, work wagons, buggies, and riders coming and going, Dave had a full-time job with watering, feeding, and bedding the animals and switching their harnesses. A familiar routine settled in at The Corners. Martha greeted the guests, making sure their rooms and meals were ready; Pearl ran the business end, collecting from the guests and paying the taxes and all the business expenses; and Dave handled the outside chores.

Whenever livery work lapsed, Dave toiled in the fields with the other hired hands. He remembered life at The Corners as "many hard years and days of plowing, sowing and reaping." In addition to music, Dave used humor and a good attitude to help him cope with life's drudgeries. The Corners house itself sat only yards from the boundary line separating Rutherford and Cannon Counties. Whenever someone asked about life on the farm, Dave replied that one of the unique aspects was that he "slept in Cannon County and ate breakfast in Rutherford County." Macon humor always included three elements: sharp wit, exaggeration, and uncommon perspectives on common things.

The same year Dave settled in at The Corners, yet another calamity struck the Macons. Lou Macon was considered the most attractive of the family's girls with long, flowing hair and dark, flashing eyes. In Nashville, she had met William A. Edgecomb. The two had fallen head over heels in love and had married in the fall of 1890. After only six months of wedded bliss, Lou's husband died suddenly in March 1891. In immediate need of a suitable interment site, the Macons buried William Edgecomb in their family plot at Mt. Olivet Cemetery in Nashville. Lou plunged into a deep depression; even the music went out of her. She relocated to New London, Connecticut, to reside with the Edgecombs, but missed her own family. Alone, depressed, and afraid, she returned to Tennessee to live at Readyville. Unfortunately, Lou's detached, depressed condition only worsened; for over fifteen years she alternated between living at The Corners and with her sister Annie at another nearby homestead.

When he was not working, Dave's Buckbee banjo was his constant companion, and he once referred to himself as "this boy banjoist." On rainy days and at night, Dave played the five-string for enjoyment and "to build up his spirits." No doubt he performed duets with sister Annie, she playing rhythm on the piano and he leading on the banjo. The closest relationship Dave enjoyed among his siblings was with the lighthearted and music-loving Annie.

Dave also encountered other amateur musicians in the area. One of these was Mazy Todd who lived in Readyville and worked at a blacksmith shop. Though talented on the banjo, Mazy made his best music on the fiddle. Along with a number of other musicians, Dave and Mazy performed in a local string band, the "Readyville Roosters." The name came from the band's willingness to accept chickens and eggs rather than cold cash as compensation for playing at local events.

But Dave's interest in music went much deeper than his own practice sessions and band work. He took a genuine interest in the deep musical traditions of Middle Tennessee, including old songs from back in the hills and tunes from the Civil War period and earlier. He seemed especially drawn to songs from the black and sacred traditions. A keen observer and prolific note taker throughout his adult life, Dave surely jotted down song titles and key phrases from the traditional works.

One song in particular caught Dave's imagination. The Readyville grist mill stood on the banks of Stones River less than a quarter-mile from The Corners. Dave frequented the mill often, and he developed a friendship there with a black millhand named Tom Davis. The extent of Tom's musical abilities is unknown, but he taught Dave a unique song about one of life's greatest concerns. It told the story of a man who was willing to beg, borrow, and steal in order to keep himself and his family fed. "Keep My Skillet Good and Greasy" would become one of Uncle Dave Macon's greatest hits.

While living and working at The Corners, Dave made his first, earnest efforts at entertaining the public. After a day of travel and a nice dinner meal, overnight guests were ready for some evening entertainment. A large, tall barn stood not far from the main house with an expansive, second-story loft for storing feed and hay. Dave constructed a small stage that extended from the high, hay loft door at the front of the barn. From this elevated perch, he played the banjo and entertained guests after dinner, receiving tips in return. Dave loved the attention and approval that performing in public engendered, and he was not satisfied with his performance until everyone was having a good time.

By the time Dave turned twenty-seven, his mother and sisters were probably wondering if he would ever marry and settle down. Jim Richardson, a young man from nearby Kittrell, some four miles west of Readyville along the main road to Murfreesboro, frequented The Corners and the Readyville mill on business, and he and Dave struck up a good friendship. Jim extended hospitality to Dave one day in 1897 by inviting him to the main Richardson homestead for Sunday dinner. The Richardson house stood on the Kittrell-Halls Hill Road less than a mile north of Kittrell, and on the appointed day, Dave arrived by buggy for the noon meal. The house was certainly full, for Patrick and Mary Richardson had a family of nine children, Jim being the oldest.

While the meal and conversation were certainly appealing, Dave's attention became focused on Jim's younger sister. Mary Matilda Richardson was already twenty years old, the eldest of the five Richardson daughters. Even at such a young age, her life was full of responsibility. Her maternal grandmother had already died, and "Tildy" had moved in with her grandfather to run the household. Henry G. Bowling owned nearly 500 acres of land in the Kittrell area and was glad to have his granddaughter around as a caretaker. In addition, Tildy still helped her mother with all the domestic chores of raising the younger Richardson children. (The Bowling home was a large, white framed house that once stood on the present-day site of the Kittrell Elementary School. The private Richardson family cemetery sits on a low knoll just behind the main school building.)

They say that, in love, opposites often attract, and surely such was the case when it came to Dave and Tildy. Despite his occasional bouts with depression, Dave was gregarious and cheerful most of the time. Quick with a smile, he was kind to strangers and eager to make new friends. In contrast, Tildy was much more reserved and aloof; some even considered her grouchy on her bad days. They were opposites in stature too. Dave was five-feet, five-inches tall with a squat frame; Tildy stood two inches taller and was slender and sinewy in build. Still, they had two important, core values in common. Both had a keen work ethic and the capacity for enduring long, dedicated hours of backbreaking labor. And over time, they would come to share a deep, personal relationship with their God.

Dave was soon going back and forth in a horse and buggy on the road between Readyville and Kittrell in frequent trips to court Miss Tildy. Before long he was completely smitten with her. In a life that had already experienced upheaval and loss, Cupid had finally come on the scene. The banjo soon became a part of the romance. According to Dave himself the "songs were sweeter, the chords were more harmonious as he played the songs for the girl of his choice." While Tildy listened courteously to her beau's playing, she would never really develop a true love and appreciation for music. They courted for more than a year, and when Dave finally asked for her hand in marriage, Tildy gladly accepted.

One particularly sad event shook Tildy as she was completing her wedding preparations. Of all her siblings, she seemed to have the closest relationship with her younger sister, Jessie. In rare family photos that survive from the period, Tildy and Jessie always appear standing close together. Three years younger than Tildy, Jessie was trim, attractive, and popular, generating interest from local men. Jessie fell ill only two months before the planned wedding and, to the family's shock, she suddenly passed away at age nineteen in September 1899. Tildy took her death hard, but decided to go ahead with the scheduled nuptials.

Dave Macon and Tildy Richardson were married on November 28. The ceremony was conducted by Rev. D. B. Vance, a Baptist minister from Woodbury, and took place in Kittrell, probably at the Richardson home. Dave was already twenty-nine and Tildy was twenty-two (born in October 1877). They were both extremely happy and, like most newlyweds, probably could not imagine the blessings they would enjoy and the challenges they would endure together.

CHAPTER 2

"From Earth to Heaven"

MR. AND MRS. D. H. MACON began married life by taking up temporary residence at The Corners. In honor of his granddaughter's wedding, and for the care she had provided to him, Henry Bowling gave Tildy a considerable dowry. A stout log cabin built in the early 1840s stood just off the Woodbury Pike, which ran through the center of the Kittrell community. The cabin was part of Henry's significant land holdings and, on a verbal agreement, he handed ownership of the cabin and ninety-five acres of surrounding farmland to the newlyweds.

Their first year of marriage was surely a busy but happy time. Dave continued his duties as a liveryman and farmhand. Meanwhile, Tildy was on the road back and forth between Readyville and Kittrell. She still tended to her grandfather's needs and assisted her mother with the younger children in the Richardson family. But her primary chore was getting the cabin ready for her and Dave. By the fall of 1900, all was set, and the newlyweds moved into their new abode. Both would call it home for the rest of their lives.

Exciting news came about the same time the couple moved to Kittrell: Tildy was pregnant! Months later, on May 19, 1901, Dave and Tildy welcomed a strapping young boy into the world. Still grieving over the death of her younger sister less than two years earlier, Tildy decided to give Jessie's name to her newborn son. The boy was named Archie Emory Jesse Macon. A single, surviving picture shows Dave and Tildy standing beside their newborn child who sits in an elaborate stroller. Dave, with a full head of hair, stands on one side of the stroller looking down at his son with obvious pride and admiration. Tildy stands opposite, displaying a trim, narrow waistline despite the recent pregnancy. Given their situation in life, the fact that the couple went to the trouble and expense to have a professional photograph made with their newborn son demonstrates obvious pride in their new family.

Two more children were born over the next five years: John Henry in June 1903 and Harry Richardson in September 1906. Both boys and their brother Archie were delivered at home under the care of a local physician. When the doctor announced that another boy had arrived, Dave always smiled broadly and replied: "Well, looks like I have another little farmhand!" If he wanted a daughter, Dave never showed disappointment at gaining another son. After each delivery, the new father asked the doctor how much he owed; the going rate was $7.50 for immediate cash payment and $10 if paid in installments. In recognition of the doctor's good care and to save some money, Dave always paid cash in full. (For a complete listing of the members of the Dave and Tildy Macon family, see Appendix B.)

Dave had reason to look forward to help from his new sons, because he found himself operating a successful, expanding business. The Macons had always been entrepreneurs and business owners, a pattern that Dave followed. During his years at The Corners, he apparently had seen a need for the regular delivery of dry goods and other materials between Murfreesboro and Woodbury. Murfreesboro had a very active train depot with surrounding warehouses and stockyards that lay along the extremely busy rail line connecting Nashville and Chattanooga. However, there was no rail spur connecting Murfreesboro and Woodbury, meaning that all supplies had to go by wagon.

By the end of 1900, the Macon Midway Mule & Mitchell Wagon Transportation Company was in full operation. The elaborate name again reflected Dave's penchant for romantic embellishment. Each word described some aspect of the business. The first word, of course, referred to Dave as the company's owner. *Midway* meant that the company's main office—the Macon homeplace—was located on the Woodbury Pike at approximately the halfway point between Murfreesboro and Woodbury. As Uncle Dave Macon explained in 1928: "Situated on the dividing line, operated by gentlemen on and up to time. Main office, eight and a quarter miles East Main Street, Murfreesboro, and ten and three-quarters miles West Main Street, Woodbury, Tennessee." *Mule* referred to Dave's preferred source of locomotion, sturdy and dependable mule teams. The *Mitchell Wagon* had developed a reputation as a prime mover during the Civil War, becoming the mainstay of Union army supply operations. With high sideboards and an even higher front bench seat, the Mitchell wagon could haul a whopping 4,000 pounds.

Like any small business owner, Dave expended considerable time and effort getting things started. He first invested in four Mitchell wagons and the mule teams to pull them. A large barn and attached corral near their cabin served as an animal care facility and a place to repack or transfer freight items. So many wagons, mules, and harnesses were too much for only one man to handle. Dave soon hired a foreman, Hatton Sanford, and it was one of the best business decisions he ever made. Sanford had courted Tildy's sister Jessie before she died, and Dave probably gained firsthand knowledge of his character and abilities during that period. Sanford worked for Dave for the next twenty years, taking only one day off the entire time to get married.

A daily work routine soon developed, which integrated family and business activities. Dave and Tildy arose each morning at 4 o'clock. He headed to the barn to feed the mules and other animals while she went to the kitchen to prepare breakfast. The growing family then ate their first meal of the day together. After breakfast, Dave harnessed the mules, hitched them to the wagons, checked the loads, and reviewed invoices and bills of lading. Meanwhile, Tildy prepared her husband a sack lunch to eat on the road and brought it to him in the barn. Hatton Sanford was always a part of these early morning preparations.

By sunrise, two wagons were underway: one headed west for Murfreesboro and the other east for Woodbury. Both would return to the start point by sundown. In this way, a Macon freight wagon passed by every home and business along the entire length of the Woodbury Pike twice each day. Over time, the hauling fleet included seven Mitchell wagons and several teams of hearty mules. Dave spent considerable time at the Murfreesboro depot waiting for arriving trains and then loading freight. Popular items included all types of textiles and building materials, farm produce, meats, and special order items. There were four key commodities not produced locally that families had to purchase: kerosene for oil lamps, sugar, coffee, and quality whiskey. Dave learned to keep extra supplies of these items on his wagons, selling them to households as needed. Dave also won a government contract to carry mail between the post offices in Murfreesboro, Readyville, and Woodbury. Pound for pound, Dave's most lucrative freight was barrels of Jack Daniel's No. 7 Tennessee Whiskey from the famed distillery in Lynchburg, Tennessee. For every single barrel of Jack Daniel's whiskey the freight line transported from the train depot in Murfreesboro to saloons in Woodbury, it earned 25 cents, a respectable sum in those days. Because of the good reputation Dave earned for reliability and fairness, and his social status as the owner of a thriving, local business, folks began to call him "Mr. Dave."

Dave was certainly aware of the historical significance the Woodbury Pike had played in the development of Middle Tennessee. Paved with crushed rock, it had become a main route southeast from Murfreesboro to McMinnville and Chattanooga. The pike was largely smooth and flat in Rutherford County with only a few turns, but a series of short, steep hills made the going more difficult in Cannon County. When conveying especially heavy loads, Dave had to up his game to make it over those hills. He would leave Kittrell with another team of mules in harness tied to the back of his wagon and following in trail. At the right time, he would halt, bring the additional mules forward and harness them in tandem at the front of the entire rig. The sight of Dave Macon urging his combined team of eight mules forward over the hills leading into Woodbury must have been something to behold.

The Woodbury Pike had been a main transit route for troop movements during the Civil War. The most striking terrain feature along the way was the vertical, bald dome of Pilot Knob, which stood between Kittrell and Readyville. During the occupation of Murfreesboro, the Union army had established a signal station atop the high hill whose bright, wigwagging flags relayed messages to far-flung northern encampments throughout Rutherford County. Dave's mother-in-law, Mary Richardson, had a particularly unique recollection from the war years. One Sunday morning she had been returning from church with her parents in a horse and buggy when a fierce-looking group of Confederate cavalrymen suddenly came galloping down the road from Murfreesboro. They shouted orders for everyone to clear the road, and her father pulled the carriage aside. Only eight years old at the time, Mary Richardson stared in wide-eyed dismay as General Nathan Bedford Forrest and his personal escort thundered past. The famed general was returning from his historic, victorious raid on Murfreesboro in July 1862.

A number of Dave Macon's lifelong personal attributes manifested themselves in those early years. Hard, physical labor outdoors had toughened him to the elements and imparted unusual vigor. Handling freight loads only further strengthened him. His sons recalled that pound for pound, their father was physically one of the strongest men they had ever seen. The wagons operated year-round, and when winter brought cold north winds and ice storms, Dave abandoned his high driver's seat in favor of walking alongside his mule teams to keep warm. He also took up pipe smoking, a habit that lasted a lifetime. Dave's strength seemed to impart a kind of gentleness. A person of even temperament, nothing much seemed to perturb him. Whenever things went wrong, as they inevitably do, Dave shrugged them off. "That's water over the dam," and "you can't cry over spilled milk," were two of his favorite expressions.

Comedy was one of his most reliable methods for dealing with others and adding levity to the incessant grind of daily work. Dave became renowned for his self-deprecating humor and a quick wit, which often conveyed real pearls of wisdom. While he was never a prankster and disliked being the butt of a joke, Dave was always listening for good jokes and stories that he could repeat to others. He delighted in proverbial tales about shady politicians, slick salesmen, firebrand preachers, overzealous lawmen, and capricious old maids. A print ad for his freight company posted in Woodbury's *Cannon Courier* contained two lines of poetic verse that typified his use of humor: "I have raised a family on this business and have got to stay. I would appreciate a part of your hauling until I pass away."

When life handed him lemons, Dave always tried to make lemonade. One day he visited a livestock farmer near Woodbury, and before long the conversation turned to horse-trading. After some shrewd negotiating, and perhaps a few drinks, the two agreed to swap a pair of mules. As it goes in horse-trading, one sought to gain an advantage over the other. The farmer succeeded in passing off a mule with the worrisome habit of breaking out of its corral and running off. The farmer's conscience bothered him, and he soon went to Kittrell to come clean and to offer to take the troublesome animal back. When the man admitted that the mule had a problem of breaking out and running off, a wry grin came to Dave's face. "I know he does," Dave replied in an effort to disarm the situation. "Every morning I break him out of the corral and run him all the way to Murfreesboro and back, and he's nary been a problem."

Mr. Dave garnered a reputation for fair dealings with everyone, especially when it came to money. He was adept at drawing up freight contracts that allowed him to make a fair profit while delivering goods to customers at the lowest prices possible. Unlike most salaried workers and farmers, he was familiar with all the expenses required to get things done: labor, fees, taxes, and transport. An emphasis on proper financial management motivated him to keep good business records. Money was a priority in Dave's life, but he maintained a very balanced attitude about the value of money. While his main aim was to provide for his family, he was always freehearted and generous when it came to providing for those less fortunate. At the same time, Dave always believed that he should be paid a decent wage for services rendered and that payment should not be delayed but made promptly. He respected moneyed people and enjoyed the company of bankers, doctors, lawyers, merchants, and other successful businessmen.

A unique incident in the spring of 1902 demonstrated Dave's proficiency as a wagoner and his empathy for others. Starting on March 28, a particularly violent storm whipped the region with torrential rains and damaging winds. For two days, some of the most violent weather anyone had ever witnessed lashed Rutherford County. Several bridges were washed out and telephone lines downed. When the storm passed after two days of tumult, Woodbury seemed totally isolated, and no word could get out regarding conditions there. One teamster who tried to go there was swept away in a flooded stream and injured.

Soon thereafter, Dave Macon believed he could make it to Woodbury with a wagonload of needed supplies. Dave knew what to do in a crisis, and he assembled the best team available. When he departed Kittrell, Dave's trusted foreman, Hatton Sanford, sat beside him on the driver's bench seat, and the strongest, steadiest team of mules from the Macon corral was under harness. The mules strained at the leather straps to pull their burden up the muddy inclines and through high standing water. The deluge had swept away a number of cabins located on streams as well as an entire black church.

Finally, Woodbury came into view. Dave and Hatton were among the first to reach the town in days. On the outskirts of Woodbury, they encountered a friendly face. Bob Vernon was a chimney builder, handyman and local musician. Concerned over Bob's well-being after the torrent, Dave asked: "Well, now Bob, how did the flood serve you?" With a sad, forlorn face, Bob replied: "Boss, all I've got is gone." Dave was fully familiar with the difficulties of life, and Bob Vernon's simple response in the face of adversity struck a chord with him. "All I've Got's Gone," which tells of the economic hardships of poor farmers and rural folk, became one of Uncle Dave Macon's earliest original songs and among the very first he ever recorded.

Music remained a big part of Dave's life. Every morning when he departed Kittrell, his banjo case was stowed securely underneath the driver's seat. To pass the time while in transit, Dave amused passersby and farmhands at work in adjacent fields with his playing and singing. When no one was around to listen, Dave entertained his mules. At one time, the best local musicians from Readyville and Kittrell formed a band to play for their own enjoyment and at certain social gatherings. The ten-man group included two banjoists, two fiddlers, a horn player, a tambourine man, two percussionists with the bones and spoons, and others playing whatever else they could get their hands on. A band portrait from 1903 shows Dave seated and striking a playing pose with the same Buckbee banjo his mother had purchased for him nearly twenty years earlier. Next to Dave sits Mazy Todd, his Readyville neighbor, holding his beloved fiddle and bow.

Mr. Dave used music to ingratiate himself with businesses and families along his delivery route. Families awaiting freight orders always received advance notification of their expected deliveries; they could hear Dave playing and singing from as far as a mile away as he approached. A booming voice, strengthened by years of shouting steering commands to mules and herding livestock, allowed Dave to project himself with remarkable volume and duration. Dave would often traverse the town squares in Murfreesboro and Woodbury atop his freight wagon, singing and playing the five-string all the while. Instead of routinely reciting a list of items to merchants during deliveries, he would convert the list into a tune, which he played on the banjo and sang. The Woodbury Pike was a tollroad in those early years and, instead of making the freight hauler stop and pay the one-cent fee, tollkeepers often raised the gate and gladly waved him through for a song.

Children living in Murfreesboro and all along the Woodbury Pike developed several strategies to entice Mr. Dave to pause and entertain them. One of the most popular was to place pails of water at roadside to invite him to stop and water his mules. While the animals drank, Dave would play a song and tell some jokes. Those children who owned musical instruments would stand at roadside with them, hoping that the freight company boss would stop and play a tune with them. People all along the freight route may have concluded that Dave Macon was a gifted banjoist and songster who just happened to operate a freight line, rather than a freight hauler who enjoyed playing and singing. If so, events of the coming decades would prove them correct.

As the Macon Midway Mule & Mitchell Wagon Transportation Company expanded its operations, the Macon household and farm grew as well. Dave and Tildy had different but complementary attitudes and outlooks, which had a great influence on the family. Dave's gregarious nature provided the home with a sense of humor, an inviting spirit, and a voice of encouragement to his sons. Tildy was the organizer and the overseer of the myriad and endless daily chores that went into taking care of the house, farm, and children.

Despite her reserved personality, she, too, laughed at Dave's jokes and funny stories. Whenever he said something a bit off-color or even outrageous, she would chide her husband by eyeing him with a tight, nervous smile, while shaking her head and exclaiming, "Oh, Dave!" As proof of their effective parenting, their sons loved and honored them very much. The children always called their father *Pap* and their mother *Mammy*.

Dave and Tildy had a good marriage, but like any couple, disagreements and arguments arose from time to time. Dave did not like those times and often sulked afterward; his cheerfulness would return once they reconciled. One time, Dave sent his older sons out to the fields to work while he stayed behind at the house for a few minutes to talk privately with Tildy about a thorny issue. An argument ensued, and Dave finally decided to just drop it and join his sons outside. When their father arrived, the boys noticed he was silent and downcast and remained that way for some time.

"Pap, is everything all right?" one finally asked out of concern. Dave stopped working and paused for a moment in deep thought before replying.

"Boys, do you know what the problem with women is?"

"No, Pap, we sure don't," a puzzled son replied.

"The problem with women is . . . sometimes you look at 'em and want 'em so bad you could just swallow them whole. And other times you wish you had!" With that pronouncement, all of them went back to work. Dave never dwelled on the particulars of unpleasant moments, but tried to learn the broader lessons from such instances before moving on from there.

The complementary nature of Dave and Tildy's parenting skills greatly manifested itself when it came to disciplining the children. While Dave cherished his role as the home's authority figure, he was an abject failure as a disciplinarian. When Archie was about six years old, he did something that infuriated his father. Dave turned him over his knee and administered a forceful spanking. The incident grated on Dave's conscience for some time. After Archie had gone to bed one night, he suddenly heard his father coming up the stairs into the finished attic where the children slept. Dave sat down on the side of the boy's bed, and as tears welled up in his eyes, apologized to Archie for once spanking him too hard and asked him to forgive him. Archie sat up in bed, and gently whispered: "Pap, there's no need to cry over such things. I'd done forgot about what happened, and I wish you'd do the same."

Miss Tildy was different. The Bible said "spare the rod and spoil the child" and that was good enough for her. And well so, for with a houseful of boys, and a husband incapable of administering discipline, someone had to do it. Tildy's preferred instrument of affliction was the switch, and the bushes behind the house provided a ready source of supply. While Tildy did not hesitate to use corporal punishment, it was always done judiciously and with careful measure after one of the boys had knowingly violated a clearly established boundary. Not following repeated instructions from Mammy was apparently the cause for most switchings.

One incident in particular became part of the family's legacy. One afternoon, her three oldest boys at the time were playing and tussling among themselves in the front yard, all the while ignoring their mother's repeated calls from inside the house to perform their chores. Her frustration finally boiled over, and Tildy stormed from the house, wading in among her sons like Samson come to slay the Philistines. Instead of the jawbone of an ass, she wielded a long, green switch. Tildy shouted at the boys while administering the spankings in turn, and the wild excitement drew the attention of their dog. The pet joined the tumult, barking loudly as it jumped up and down and kicked with excitement. In a frenzy, Tildy grabbed the dog by the collar and proceeded to give it a thrashing as well. The odd sight of their mother spanking the family dog caused the boys to burst into sidesplitting laughter. Their sudden amusement caught Tildy's attention, and a pause in the action made her realize the absurdity of the whole situation. Mother and sons stood in the front yard sharing a good laugh. Tildy tossed the switch aside and strode back into the house in complete defeat, content to allow herself to return to her chores and the boys to their playing.

Procuring and preparing food was a top priority at the Macon homestead. Tildy cooked a griddle of twelve hoecakes every single day for the boys to munch on. The basic, main meal of the day consisted of boiled or fried potatoes, pinto or green beans, a slice of meat, and a seasonal fruit or vegetable, all complemented with cornbread. Dave himself enjoyed salted, country ham as a main staple, eating it nearly every day of his life. He organized a "meat club" among the farmers in Readyville and Kittrell, which allowed its members to barter and exchange for poultry, pork, and beef. Dave set aside a hog every year for each member of the family. Killing time was always in early December, providing enough butchered hog parts to fill the Macons' smokehouse to overflowing.

Tildy threw herself entirely into the tasks of raising her sons and running a large farm, and her capacity for work was legendary. Once in late summer, she completely organized the house and her sons for a marathon canning session. After a week of intense labor, the kitchen and attic were stacked full with 700 jars of canned fruits and vegetables, sustenance for the coming winter. During those rare moments of rest and leisure, Tildy relaxed by releasing her mind and transferring her nervous energy to her hands. Flowers brought her delight, and the front porch and yard were always adorned with the blossoms of the season. She enjoyed working on crafts while rocking in her favorite, white rocking chair. Tildy specialized in detailed crochet and needlework, making beautiful centerpieces, coverlets for small tables, and doilies for vases. It is believed she pieced together as many as 200 tops for quilts.

To accommodate the growing family, the household and farm had to expand. A common practice in the South at the time was to use an existing cabin as the basis for building a much larger house. The small cabin Dave and Tildy had first lived in was covered with plank siding and a new, long wing added to the west end of the structure. A vaulted roof with a large, single dormer crowned the extended house and enclosed a finished upstairs attic. The attic became living and sleeping quarters for the boys and provided storage space. In the finest southern tradition, a covered porch lined the entire front of the new house and became the focal point of family life.

Dave supervised the construction of additional outbuildings around the existing house and barn. A number of stout, wooden sheds sprang up that provided storage space for tools, supplies, and farm implements. His favorite outbuilding was the smokehouse, which stood closest to the back of the house for easy access from the kitchen. Dave was fearful of fire all of his life, always taking measures to protect his family and property from the damage and loss of fires. The sheds were built with enough space between them so that if one did catch fire another would not be consumed. Eventually, an auto garage stood on the property.

The Macon farm also expanded into a considerable agricultural enterprise. By 1914, Dave was able to accrue adjacent land parcels for tilling and grazing until the farm comprised a total of nearly 300 acres. The years at Macon Manor in McMinnville and at The Corners in Readyville had taught him how to work the land. He had a reputation for being able to plow the longest, straightest furrows in Rutherford County using a mule rather than a horse. Cash crops included corn, cotton, and wheat. Small herds of cattle and hogs provided milk, meat, and pork for the family.

As the boys grew older, they became an integral part of running the freight business and the farm. As soon as he was old enough to sit up on a wagon seat, Archie began to ride along with his father on freight runs. It was probably during one of these freight runs when Dave tried to teach his eldest son the banjo, but Archie was not born with a musician's aptitude, and the only instrument he ever learned to play was the harmonica. However, Dave did teach him all about handling mules and horses and how to drive a team. When he got older, Archie assumed responsibility for taking care of the animals. Dave eventually listed his oldest son as a business partner with the title "yard and feed boss." Harry Macon inherited his father's love of wagons, a trait that would lead him to a lifetime in the transportation industry. John Macon had a knack for working with hand tools, especially cutting devices. He enjoyed whittling and became a gifted wood carver. All three boys learned the skills necessary to run the farm.

To provide the additional labor needed for the largest, most difficult farming jobs, Dave turned to his neighbors. He often hired numbers of local, black men for such demanding projects as rock-fence building, clearing land, and construction jobs. He always treated his black neighbors fairly and paid their wages promptly. The black families living in Kittrell and Readyville liked and respected Dave, calling him "boss man." Dave developed sharecropping arrangements with others, both black and white, for the tillage, planting, and harvesting of the major crops.

Dave and Tildy both seemed uncomfortable with the newfangled technology that was coming to rural America. Electrification was sweeping the country, threatening the great power and wealth of the companies that produced and distributed kerosene for oil lamps. John D. Rockefeller's colossal Standard Oil Company assured housewives that electricity, outlets, and wiring were all dangerous, posing real threats to their homes and children. According to the petroleum industry, a single electric spark could set a house afire in a moment, destroying a family's possessions and killing everyone in a single, fiery conflagration. Only safe, reliable kerosene could provide the warmth and light families needed. Dave probably acknowledged that electricity had its dangers but was willing to make the upgrade. But Tildy held the line; there was no way she would allow "the spark" to be introduced into her home. In her mind, there was little difference between the flash and zap of high voltage electricity and the raw, destructive power of lightning. Oil lamps continued to light the Macon household for years after other neighbors had converted to electricity. However, telephones seemed to pose no apparent threat, and the house was soon equipped with the convenience of a new phone.

Another string of sad events hit the Macon clan during 1905–1908. In May 1905, Sam Macon, Dave's older brother, died unexpectedly in Bentonville,

Arkansas. The following year, his mother passed away at age sixty-eight. A woman who had courageously endured the hardships of the Civil War, Reconstruction and her husband's sudden death, Martha Macon passed away quietly at The Corners on November 6, 1906, after a short illness. Before long, more bad news came from Arkansas. Emory John Macon had been adversely affected by his brother Sam's death, and after his mother also passed away, he plunged into a deep depression. John suffered for eighteen months with no improvement to his condition, and no longer willing to endure life's hardships, he took his own life in Bentonville on April 11, 1908. Both John and Sam Macon were bachelors who passed their life's savings to their siblings and others. Dave was named as a beneficiary in at least two of the three wills of his mother and two brothers, receiving payments of at least $5,000 and perhaps more. Martha's large china hutch from the Broadway House and the square piano she had purchased for her home in the 1870s went to Kittrell to help furnish Dave and Tildy's house additions.

A fourth shoe fell in 1907. Lou Macon, mentally unbalanced by her new husband's sudden death nearly two decades earlier, had stayed with her mother and Pearl at The Corners and at other times lived nearby with her sister Annie. But Lou's health did not improve, and it became more and more challenging for the family to care for her. One night Annie hosted a dinner party for the neighbors, and in the middle of the evening, Lou came down the stairway barefoot and dressed only in a nightgown with her hair greatly disheveled. She helped herself to some food without saying a single word to anyone. The whole embarrassing event made the Macon sisters realize that Lou needed a level of care and treatment they could no longer provide.

Martha Macon may have refused to send her daughter away while she was still alive, but Martha's death permitted the Macon sisters to do what they thought best about Lou's sad situation. They soon committed her to Central State Hospital in Nashville, one of three mental health facilities Tennessee operated at the time. Lou Macon would remain a patient there on and off for the next thirty-five years. Thus, by the time he was thirty-seven years old, Dave Macon had lost both parents and half of his ten siblings; three brothers and one sister were already dead and another sister was in an insane asylum.

A somewhat unusual series of events transpired in the middle of these family losses. When Sam Macon died in Arkansas, he left instructions that his body was to be brought home for burial. Pearl Macon immediately swung into action. An empty plot was still available at Mt. Olivet Cemetery in

Nashville, but the bitter memories of those years prevented Pearl from burying her brother there. Within days, she had purchased a new family plot in Evergreen Cemetery in Murfreesboro, and Sam was soon interred there. Not long thereafter, Pearl petitioned the courts to have Captain John's body exhumed and moved from Nashville to Murfreesboro. Martha objected, but Pearl persisted and proceeded with the reburial. Pearl probably observed Martha's own advanced age and failing health and was unwilling to see her mother interred in Nashville alongside her father. Pearl's plan worked, and when the time came, Martha was buried next to her beloved Captain John in Murfreesboro. Fate added one last twist to this story. After suffering through a failed marriage and a bitter divorce, which saw her lose contact with her only two children, Pearl herself suddenly passed away in 1916 at age thirty-eight. She was buried at her mother's feet in Evergreen Cemetery in the very soil she had purchased eleven years earlier.

But the circle remains unbroken, and where life ebbed away in one place, new life sprang forth in another. In 1908, Tildy gave birth to another son, Glen Samuel. He would eventually exhibit a penchant for books, sports, and music. A fifth son, Dorris Vanderbilt, was born in 1910. He had a knack for domestic chores, often working beside his mother in the kitchen and helping to tend the family's garden. Dorris became a respectable guitar player and vocalist, talents that would eventually make him a Grand Ole Opry mainstay. Dave and Tildy's sixth son, Esten Gray, was born in 1913. The baby was soon stricken with erysipelas and on death's door. Esten did recover, but not before the infectious brain disease took the vision in his right eye. The handicap prevented him from performing most manual labor, and he thrived on academics, teaching, journalism, and preaching.

Dave's life took a new turn about this time: he got religion. The specific reasons why are uncertain, but a few possibilities stand out. The deaths in his own family may have made Dave more cognizant of the fragile nature of life. Furthermore, he was fast coming up on forty and certainly more aware of the passage of time and his own mortality. As a father with a growing family, he may have wanted an active church life as a positive influence on his children. Perhaps the inspirational evangelist, Sam Jones, had planted a seed in Dave Macon during the great Nashville tent revivals of 1885 that did not yield its fruit until twenty years later.

Traditionally, the Macon family had been members of the Methodist church, a practice Dave continued. He began attending Haynes Chapel Methodist Church, which owed its beginnings to Sam Jones. It was a small country church on the Woodbury Pike about three miles west of Kittrell. The year before he burst forth onto the scene in downtown Nashville, Sam Jones had preached a revival in Murfreesboro. Not long afterward, attendees of those meetings decided to organize a new congregation and raise their own church along the Woodbury Pike. Two local men, J. C. Haynes and John Coleman, took the lead in procuring the land, raising money, and receiving donated materials. The church was built with volunteer labor and dedicated in August 1887, named in honor of J. C. Haynes.

Dave Macon was not a man of half measures, and when he did something, he went big. His personal search for the full blessings and truth of the gospel and the religious exercise of his own faith became a big priority. In 1905, Dave made his public profession of faith in Methodism at Haynes Chapel. At the time, the Methodists in the area organized large baptismal events at a central location, and Dave and his oldest son Archie were baptized together with a group of other new converts along the banks of Cripple Creek near Kittrell. He helped with the music at church, playing hymns on the banjo. His favorite sacred song at the time was a contemporary tune, "The Un-clouded Day," which spoke of a perfect, heavenly home. The congregation soon discovered that Dave had a talent for public speaking, and they often called on him to teach classes or to deliver an occasional sermon. When an elder passed away in the black community, the relatives often called upon Mr. Dave to attend the funeral and give the eulogy. In addition to partici-pating in church activities, Dave took up Bible study. He had a voracious appetite for reading and studying the Scriptures, becoming an amateur Bible historian and theologian. He always welcomed an opportunity to discuss the Scriptures with others and formed the habit of reading a chapter a day from the Bible, a practice he maintained for the rest of his life. Dave acquired an oversized print of the classic religious painting *Christ in Gethsemane* by German master Heinrich Hofmann and hung it above the fireplace where it remained for decades.

The New Testament taught that "faith without works is dead," and Dave took the lesson to heart. In 1916, the congregation decided they needed a new church organ, and Dave led the effort to raise the $40 necessary for the purchase. All along his freight run he told businesses and families of the fund-raising effort. Dave invited people to donate the loose change from their own purchases and deliveries toward the organ's acquisition, and most gladly obliged. When the financial goal was nearly met, Dave decided to donate the balance himself, and he placed the order. When it finally arrived at the train depot in Murfreesboro, Dave picked up the new organ using one of his freight wagons and delivered it to Haynes Chapel. A group of men were standing by at the church, and Dave supervised them in muscling the heavy organ from his Mitchell wagon, up the front stairs, and to the front of the sanctuary. They nudged the organ into its final position, making sure it was level. Dave then sat down, flipped open the keyboard lid, pumped the pedals to fill the bellows and played "What a Friend We Have in Jesus," the first hymn performed on Haynes Chapel's new organ.

That same year, Dave took the rather remarkable step of providing a final resting place for all of his family members and many of their progeny. A small, local cemetery had been organized years earlier along the Woodbury Pike, just down the road from Haynes Chapel. In June 1916, Dave paid $20 to purchase a 6,000-square-foot corner section of the Freeman & Coleman Graveyard. The rectangular tract was then divided into two rows of graves, for a total of fifty plots. Eight years later, the first family member was laid to rest there under sad, surprising circumstances.

Throughout her life, Tildy remained true to the Church of Christ, a southern, religious restoration movement that differentiated itself from other Protestant denominations. In fact, the Church of Christ eschewed denominationalism, believing that such great reformers as Martin Luther, John Calvin, and John Wesley had distorted the original gospel message with their own human beliefs and practices. Members of the Church of Christ discarded all creeds and doctrines of men. They considered Jesus himself as their founder, with the Apostle Paul as the church's original organizer. The sole guide for doctrine, teaching, and everyday living was the New Testament. A key, doctrinal concept was for the church "to speak where the Bible speaks and be silent where the Bible is silent." The Church of Christ prohibited the use of musical instruments as part of worship services, relying instead on a capella choirs to produce uplifting, intricate harmonies. Smoking, drinking, gambling, cursing, and dancing were all serious sins that could send offenders straight to hell. Many Church of Christ members at the time contended that their organization was the only true Christian church, and anyone outside their fold was inviting eternal damnation.

Since her youth, Tildy had been a member of Science Hill Church of Christ. The large, two-story framed building sat along the Woodbury Pike near the base of Pilot Knob. The name "Science Hill" came from the fact that the church had sponsored and housed a local academy with an emphasis on mathematics and science. The ample structure served as church, school, and public meeting hall. In addition to an expansive sanctuary on the main floor, a loft provided additional seating.

The Church of Christ's claim at the time as the only true bearer of an uncorrupted gospel message prevented Tildy from any meaningful participation in Methodism. She and Dave remained members of their respective congregations and fully supported one another in that arrangement. The family often alternated its participation in worship services: one Sunday at Haynes Chapel, the next at Science Hill. Despite the religious differences, Christian principles of love, fellowship, faith, and prayer were very much a part of home life. The children were left to make their own decisions regarding their church of choice. Archie was the first to make a decision, becoming a lifetime Methodist and an active member at Haynes Chapel alongside his father.

Despite a busy work schedule and the responsibilities of family, Dave began to pursue the calling of a part-time entertainer. Given his innate abilities to sing, play, and relate funny jokes and stories, Dave began to receive invitations to perform at local events throughout Rutherford and Cannon Counties in Middle Tennessee. He was a favorite at family reunions, picnics, baseball games, and fund-raisers. He also became a respectable square-dance caller, shouting the dance moves even as he played on the banjo. When businessmen and local politicians needed to drum up a larger crowd, they invited Dave Macon to their festivities, and he played at auctions, storefront openings, and political rallies. He often performed for a modest fee; sometimes a hat or basket was passed for tips. At other times, Dave played for a meal or even performed for free.

One of his earliest, organized public performances occurred at a large farm on Franklin Road about five miles west of Murfreesboro. The farmer had died unexpectedly in a work accident, and Dave agreed to perform there as a fund-raiser for the widow and orphans. An empty hay wagon served as an elevated stage platform, and neighbors positioned lanterns and torches to illuminate the evening performance. A respectable crowd showed up, and the concert was certainly enjoyed, but when a collection plate was passed for donations, the results were less than expected. When Dave heard the numbers, he waived his performance fee and freely donated his money to the needy family.

The basic performing elements that Uncle Dave Macon employed throughout his public career emerged during these early performances.

More than anything else, Dave exuded energy, excitement, and enthusiasm. His performances usually started with a single, loud rap on the banjo strings followed by an exuberant, shouted greeting. He immediately broke into song, foregoing any other preliminaries. The sudden burst of energy gripped the audience's attention, preparing them for more. Once the show started, Dave was constantly in motion as he played, sang, twirled the banjo, danced, told jokes, related funny stories, and peppered the audience with witticisms. The crowd had to remain focused on him just to keep up with the onstage antics. Right in the middle of a song, Dave would set the banjo on the floor with the neck upright, whip off his hat, and fan the instrument vigorously, as if trying to keep it from overheating, all the while continuing to pick the strings with his left, fretting hand. Instrumental music by solo fiddlers and traditional string bands was in vogue at the time, but Dave was both musician and vocalist, and the crowds delighted in the novelty of his ballads, love songs, protest tunes, and sacred hymns.

Dave had an unusually powerful voice, especially when he shouted. In the days before microphones, sound systems, and amplifiers, Dave's strong vocals allowed him to command enclosed spaces with authority and outdoor listeners to hear him without straining their ears. The performances were as much physical as musical. Dave would stick out his tongue, bug his eyes, imitate animal noises, grin excitedly, and rock back and forth and side to side as he talked, played, and twirled his banjo. When he told funny stories, Dave would throw his voice to satirize the sex and deportment of the particular person speaking in the moment. The often sensitive topics of politics and religion were not off limits, but fair grist for the mill. When he poked fun at crooked politicians, stupid laws, holier-than-thou preachers, and backslid sinners, the crowd would nod their approval or clap enthusiastically. In response, Dave would thrust out his chin and shout with gusto: "You know I'm right! You know I'm right!"

Dave was one of those exceptionally gifted entertainers who had an intuitive, almost mystical connection to his audience. Whenever his planned songs or spoken routines failed to strike a chord with listeners, he could turn on a dime to other material in the hopes of eliciting a better response. Dave was not happy with himself until everyone was smiling, clapping, and having a good time. Yet he was careful not to give them too much. Performances usually lasted about an hour. When the excitement reached a fever pitch, Dave played a bit longer and then suddenly closed out. "Leave 'em wanting some more" was his private mantra for public performances, as he hoped to be invited back for future engagements.

Dave Macon's performance method was cut from vaudeville whole cloth and heavily influenced by the actors, musicians, and singers he had observed in Nashville as a teenager. Vaudeville shows had an opening act followed by a series of different performers, all building toward a climax with a main, featured artist. Dave's loud shouts and banjo rapping at the start of a performance served as a curtain call. Subsequent songs, jokes, and philosophizing mimicked the musicians and comedians of vaudeville, giving his audiences a varied entertainment experience. All of his playing, singing, and stage antics set the crowd up for a final crescendo, usually a set of two or three closing numbers. In all, Dave Macon was a complete vaudeville show all rolled into one, and he possessed the vocals, musical abilities, energy, and drive to pull it off.

Dave was also busy compiling a treasury of local, traditional, and sacred tunes. He picked up dozens of old Middle Tennessee folk songs, including "Sail Away Ladies," "Whoa Mule," and "Rabbit in the Pea Patch." The earliest performances surely included such songs, as well as those Dave had learned as a teenager in Nashville. He drew a great deal from black traditional tunes, and their unique rhythm and lyricism distinctly influenced his music and singing. For example, in many songs Dave pronounced "I am going" as "I's gwine." He also began to write some of his own material, which would burst forth onto the music scene in coming years. Dave noticed that people reveled in contemporary commentary about news and public personalities, whether those events originated at the local, state, or national level. He dabbled with new protest and comedic tunes that lampooned political feuds, labor disputes, and public scandals. Traditional hymns were always on Dave's play list, and he began to try his hand at new worship songs based on Christ's parables and the Bible's most well-known stories.

Success at local venues fueled Dave's imagination and ego, and he began to entertain thoughts of going professional. But there was a considerable stumbling block in his mind: could he make enough money to maintain the comfortable lifestyle to which his wife and children had become accustomed? That was the key question. A well-to-do farmer once asked Dave how much he would charge to play at a private family birthday party. Perhaps not too interested in performing at such an intimate venue, Dave asked the farmer for $15, an exorbitant price at the time. He was totally taken aback when the farmer agreed, and the incident may have planted in Dave's mind the assurance that he indeed might be able to make a living as a professional musician and entertainer.

While the Macon business, farm, and household may have given the outward impression that all was well, some daunting personal problems were starting to affect the entire family. Dave had always been prone to occasional fits of melancholy and, as he grew older, the malady grew into deeper bouts of depression. The episodes were unpredictable and infrequent, but when depression did occur, it hit Dave hard. A dispute on Tildy's side of the family presented the Macons with an unexpected and significant financial challenge, which seemed to exacerbate Dave's tendency toward depression.

Henry Bowling, Tildy's grandfather, died in 1912 and, as the family went about reconciling the disposition of his land holdings, the Bowlings questioned Dave and Tildy regarding the cabin and acreage they had received as a dowry in 1899. The couple both testified to the validity of the gift, but when the Bowlings demanded to see paperwork verifying the legal transfer of ownership, Dave and Tildy could not produce it. No doubt the dowry was legitimate, but it was based on an oral contract without proper documentation. The ninety-five acres and house gifted to Tildy was deeded in her name separate from the family's other real estate holdings, and in 1912 the dowry was worth an estimated $1,200. The Bowlings demanded that the dowry gift be purchased outright, with the proceeds paid to Henry Bowling's estate. Trying to keep peace in the extended family, Dave and Tildy took out a loan to pay for the homestead they had already occupied for a dozen years. The perceived injustice and financial burden deeply disturbed Dave and, before long, his occasional fits of melancholy intensified into odd and troubling behavior.

When Dave was well, few could match his good nature and joviality, but when depression hit, he descended into a gloomy, dark place where the rest of the world seemed beyond normal reach. At times, he would sit motionless for hours, staring out the window. At night, he would sit up all alone, positioned in his favorite chair near the fireplace, staring aimlessly into the fading fire or out the window into the darkness. When Tildy once checked on her husband at night, Dave murmured that he hoped sunrise would never come. The family physician finally examined Dave in the middle of one of his bouts. Afterward, the doctor confided to one of his own family members: "Well, Dave's going down again. He's just sitting there, not talking, just staring into space."

On occasion, his sense of detachment overwhelmed him. One incident was particularly disturbing. A neighbor was passing by the house one day, and to his dismay, he saw Dave sitting astride the high crown of the barn's roof. Concerned for Dave's safety, the neighbor approached and shouted up to ask if everything was all right. Dave called back that he was fine and just wanted to be left alone; he had climbed up onto the high rooftop to get away from everybody and everything. On a few occasions, he spoke of ending it all by hanging himself in the barn, but no suicide attempt was ever made. While it is impossible to make any meaningful diagnosis so many years after the fact, Dave's behavior and demeanor while ill seems to indicate that he suffered from some form of manic depression.

At the same time, alcoholism got its grip on him, with Dave becoming a binge drinker when the urge hit. Whenever he drank to excess, another personality emerged. Uncle Dave Macon would one day sing:

Whiskey is a beverage
Which works upon the mind.
Makes both men and women
Do things they're not inclined.

In fact, those words were autobiographical. While sober, no one was more jovial or good natured than Dave Macon, but when the whiskey took over, he transformed into a bitter, frustrated man. He would sit in his chair for hours, recalling past perceived injustices and often breaking down in tears. Distress over the money owed to the Bowlings was a common theme during those bouts of self-pity. At his worst, he lashed out verbally at friends, family, and relatives, leveling the harshest criticisms of their personal behavior and mannerisms. Dave abhorred violence—he would get into only two physical altercations his entire life, both fueled by alcohol—and there is no evidence whatsoever that he was physically abusive toward his wife and children. Still, his drinking placed a great deal of stress upon Tildy, to the point that the boys began to notice. Dave's drinking became the basis for a serious, festering resentment among the children regarding their father's drunken demeanor toward their mother. Furthermore, he made the imprudent decision to drink in front of his young sons, a choice that would carry devastating consequences for some of them.

Even worse, he began to drink heavily whenever one of his psychiatric episodes hit. Perhaps hoping to escape the numbness of his depression, Dave plied himself with excessive amounts of whiskey. He would often wind up in bed for periods as long as two or three days. He ate nothing the whole time, drifting in and out of consciousness, and whenever he awoke, he craved another drink. When the bottle ran dry, he would cry for Tildy or one of the boys to bring him another bottle of Jack Daniel's Tennessee Whiskey, his alcoholic beverage of choice. Apparently they took him liquor in the hopes that his behavior would at least not worsen.

Curiously, the dire psychiatric and alcoholic episodes ended as fast as they began. Dave would unexpectedly sit up in his chair or on the side of the bed and call for his banjo. He would begin to play, and the action seemed to ease and even hasten his transition back to normalcy. When the boys heard him playing, they knew that Pap was in the clear. No matter how long the depression and boozing lasted, Dave was always up the next morning following his rebound, fully dressed and ready to go back to work as if nothing had happened.

But sometimes Dave got so bad that Tildy reached her wit's end and, during the first two decades of their marriage, she was forced to commit him three times for mental health treatment. In 1906, Tildy committed her husband to the West Tennessee Hospital for the Insane in Bolivar. The nature of his treatments and rehabilitation remains unknown, especially given the relatively backward state of mental health treatment regimes in those days. But it was surely not pleasant, and the length of his first stay is unknown.

In February 1913, Bob Macon came all the way from Oklahoma on vacation to visit his brothers and sisters. If Bob was hoping to have some rest and relaxation while in Tennessee, he was in for a shock. When he arrived in Kittrell, Dave was in the middle of one of his worst fits of depression. Tildy informed her brother-in-law that Dave was sick, that he had been hospitalized previously for depression, and that he needed to go again for treatment. With no one else available to drive Dave to Central State Hospital in Nashville, Bob dutifully volunteered to take his brother.

When they arrived at the patient receiving area at Central State, Dave convinced Bob to stay in the car while he went inside to make sure the hospital was ready to admit him. At the receiving desk, Dave told the staff that his brother was outside in the car, bad off and in dire need of help. He cautioned them that Bob would certainly refuse to come inside, but they should ignore his protests and admit him immediately. A number of male nurses went to the car and collared Bob, who rightly protested, exclaiming that they had the wrong Macon. Bob had no choice but to go along for the moment and soon found himself confined in a mental ward and surrounded by other patients.

Exactly how Dave got home is uncertain, but he did return to Kittrell later that same day. Tildy must have been totally perplexed as to what had occurred, but just before bedtime, an ambulance arrived from Nashville with Bob. For several hours Bob had pleaded with doctors and nurses that Dave had tricked them all, and by dinner time, he had finally convinced them that they had seized the wrong man. The jig was up, and Dave reluctantly agreed to return to Central State in the ambulance that night.

At first glance, the whole episode has the ring of boisterous slapstick comedy, but a second look reveals a more disconcerting incident. Dave knew that what faced him at Central State was far from pleasant and he sought to avoid it, even to the extent that he was willing to play a cruel prank on his own brother. It showed the powerful grip that depression had on Dave's mind, clouding his judgment and altering his personality. Dave and Bob's brotherly love somehow survived the ordeal intact, and a future visit to Bob's ranch in Oklahoma would one day change Dave's life forever.

Dave's second hospital stay lasted thirteen weeks in the very same facility where his sister Lou was already a resident patient. Doctors and nurses learned that the key to Dave's recovery was getting him dried out. Just as he did at home, Dave sat up on the side of the bed when his recovery began and asked the nurses and staff to get him a banjo. Soon the mental ward was filled with the atypical sounds of Dave's playing and singing. Doctors probably concluded that the best treatment for Dave Macon's depression came from neither a whiskey nor a serum bottle, nor from a cardboard pillbox, but from a five-string banjo.

In early May 1919, Dave unexpectedly sank into his worst bout of depression. Tildy immediately saw that her husband once again needed hospitalization. On top of it all, at age forty-one she was in the late stages of the third trimester of her seventh pregnancy. Unable to provide the care and observation Dave needed, and concerned over the well-being of her unborn child, Tildy quickly called a neighbor. She begged him to come in his Model T and to take her husband to the hospital. When the car arrived at the house awhile later, Dave was in a deep depression and consumed with alcohol. He had once evaded hospital admission by trickery, but now he was ready to fight. When the neighbor and the older sons tried to force Dave into the vehicle, he went completely berserk. His exceptional strength, further fueled by an alcoholic buzz, was too much for them, and they were unable to overpower him. An awkward standoff ensued.

Not one to be easily deterred, Tildy immediately phoned Kittrell's squire who arrived shortly with a group of local men. Their pleading was to no avail, and the lawman and his companions soon tackled Dave, overpowered him, placed him in handcuffs, and forced him into the Model T. The squire got into the back seat alongside Dave to make sure they all arrived in Nashville safely. Tildy remained in the front yard the whole time, witnessing the entire, disturbing scene with Archie at her side. As the car prepared to depart, Tildy wrung her hands in utter despair as tears welled up in her eyes. Finally the car drove away. After several minutes on the road, Dave calmed down. He knew the squire well and asked if he would please remove the handcuffs. After Dave swore an oath that he would behave and harm no one, the squire removed the restraints, and they arrived at Central State without incident.

Back at the house, the other neighbor men who had come to the house quickly said their goodbyes and left. When they were alone at last, Archie stepped close to his mother, clasping her trembling hands in his own. "Mammy," he began in a low, earnest voice, "if ever I have a home of my own, there's no whiskey a-comin' in it!" Archie would be good to his promise; he remained a teetotaler for the rest of his life.

Tildy had little time to worry about her husband's condition, because within days she realized the baby was ready to come. In his father's absence, Archie assured his mother that he would remain close at her side during the delivery. But Tildy was self-conscious about her condition and did not want her eighteen-year-old son to see her in the throes of delivery. She asked him to pack up the older children and to go stay with their Richardson relatives for a few days. Archie refused, pledging to his mother that he would not abandon her like his father had done. Tildy would have none of it. She roared back, ordering Archie and the older boys to leave and go stay with their relations. Before the boys left, Tildy told Archie to ask the Richardson womenfolk to come to the house without delay.

Tildy's sisters, sisters-in-law, and nieces soon converged on the house, making preparations for the delivery while caring for the younger boys. Before long, Tildy went into labor for the seventh time, and the doctor came to the house. On May 12, 1919, Paul Franklin was born during a routine delivery. Dave and Tildy were now the proud parents of seven sons.

Meanwhile, Dave was under treatment at Central State, drying out and slowly regaining his wits. At one point, he again called for a banjo. By the end of his third stay, which lasted thirty days, those at Central State had come to realize that Dave Macon was a man of exceptional musical and performance talent. Someone suggested that before he was released, Dave should put on a show. Never one to turn down an invitation to perform, Dave gladly accepted. A ward was rearranged as an auditorium, and Dave put on a concert for doctors, nurses, staff, and even patients. In all likelihood, Dave's sister Lou was present. At least for a time, song and laughter broke out at Central State, drowning out the pain and anguish. Immediately afterward, Dave was released and on his way home in an ambulance. He must have felt good, having just been released from the asylum and still basking in the glow of approval from his performance. On top of it all, he was expecting a loving reunion with his family.

What happened next snapped Dave out of his euphoria and rocked him back on his heels. The ambulance pulled into the front yard in Kittrell, and all Dave saw was Tildy sitting alone on the front porch in the warm weather holding their newborn child. He stepped from the vehicle, looking at his wife and new son without a word. The ambulance drove away, leaving Dave alone in the yard. The full realization that he had been absent during the birth was surely very humiliating. He finally screwed up the courage to approach the house. The exact words exchanged that day on the front porch were never recorded, but Dave finally realized that the situation with his depression and drinking had to change. He determined to get a grip on himself as best he could and resolved to never again be hospitalized for depression. When Dave Macon made a solemn promise, you could count on him; he was never again admitted to Central State.

A second, jarring event occurred only a few months later. Most published accounts of Uncle Dave Macon's life state that his first, organized public performance occurred at Morrison, Tennessee, in 1921 at a church fund-raiser. In fact, Dave Macon's first public event outside Rutherford and Cannon Counties came in the latter half of 1919 at Liberty, Tennessee. Instead of an inspiring debut, the performance was a debacle that almost quashed the career of one of America's greatest showmen, even before it began.

Liberty was a small town in Dekalb County, which lay some twenty-five miles northeast of Kittrell by road. Why Dave decided to put on a show there is unclear, but the timing suggests that as early as 1919 he was earnestly planning on becoming a full-time entertainer. The Liberty foray was no doubt an experiment to introduce him to the challenges and benefits of performing on the road. Locals organized and promoted the event, which was held in a schoolhouse. The exact date remains unknown, but the performance probably took place either right before or just following harvest time.

Dave went to Liberty in a Ford Model T driven by a neighbor. Upon arrival, all arrangements were ready for the evening performance, and folks were already starting to show up. Dave tuned up his banjo and probably went through a few songs to warm up. By showtime, the one-room schoolhouse was packed. One of the organizers produced a straight-back chair, placing it at the head of the large, open room.

At the appointed time, Dave stepped forward, took his seat, and the show began. Dave started out strong and then got even stronger. Before long he was twirling his banjo and dancing around at the front of the room while playing and singing. Between songs he told hilarious jokes and made biting, witty remarks about the news and personalities of the day. Dave's energy was infectious, and the crowd loved it. Before long they were whooping and hollering along with the strange, unique showman from Rutherford County. At the very height of the frenzy, organizers passed a collection plate so the crowd could make a donation.

About this time, Liberty's overzealous constable happened to pass by on his rounds, and the unanticipated ruckus from the schoolhouse drew his attention. There was way too much noise coming from inside for that time of night! The constable charged into the building and was shocked by what he saw. Folks were out of order with all of the laughing and clapping; some of them were even up and dancing around! There was a good chance some men were passing around open whiskey bottles at the back of the room.

The constable's reputation as a stickler for law and order surely preceded him. At the sight of the lawman, people sprang from their seats and dashed from the room; others may have dived out through open windows. In short order, the room was vacant except for Dave and the constable. The officer did not recognize the banjoist and pointed, accusing questions flew fast and furious. The constable then whipped out a citation book and began scribbling a series of trumped-up charges: disturbing the peace, performing without a proper permit, serving alcohol without a permit, inciting a riot, contributing to the delinquency of minors, and on and on and on. All the while, Dave kept his mouth shut, not an easy accomplishment for him.

In the end, the constable presented Dave with a citation with fines that added up to the considerable sum of $17.50. Dave found the plate filled with donations and meticulously counted the cash. By the time he counted out the full penalty, only a few odd coins remained in the plate. The constable took the money, marked the ticket paid and told Dave to get out of town. He gathered up his banjo and stalked from the room. Outside, a group of men lingered near the school's front porch in the dark, waiting to see what had happened. When Dave stepped outside, they saw the somber look on his face.

"Mr. Macon, what happened?" one of them asked anxiously. But Dave was in no mood to discuss the humiliation and embarrassment of what had just transpired. He stood silent for a moment before answering.

"Boys, you have a problem here in Liberty!"

"What's that, Mr. Macon?"

"They named this place wrong! They named it Liberty, but a man ain't got no liberty here. Yes, sir, you have to pay your way through here!" Without another word, Dave and his driver got in the car and left.

Dave sat silent and brooding through the long drive back home, no doubt stung by the evening's events. A law-abiding person, Dave had never been accosted in such a way by a lawman. When the car finally pulled into the front yard in Kittrell, he was still downcast. Dave told the driver he needed to talk to someone before going inside and asked the man to get Archie. Despite the late hour, Archie soon came outside. He stood beside the Model T in the dark while his father remained in the passenger seat. In hushed tones, Dave told his teenage son what had happened, wanting to get things off his chest before he went inside to face Miss Tildy. It would not be the last time Dave would turn to his oldest son in confidence. Before the conversation ended, Dave decided that discretion was the better part of valor.

"Arch, if your mother ever finds out about this, I'm done for!" Dave declared. "If she finds me out, she would never, ever let me travel and perform." In the dark of the night, the two vowed a code of silence, swearing to one another to never let Miss Tildy know about the debacle in Liberty. If she ever found out—and she probably did—it was never from her husband or oldest son.

Lizzie Weeks was born in Kittrell in 1893 and lived there until she was well up into her twenties. Her parents were regular members at Haynes Chapel, and Lizzie made her profession of faith in Methodism there at age ten. The family attended Sunday services once a month, walking five miles one way to church. Lizzie always preferred to wear her best dress shoes to church, but after only a mile the shoes hurt her feet, and she walked the rest of the way barefoot. By the time Lizzie was a teenager, her father and Dave were "big chums," and one Sunday the Macons invited the Weeks family to have lunch at their house following church.

When they all sat down to eat, Lizzie noticed that their host seemed preoccupied. On several occasions, Dave pulled out a gold pocket watch to check the time. At 1 o'clock, he suddenly announced that everyone was to go outside onto the front porch so they would not miss the spectacle. They all headed outdoors, and moments later, as if on cue, a strange, mechanical whirling sound was heard out on the Woodbury Pike, coming from the direction of Murfreesboro. Suddenly, a new Ford Model T appeared, rolling along effortlessly at high speed. A well-heeled man in Murfreesboro had just purchased one of the automobiles, and Dave had noticed him passing through Kittrell on fun, recreational drives at the very same hour on previous Sundays.

"Here it comes, and there it goes!" Dave called out in excitement. "Look how fast it goes!" Lizzie stood on the Macons' front porch staring in shocked disbelief at the horseless carriage. How could a contraption go so fast without being harnessed to a team of mules or horses? "The car was going about 10 mph," Lizzie recalled with a laugh and a smile many decades later. "That was the first time I ever saw a car." Lizzie Weeks would live to be 100, and one of the most cherished memories of her long life was the Sunday afternoon she stood on Dave Macon's front porch as a teenager and watched a Ford Model T roll past.

A new era was dawning in America. As the twentieth century unfolded, Americans were a people on the move. Henry Ford had introduced the revolutionary Model T, a mechanically reliable, mass-produced automobile that was affordably priced to allow most families to own one. The airplane was coming of age, especially following its extensive use in World War I. Commercial radio was in its earliest stages, with only a handful of broadcasting powerhouses transmitting signals from major cities in the Northeast and the Midwest, but a national network of radio stations was not far off.

One of the most noticeable technological advances was the widespread debut of the motorized truck. Trucks had proven themselves more efficient than horses and mules in hauling military supplies during World War I. In the war's aftermath, motorized delivery trucks began to replace horse- or mule-drawn transportation throughout America. Dave Macon would have nothing of it. He was distrustful of complex mechanical devices, especially those that put life and limb at risk when they failed. A man could depend on a horse or a mule to let him know when something was wrong, but trucks and cars could break down or blow a tire without warning. Even worse, if a Model T's engine backfired while starting it with a hand crank, the reverse torque could break an arm or shatter a wrist. As proof of his convictions, Dave never learned to drive an automobile.

In 1920, a competing freight line in Rutherford County made the change-over from mules and wagons to trucks. Shortly thereafter, the company's owner approached Dave about making the same transition and combining their efforts into a larger enterprise. His answer was brief and to the point, a vintage Macon-style response: "Boys, you can keep your trucks; just give me my banjo!" At midyear Dave closed the Macon Midway Mule & Mitchell Wagon Transportation Company rather than modernizing to truck transport.

Eight years later, Uncle Dave Macon sat down before a microphone in a recording studio in Chicago to cut the record "From Earth to Heaven." The autobiographical ballad told of his years of wagoning, his trust in animals, and his suspicion of mechanical contraptions. An Uncle Dave classic, the song's main lyrics are worth recounting:

> Been wagoning for over twenty years
> And living on the farm.
> I'll bet a hundred dollars to a half a ginger cake
> I'll be here when the trucks is gone.
>
> An auto truck has a guiding wheel
> While I hold my lines.
> Oh when my feet and body get cold
> I'm a walking half the time.
> I speak right to my power,
> They understand my talk,
> And when I holler, way get right,
> They know how just to walk.
>
> Says an auto-truck runs quick and fast
> A wagon hasn't the speed.
> Four good mules and a Mitchell wagon
> Is the safest, yes indeed!

I'm on my way to heaven,
Let me tell you just how I feel.
I'd rather ride a wagon and go to heaven
Than to hell in an automobile!

With his business closed, Dave entered a brief period of uneasy retirement. The lure of becoming a professional entertainer had a grip on him that would just not let go. One day, Dave traveled to Woodbury to visit his oldest brother Van and to discuss the matter. Dave trusted Van's judgment, though they were polar opposites in terms of personality. A niece once observed that "Uncle Van" was "as mean as a hornet," especially compared to her friendly and jovial "Uncle Dave." Van sat serious and silent as Dave explained his desire to become a full-time entertainer. When his younger brother finally finished, Van let loose. Dave was just too old to consider anything like becoming an entertainer, especially with all of the travel involved. Van discouraged Dave from pursuing his dream, especially at his age, and recommended that he concentrate his efforts on farming, raising his children, and otherwise enjoying his retirement. If Dave wanted to entertain, he could continue to play locally. Dave probably left Van's house downcast and discouraged, but he had the fire in the belly when it came to performing, and he was not so easily dissuaded.

By the time he turned fifty years old in 1920, Dave Macon was well-established and prospering. He had a good marriage and seven sons to show for it. The freight company had done well, and with the benefit of inheritances from his mother and deceased brothers, the family was financially secure. His house and farmlands were worth an estimated $8,500. Still, irregular fits of melancholy and bouts with alcoholism continued to plague him. He thoroughly enjoyed playing locally and had earned some regional notoriety with his part-time music career. Nothing pleased him more than putting a smile on other peoples' faces, whether it was with music, jokes, or witty commentary. As Dave Macon entered middle age, the only thing that eluded him was the full expression of his natural desires to play for larger audiences and to gain greater fame and recognition. Those desires were about to be satisfied beyond his wildest dreams.

FIGURE 1. Captain John Macon survived the battles of Perryville, Shiloh, and Stones River, as well as the rigors of Reconstruction, only to die in a street brawl in downtown Nashville. He always maintained a positive attitude in the face of life's challenges, a trait he passed on to his son Dave. (Macon-Doubler Family)

FIGURE 2. Born in 1838, Martha Ann Ramsey Macon bore eleven children and endured the Civil War, Reconstruction, and her husband's untimely death in 1886. Though Martha encouraged her son Dave to develop his musical talents, she passed away before Uncle Dave Macon became a nationally recognized entertainer. (Macon-Doubler Family)

FIGURE 3. Uncle Dave as a child outside Macon Manor at Smartt Station, Tennessee, circa 1875. The photograph was kept for decades among the pages of the Macon family Bible, making it perhaps the rarest Uncle Dave image of them all. (Macon-Doubler Family)

FIGURE 4. Young Dave stands next to his eldest brother, Van, in Nashville, circa 1884. After Captain John's death, Van became the patriarch of the Macon family and one of Dave's lifelong confidants. Van would one day discourage his younger brother from becoming a professional entertainer. (Macon-Doubler Family)

FIGURE 5. Uncle Dave Macon's songbook from the 1930s. An image of him holding a banjo at age sixteen while living in Nashville graces the front cover. The upper, facsimile signature is part of the cover design; the lower, genuine signature was added in his own hand for a relative. It is the only signed copy of an Uncle Dave Macon songbook known to exist. (Macon-Doubler Family)

FIGURE 6. The Corners house in Readyville, Tennessee. Martha Macon purchased the home and surrounding acreage in late 1887 following her husband's death. Uncle Dave further developed his musical skills here while helping his mother run the house as an inn and boarding house. The barn and loft from which a young Uncle Dave performed for travelers and overnight guests no longer stands. (Macon-Doubler Family)

FIGURE 7. Dave and Tildy Macon pose with their first child, Archie, who was born in May 1901. Dave looks down at his new son with pride and admiration. The eldest of seven sons eventually born to the couple, Archie would become a lifelong friend and the closest confidant to his father. (Macon-Doubler Family)

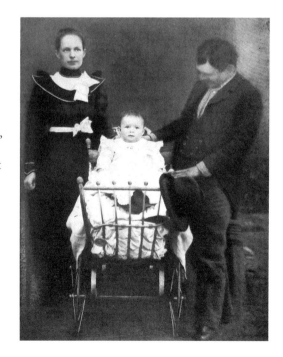

FIGURE 8. Uncle Dave was a devoted Methodist for much of his life and a member of Haynes Chapel Methodist Church on the Woodbury Road. A generous man, he twice paid in full to have the roof replaced on the building. Uncle Dave is buried nearby in Coleman Cemetery. Haynes Chapel as it appears today. (Macon-Doubler Family)

FIGURE 9. The town square in Murfreesboro, Tennessee, on a busy day in September 1920. The mix of motorized and animal-drawn transport present illustrates the dilemma Dave Macon faced in the decision to upgrade his freight hauling business from mules to trucks. The same year this picture was taken, Dave abandoned the hauling business in favor of his banjo, striking out on his own to become a professional entertainer. (Shacklett Photography)

FIGURE 10. A bareheaded Uncle Dave at a local performance at the very start of his entertainment career. In fact, this photo may have been taken during his crucial trip to Oklahoma in the summer of 1920. His thumb and two-finger picking style is evident as he holds a unique seven-string banjo. (Macon-Doubler Family)

FIGURE 11. W. G. Thuss (left) posing with the new, rising entertainer, Uncle Dave Macon. Thuss was a prominent Nashville photographer who was hoping to build personal and professional ties with the music star. (Macon-Doubler Family)

FIGURE 12. A successful fund-raiser in 1921, which garnered enough money to replace two sets of front, double doors at the Methodist Church in Morrison, Tennessee, helped to convince Uncle Dave that he really could make it as a professional performer. The doors are still there, opening wide to welcome worshippers whenever services are held. (Macon-Doubler Family)

FIGURE 13. Uncle Dave appears in a rube costume for a promotional shot for Loew's Theaters. While some performers balked at wearing such stage garb, Uncle Dave didn't care as long as he got to perform and was paid. (Vanderbilt University Special Collections and University Archives)

FIGURE 14. When Uncle Dave began his music career, he still had small children at home. Uncle Dave is seated between his two youngest, Esten (left) and Paul (right). Miss Tildy stands at back right. Miss Tildy's mother, Mary Richardson (in hat), stands beside her eldest daughter. Uncle Dave and his mother-in-law had a particularly close relationship. After Tildy's death, Uncle Dave and Mrs. Richardson maintained a gracious friendship until she passed away in 1947. (Macon-Doubler Family)

FIGURE 15. Uncle Dave poses for a studio shot in Tampa, Florida, a year or so before joining the Grand Ole Opry in 1926. The more rustic, country garb was meant to emphasize the traditional roots and sounds of old-time music. The cocked hat became an Uncle Dave trademark. (Macon-Doubler Family)

FIGURE 16. Sid Harkreader was an outstanding fiddler and one of Uncle Dave's most long-serving musical partners. The duo eventually split but remained lifelong friends, still performing and recording together on occasion. (Grand Ole Opry, LLC)

FIGURE 17. The "Solemn Old Judge" of the Grand Ole Opry, George D. Hay. A brilliant publicist and radio announcer, Hay and Uncle Dave became close friends and were widely recognized as the two driving forces in the establishment and success of the early Opry. (Grand Ole Opry, LLC)

FIGURE 18. With increased national exposure, Uncle Dave began endorsing products in nationwide advertising campaigns. He and Sam McGee pose for a photograph for the catalog of the Gibson Mandolin-Guitar Manufacturing Company, as the corporation was known at the time. The picture was taken at Wagner Studios in Cullman, Alabama, in 1928. (Macon-Doubler Family)

FIGURE 19. A recently discovered and never before published image of Uncle Dave taken at a performance venue. The candid shot captures the big grin and piercing brown eyes, which allowed the Dixie Dewdrop to establish a direct, personal connection with audience members during live performances. (Macon-Doubler Family)

FIGURE 20. Uncle Dave and Dorris pose for a WSM promotional shot in the early 1930s. WSM reproduced this photograph by the thousands on heavy gauge paper to send to the many listeners who wrote in requesting a photo of the performers. Uncle Dave and Dorris often signed such photos before they went out in the mail. (Grand Ole Opry, LLC)

FIGURE 21. Uncle Dave regularly stayed at the homes of promoters or other musicians while on tour, doting on the children like an affectionate grandfather. Two unidentified mothers and their children pose with the visiting Opry superstar. Even in casual, personal photos, Uncle Dave positioned himself at the center of attention. (Macon-Doubler Family)

FIGURE 22. The Macon family home in Kittrell, Tennessee. It was placed on the National Register of Historic Places in 1974. (Macon-Doubler Family)

FIGURE 23. Uncle Dave befriended DeFord Bailey, a master harmonica player and the first black performer on the Opry, who toured with the Dixie Dewdrop. DeFord was sometimes refused meals or accommodations at hotels while touring in the segregated South. On those occasions, Uncle Dave informed hotel managers that DeFord was his personal valet, allowing the harmonicist to be fed and roomed. DeFord Bailey was inducted into the Country Music Hall of Fame in 2005. (Grand Ole Opry, LLC)

FIGURE 24. Uncle Dave with his close friends, the Delmore Brothers. Alton (right) was an inspired, prolific songwriter who composed over 1,000 songs. Rabon (left) was the duo's mainstay when it came to picking. The Delmore Brothers had an uneasy relationship with WSM management, and the trio had their best times together when they were on the road and far from Nashville. All three would become members of the Country Music Hall of Fame. (Grand Ole Opry, LLC)

BACKUSBURG HOMECOMING

WSM's "Grand Ole Opry" Units from Nashville
═══Announcer and All in Person═══

GRAND OLD OPRY WSM

HERBERT WILLIAMS, *Promoter*

★★★★★★★★★★★★★★★★★★★★★★★★★★★★★

"Solemn Old Judge," himself, Chief Master of Ceremonies, Assisted by two others

Tennessee Mountaineer Bands, string music.
Uncle Dave Macon and Sam McGhee.
Paul Warmack and his Gully Jumpers.
The famous "Fruit Jar Drinkers," fastest band in America.
Robert Lund, talking blues expert.
Black-face negro minstrels.
DeFord Bailey, the Pan-American Harmonica King.
Thirty-piece Band, dance orchestra from Paducah.
Several of the best quartettes in the state, including May-
   field Male Quartette and WSM's Mixed Quartette,
   composed of Christine Lamb, Margaret Ackerman, Ovid
   Collins, and George Nevins.
Speech by Hon. Boris Gregory, Congressman, Washington.
Also short speeches, baseball, barbecue, ice cream, drinks.
Airtight radio schedule program from 8:00 until sun-
   down 4th of July every year, so come very early.

★★★★★★★★★★★★★★★★★★★★★★★★★★★★★

*The one chance in a lifetime to see the artists of
WSM, one of the strongest and richest radio
stations in the world. Tune in WSM or WPAD
for further announcements.*

★★★★★★★★★★★★★★★★★★★★★★★★★★★★★

UNCLE DAVE MACON, *"Funniest Man in the World"*

*Come via Mayfield or Murray to Coldwater. Easy car distance and good
road. If rained out on Wednesday, July 4th, come Wednesday, July 11th.*
If again rained out, come first fair Wednesday

BIGGEST JULY 4th Celebration in State

FIGURE 25. The official poster of the Backusburg Musicale, America's first
organized summer music festival held in western Kentucky on July 4, 1934.
Uncle Dave was the event's headliner, billed as the "Funniest Man in the World."
An elaborate slate of Opry stars, other entertainers, and various amusements
attracted 20,000 festival goers. (John Doubler Collection)

FIGURE 26. The official Grand Ole Opry cast shot from 1935. The "brain trust" of the Opry is positioned at center stage: Judge Hay stands to the right of the fireplace with pipe, Uncle Dave is seated before Judge Hay with his left foot in motion, and Dr. Humphrey Bate sits across from Uncle Dave in hat and tie. The Delmore Brothers lie prone at front, center stage. Seated on the right side of the stage are Dorris Macon, fiddlers Sid Harkreader and Arthur Smith, Sam and Kirk McGee, and DeFord Bailey. This image captures one of the greatest concentrations of old-time and country music talent ever assembled. (Grand Ole Opry, LLC)

FIGURE 27. When Uncle Dave stopped there for a show, the residents of Brownstown, Illinois, had converted and decorated an old laundry cart into a makeshift version of a cargo wagon to honor his early career as a freight hauler. The Dixie Dewdrop enthusiastically embraced the gimmick, posing for several shots with the wagon and mule. (Macon-Doubler Family)

FIGURE 28. Miss Tildy enjoys the sunlight outside her home the year before she passed away. In her last years, she was largely confined to the front parlor of the house, where she sat in a large, white rocking chair while supervising house and farm work and piecing quilt tops. (Macon-Doubler Family)

FIGURE 29. During the 1940s, Uncle Dave toured with the new generation of Opry stars. The Dixie Dewdrop poses with Bill Monroe and an unidentified female admirer during an appearance in North Carolina. (Macon-Doubler Family)

FIGURE 30. Uncle Dave and Judge Hay at Ryman Auditorium the night of the celebration of the Opry's 25th Anniversary in November 1950. They were already publicly acknowledged as the founders of what would become America's longest running radio show. (Grand Ole Opry, LLC)

FIGURE 31. A group of admirers stops at Uncle Dave's house. He loved for people to visit and often put on an entire show just for them. The back of the photo contains an inscription in the Dixie Dewdrop's own handwriting: "From Pikeville, Tenn. Four Lady Friends who stopped to see me on Dec. 3rd 1950." (Macon-Doubler Family)

FIGURE 32. The final resting place of Dave and Tildy Macon at Coleman Cemetery five miles east of downtown Murfreesboro. Uncle Dave himself composed the inspirational epitaph to his beloved departed Tildy. The inscription on Uncle Dave's headstone—*The World's Most Outstanding Banjoist*—was inspired by a motto on his banjo case from early in his entertainment career. (Macon-Doubler Family)

FIGURE 33. A Tennessee Historical Commission roadside marker at Coleman Cemetery honors Uncle Dave's life, recognizing him as a "country music immortal." (Macon-Doubler Family)

FIGURE 34. Many of Uncle Dave's personal effects from the Macon home in Kittrell are on display at the Museum of Appalachia in Clinton, Tennessee. (Macon-Doubler Family)

FIGURE 35. Archie Macon stands at the Uncle Dave Macon monument just east of Woodbury, Tennessee, along U.S. Route 70S. Before his death in 1978, Archie became a great advocate of his father's life and legacy, speaking freely to historians and country music fans about his famous father. (Macon-Doubler Family)

CHAPTER 3

"Keep My Skillet Good and Greasy"

THE SPARK THAT FIRED one of America's most remarkable entertainment careers came from an unlikely source: a dire medical diagnosis. Throughout the spring and early summer of 1920, Annie Macon watched in alarm as her youngest child seemed to melt away right before her eyes. At twenty years old, the young man suffered frequent spells of coughing, hacking, and choking and often had difficulty breathing. Annie finally took her son to a specialist who came to a troubling conclusion. The young man had an acute case of asthma and was experiencing extreme, allergic reactions to the many tree and grass pollens found in Middle Tennessee. The doctor's recommended treatment regimen was even more jarring. The patient had to be removed from Tennessee to a dryer, milder climate for an extended period of rest and recuperation, and if that did not occur, there was a very real chance of further wasting and even death.

Shocked by the diagnosis and the need to relocate her child elsewhere, Annie turned to her brothers for help. She quickly contacted Bob in Oklahoma, asking permission to bring her sickly son for an extended period of rehabilitation in the drier climate. When Bob readily agreed, Annie set the wheels in motion for the lengthy trip. Concerned over the challenges of traveling alone with a near invalid, she asked Dave if he could go along too. With his freight business closed, Dave had time for such an excursion, and with Tildy's blessing, he agreed to escort Annie and her son. A few days later, the three stood on the platform at the Murfreesboro train depot, their luggage stacked on a nearby freight cart. The train that would carry them to Nashville and points westward soon arrived, and as they mounted the steps of their assigned coach, Dave climbed aboard lugging his banjo and case.

By all accounts, the trip to Vinita, Oklahoma, in July 1920 was the first time Dave had ever traveled beyond Tennessee. He found the trip both refreshing and relaxing. For the first time in twenty years, he was free from the daily grind of responsibilities imposed by his family, farm, and business. He enjoyed the companionship of his sister and nephew as he took in the new sights along the route. Most of all, Dave had uninterrupted time to concentrate on his music. Years later, he recalled that he "gave himself up almost entirely to his favorite past time, that of playing and singing on the banjo." At other times, he wrote out verses to new songs and worked on the melodies, often with his sister's help. All the while, Dave continued to mull over his plans for becoming a full-time entertainer.

After a day or two of rail travel, the trio arrived in Vinita. Bob welcomed them to his ranch at Pensacola, a few miles southeast of Vinita. The first priority was to settle Annie's sick son into his new living quarters. A few days later, Bob hosted a barbeque in honor of his Tennessee relations, and many friends and neighbors attended. Someone invited Dave to provide entertainment, and before long he was playing, singing, and cracking jokes. An elderly lady present was especially taken with Dave's musical abilities. Her church was in the last stages of organizing a fund-raiser toward building a new parsonage, but had not yet booked a suitable entertainer. Would Dave be willing to put on a performance? He gladly agreed, and a few days later played at a local school where the fund-raiser was held. It must have been a remarkable show because requests for him to appear at other venues began to pour in at Bob's ranch.

An intended stay of two weeks turned into a monthlong visit. Dave entertained at many places in the northeastern corner of Oklahoma and may have even ventured across the state line to perform in Arkansas. The experience taught him a vital lesson. The mix of old-time and comedy songs, along with sacred hymns, which entertained Tennesseans, appealed just as much to Oklahomans. Dave's banjo twirling, jokes, commentaries, and other stage antics drew the same applause and laughter as they had back home. When an offering plate was passed at the height of the performance, it usually took in a respectable amount of money. Dave saw that his performances had a certain, wide attraction, and it boosted his confidence.

To ease the burden on Bob's family of the unexpected, extended stay, Dave and Annie moved to a hotel in Vinita at the end of the second week of their visit. Having lived for four years in the Broadway House in downtown Nashville as a teenager, Dave was always at ease during extended hotel stays.

Most of the time he was on the road, going to and from bookings. On those afternoons and evenings when he was in Vinita, Dave played and entertained on the hotel veranda for other guests and local townspeople.

However, the most memorable moment of the trip did not occur at one of Dave's shows but in the hotel lobby. One day a fellow guest unexpectedly approached and declared that the Tennessean had literally saved his life. When a surprised Dave asked what he meant, the gentleman answered:

> I was so blue and down and out I did not care to live any longer. But by seeing you at your age act out as well as playing and singing on your banjo at the same time, my spirits just rose and refreshed my whole soul and body and has given me hope to go on with life's duties.

It was an encounter that Dave never forgot. Aware that he possessed a gift for entertaining, Dave perhaps did not fully realize the great influence his music could have on listeners. The man's words were powerful testimony to the positive, therapeutic efficacy of Dave's songs and showmanship.

Eventually, the Oklahoma excursion came to an end. Dave and Annie said farewell to brother Bob, leaving Annie's son in his good care. On the trip home, Dave had time to reflect on the practice sessions and concerts of the past month. No doubt the encounter with the stranger—whose life was changed by his music— left a strong, lingering impression. If Dave needed further assurance of his ability to become a full-time entertainer, it came in the form of the cash he carried home from his Oklahoma performances. Within days of his return to Tennessee, Dave Macon began planning in earnest for the launch of his musical career.

Bessie Moore sat at her desk in a one-room schoolhouse in Smyrna, Tennessee, some twenty miles southeast of Nashville, completely absorbed in her studies. It was an unusually warm spring day, and all the school's windows and doors were open in order to cool the building. Bessie sat near an open window enjoying the sunlight and the wafting breeze when suddenly a figure appeared at the window sill. The third-grader looked up from her papers, and when she recognized the man, her face lit up.

"Hi, Uncle Dave!" the little girl cried.

"Hello, Miss Bessie," Dave replied with a grin. "You've let your hair grow out, I see, and it surely looks fine." Bessie was thrilled that Uncle Dave had noticed her new hairstyle. It was not the first time the two had met. Months earlier, Uncle Dave had put on a concert in Murfreesboro, using the flatbed of a delivery truck for a stage. Bessie had been in attendance and had thoroughly enjoyed the show.

Uncle Dave called to the teacher at the head of the classroom, asking if it would be possible for him to play a few tunes for the children. He was booked for a show at that same school the following evening and wanted to play for the students in hopes they would convince their parents to bring them to the performance. The children were due for recess, and the teacher agreed to let Dave put on a short demonstration. Uncle Dave took a seat beneath a shade tree near the schoolhouse, and before long he had an audience. Children streamed from the school's doors and gathered around him in anticipation. Others watched from open windows or sat on the windowsills. He performed a few tunes as he joked and cut up with the youngsters, inviting all of them to come to the show the following night.

Bessie went home late that afternoon determined to convince her parents to bring her to the show. Over supper, she told her father that Uncle Dave Macon had come to her school that afternoon to invite the children to attend his program. Possibly interested, Bessie's father asked who else was to appear, and she replied that Uncle Dave was going to perform all by himself.

"Ain't no one man who can put on a whole show by himself!" her father growled with a frown.

"Uncle Dave Macon can!" Bessie replied enthusiastically.

The aspiring performer who came on the scene in the spring of 1921 was an improved, polished version of the amateur troubadour who had previously entertained throughout Rutherford County. In the weeks following his return from Oklahoma, Dave put additional thought into the specific techniques that he would employ as a professional. Perhaps recalling the early years in Nashville, when he had observed entertainers rehearsing in the basement of the Broadway House and applying their craft at tent and medicine shows, circuses, and on the streets, Dave desired to project more than just vocals and instrumentals. A professional performer needed a persona, a distinct style and presence that would further capture the audience's fancy and make them want to come back for more.

Dave realized that it was important for a performer to be seen as well as heard. Casual clothes were simply inadequate for an aspiring, professional entertainer who wanted to impress an audience. He decided to wear dark, quality three-piece suits with all the accoutrements a well-heeled gentleman should display. Starched white shirts, often adorned with fancy woven designs, and dress ties accented his expensive suits. A golden watch chain hung at his waist, attached to a large, gold Elgin pocket watch. A large, black plug hat set at a jaunty angle became his standard headgear, which he wore in public at all times, whether he was performing or not. Dave purchased black, high-top shoes, which became his favored footgear for the remainder of his life.

Desiring to improve the sound of his playing, Dave purchased two additional banjos. The first was a standard production Lyon & Healy. The other was a heavier Slingerland of excellent quality and construction. The Slingerland's open backing included a metal brace that connected the lower neck with a wooden dowling, which reinforced the banjo's pot. The brace gave the instrument increased rigidity and durability and could serve as a handhold during Dave's banjo twirling. The Slingerland was probably his favorite instrument in the early years. When he posed for a widely circulated promotional shot in the early 1920s, with a big grin on his face while seated in a fancy chair with his left leg cocked high in the air, Dave held his beloved Slingerland. From the beginning, Dave routinely toted three banjos to performances, with one each tuned in the keys of C, F, and G, thereby allowing him to switch from song to song without having to pause to retune his instrument. Audiences noticed that each banjo had a different colored ribbon wrapped around its head, probably thinking that they were only decorations to add pizzaz to the act. But as always, there was a method to Dave's madness, and the three ribbon colors—yellow, red, and blue—corresponded to the key tuned on each banjo. The color code system allowed him to switch banjos quickly without having to pause to determine which instrument was which.

More significant than improvements to his clothing and instruments, Dave believed that a performer needed a distinctive stage name. In the segregated South, the terms "uncle" and "aunt" were common, accepted usages, especially during public conversations between the races. Apparently, black children in Kittrell and Readyville were the first to call the banjoist "Uncle Dave Macon," and Dave quickly adopted the moniker. He understood the social power and advantages of such a title. An uncle was someone who could be trusted and possessed wisdom regarding worldly and perhaps even spiritual matters. As Uncle Dave Macon, he sought to foster closer familial and emotional ties with his audiences and fans as he enthralled and entertained them with songs, jokes, and stories.

Confident in his abilities to manage his own business affairs and finances, based on twenty years of success as a business owner and farmer, Dave decided against hiring a talent manager, a booking agent, or even an accountant. From the beginning, he personally managed the details of promoting his act, booking locations, settling the financials, and making travel arrangements. In the process, Dave developed a rapport with local organizers and other men of influence. These associations developed into an extensive, informal network of promoters, which grew throughout Tennessee, Kentucky, and Alabama. When Dave put money in their pockets, local publicists were always eager to invite him back for more.

By acting as his own agent, Dave imposed upon himself endless hours of work by telephone and correspondence. By habit, Dave was a chronic notetaker. The wall surrounding his easy chair in the main room at his home was wallpapered with calendars on which he annotated his appearances and travel plans. For most, such work might have been drudgery, but for Dave, all efforts at advancing his fledgling career were a delight. The small post office in Readyville became a conduit for his voluminous correspondence, and the Readyville address led many to believe that Uncle Dave lived there instead of a few miles away in Kittrell.

Uncle Dave Macon's first appearances as an aspiring professional took place in early 1921 at Lascassas, Walter Hill, and Smyrna in the northern tier of Rutherford County. He was well received, and word soon spread throughout adjacent counties that a talented and funny entertainer was available for local shows. In the following months, Uncle Dave appeared at schools, churches, and outdoor concerts in several surrounding counties. An appearance at Morrison, Tennessee, about thirty miles south of Kittrell, held special significance. The small town was in Warren County and not far from where Uncle Dave had been reared. A Methodist Church there needed to replace two sets of front double doors and organized a fund-raiser. As Dave performed, a church collection plate made the rounds, garnering the $17 required for the new doors and a fee for his performance. In his mind, Dave considered the success at Morrison a breakthrough event, proving that he should continue his pursuit of an entertainment career.

The only advertising done in those first years was by word of mouth. Uncle Dave and local organizers eventually employed handbills, posters, and newspaper advertising to promote shows, but the only visual advertising he employed at first was to decorate his banjo cases. Along the neck appeared two lines of block lettering. The top line read *Uncle Dave Macon* with the inscription just below delivering the punch line: *The World's Most Outstanding Banjoist*. Whenever he first arrived in a community for a scheduled show, Dave made the rounds to stores, schools, and courthouse squares to promote himself, inviting other offers for performances and playing for the public at every opportunity. Busking on the lawns of county courthouses was a favorite technique, which garnered extra money and free publicity. When bad weather and other unexpected circumstances either postponed or canceled shows, he sought to play at alternative venues.

Local organizers often provided meals and lodging and even invited Uncle Dave to stay at their homes. One time, the young son of a promoter where he was staying was too sick to attend Uncle Dave's concert, and the notion of missing the show distressed the youngster just as much as the illness. Late that night, Dave and the boy's father returned home to find the youth in bed but still not asleep. Uncle Dave pulled up a chair beside the boy's bed and put on a second, private show just for him.

On another occasion very early in his career, Uncle Dave stayed the night at the Sam Davis home in Smyrna, Tennessee, years before the site became a state historic landmark. Sam Davis was well known in the region as a scout in the Confederate army who was captured and hanged as a spy. Offered a stay of execution if he would only reveal the identity of the Union soldier who had provided him stolen documents, Davis went to the gallows rather than exposing the informant's identity. While Uncle Dave was at the house, a member of the Davis family showed up with a banjo. The two were soon playing together, and as Uncle Dave listened, the man performed a popular, comedic song from the Civil War. He was so impressed with the tune that he sat down with the musician and wrote out the lyrics. Four years later, Uncle Dave would record the song as the "All Go-Hungry Hash House."

Adeline King, whose family lived in a remote area of Cannon County, penned an intimate portrait of one of Uncle Dave's earliest performances. He was to play at a nearby schoolhouse and had arranged to eat and sleep with the Kings. In return, the entire family could attend the show at no charge. Uncle Dave arrived in late afternoon with two of his young sons and made himself at home. A teenager at the time, Adeline recalled every detail of the visit:

> Uncle Dave was a hefty, energetic man, completely an extrovert. His hair and whiskers were white. He talked all the time, telling tales and laughing heartily at his own stories, slapping his thigh or whamming the shoulder of the person next to him. He and his sons ate as heartily as they roared their songs; and Mother's ham and biscuits and blackberry jam vanished quickly from the table.

At the performance, Uncle Dave "picked and sang and roared" as he worked the banjo and the crowd. Some people sang along, and Adeline was surprised by the volume of noise. Writing decades afterward, she clearly remembered the uproar: "People who today may worry about how loud teenagers like their music, probably never attended one of Uncle Dave's 'jams.'" At show's end, a hat was passed, and people tossed in nickels, dimes, and even quarters "as generously as they were available." That night Uncle Dave and his sons slept in an upstairs bedroom, the house rumbling with their snores, which were just "as sonorous as their picking and singing had been." The next morning, more ham, biscuits, and blackberry jam disappeared before the Macons headed home.

The man who distrusted automobiles and could not drive had to count on others to get him to his appearances, so transportation posed a significant challenge. Uncle Dave managed to cobble together a patchwork solution. At the start of the week, one of Uncle Dave's older sons or a neighbor drove him to his first engagement. From there, promoters carried him to subsequent performances. A few days later, when the string of bookings ended, a family member or neighbor would drive to the site of the last performance and return Dave to Kittrell. Uncle Dave tried to travel light, but all the necessities of staying on the road for several days while performing multiple shows resulted in considerable baggage. He used a suitcase or small trunk to carry clothes and other necessities. A small, black bag, which resembled a country doctor's carrying case, was always within reach. Inside were business papers, pens and pencils, money, reading glasses, scratch paper, and a fifth of Jack Daniel's whiskey. Uncle Dave always referred to the black bag as his "grip."

Uncle Dave's oldest son was just learning to drive in 1921, and when a show was booked in nearby Woodbury, a neighbor let Archie borrow a Model T to drive his father there. When the day came, Uncle Dave climbed into the car, stacking his three banjos in the back seat. The Model T had a tricky shift lever at the driver's left knee, which controlled both the transmission and park brake. The two left the house without Archie realizing the park brake was still partially engaged. Halfway to Woodbury, they smelled something burning, and before long, smoke billowed from the brakes. Archie suddenly swerved to roadside and slammed on the brakes, bringing the Model T to a shuddering stop. Uncle Dave slung open the passenger door and jumped out shouting, "Get those banjos out of there!" A quick inspection revealed the minor problem. Archie fully released the park brake, and father and son were soon on their way. Years later, Archie laughed at the memory of the mishap, recalling that he had never seen his father move faster than the day Uncle Dave thought his banjos were going to be incinerated. The incident further cemented his father's inherent mistrust of complicated, mechanical contraptions.

One embarrassing incident resulted in a major change to business practices. Uncle Dave started out following Annie's advice to gather proceeds by passing a collection plate. This tactic worked for a while. At the height of the show, promoters would pass plates for audiences to make a donation. Dave would pause for a moment to thank the crowd for their generosity and to tell them how much he enjoyed them and their community. But finally Dave's penchant for exaggeration got the best of him. While the collection was being gathered, he started to tell audiences that his wife and children were at home barefooted and needed all of the financial support the crowd could muster. On more than one occasion, he even shed some crocodile tears during the appeal, wiping his eyes with a handkerchief as he spoke.

To some listeners, the appeal made no sense. Before them stood an entertainer equipped with three banjos and sporting a classy suit with a gold watch, big hat, and shiny shoes. He usually arrived and departed riding in a nice automobile. In every way, Dave Macon appeared to possess much more than the rural, working poor who flocked to his performances. One night immediately following a show, a group of men approached Uncle Dave to question the veracity of his earnest appeal for funds. Always one with a ready answer, Uncle Dave replied that his wife and children were indeed barefooted because at that time of night they were at home and in bed.

The lame explanation did not sit well with those fans, and the situation was very embarrassing. Realizing that news of the incident and continued monetary appeals could damage his reputation, the collection plates were dropped immediately. Instead, Uncle Dave developed a simple ticketing strategy with fixed pricing paid to promoters in advance or at the door with him receiving an agreed-upon percentage of the total take. The pricing strategy was based on both geography and social status. Farmers, laborers, and their families in rural locations paid ten cents each to attend shows, with city slickers paying twenty-five cents per ticket. The ticketing plan worked well, and Uncle Dave employed it without modification for many years.

Within a few months, Uncle Dave had achieved early success as an aspiring, professional entertainer. He was making enough money with frequent, small venue appearances not only to cover all his expenses but to maintain his family's lifestyle. People responded positively to his unique, dynamic personality as well as his songs, jokes, and observations on life, politics, and religion, and they were willing to pay to hear them. In the course of his first months of touring, he had appeared at rural venues in Middle Tennessee, southern Kentucky, and northern Alabama. But it still wasn't enough. Dave longed to appear at theaters, halls, and churches in the Southeast's largest cities. There he could attract larger audiences who had the means to purchase more expensive tickets, all while developing a larger fan base and welcoming opportunities to play at similar venues in other cities. Uncle Dave Macon was determined to take his act to the next level, and in order to make that happen, he headed to Nashville.

The repetitive performance of seemingly mundane tasks can sometimes lead to spectacular results, and for Sidney J. Harkreader, that mundane task was getting a haircut. On a beautiful day in the early fall of 1921, Sid walked into Melton's Barbershop at the corner of 2nd Avenue and Broadway in downtown Nashville, and what he saw there knocked him for a loop. A middle-aged banjo picker was strolling about the shop playing and grinning. At one time the songster strummed the banjo's strings with the stiff brim of his hat, and then with a flourish, placed the hat back on his head at a cocked angle. The whole barbershop roared with laughter at the playing and various antics. Sid had never before seen anything like it. He found an empty seat along the wall of the establishment, sat down, and, turning to the fellow next to him, asked: "Who is that?"

"That's Uncle Dave Macon from Rutherford County!" came the reply. Sid settled back into his chair, intently studying the unique character. Uncle Dave wore a pink shirt with sleeve holders and sported long sideburns, a goatee, and chin whiskers. Whenever he grinned, gold teeth flashed from between his lips. As he sat playing, Uncle Dave slung the banjo around and beneath his legs, with the instrument keeping perfect rhythm and sound as it spun. An aspiring musician himself, Sid had walked into Melton's with his own fiddle and case tucked underneath his arm, and he soon pulled out his favorite instrument. Sid stepped forward slowly with his fiddle and bow in hand, and when Uncle Dave indicated that he was willing for the fiddler to join in, Sid moved closer and cut loose. Within minutes, Melton's Barbershop more resembled a Friday night hoedown than a business establishment. All of the customers were in stitches, and passersby began to crowd inside whether or not they needed a haircut. After a few more tunes, the two musicians finally took a short break.

"You sure do play that fiddle," Uncle Dave said to the younger musician. "Do you play a guitar?" When Sid replied that he played the guitar as well, Uncle Dave suggested that perhaps they could get together to perform at some shows. Meanwhile, several patrons rose from the barber chairs to be brushed off and to pay their bills. One of them indicated that he would like to speak with Uncle Dave and Sid privately. In a corner of the barbershop, the individual introduced himself as Ediston A. Vinson, the manager of the Loew's Vendomme Theater on Church Street in downtown Nashville. He had very much enjoyed their impromptu performance and was interested in booking them to play onstage. Vinson asked the duo to come to his office the next afternoon to discuss the possibilities of a contract.

Over the following hours, Uncle Dave got to know the young fiddler. Sidney J. Harkreader hailed from Gladeville, a small community near Lebanon, Tennessee, which lay twenty miles due east of Nashville. Born into abject poverty in 1898, his early life consisted of an incessant grind of demanding farm and house chores. Music was the family's preferred relief from backbreaking work, and Sid had demonstrated natural abilities at playing and singing. His first fiddle was a homemade affair his father assembled from dried cornstalks, broom wire, and horse hair. By age fifteen, Sid had collected enough money from trapping rabbits to order a fiddle from the Sears and Roebuck catalog for $3.95. The first fiddle tunes he learned were "Swanee River" and "Home Sweet Home." Sid believed that his natural ability on the fiddle was a gift from God, and before long, he was playing at events throughout his native Wilson County, receiving meals and petty cash as compensation. By age twenty-three, Sid believed the fiddle could free him from poverty, and he developed a burning desire to become a full-time musician. He headed to Nashville seeking opportunities, promoting himself as "Fiddlin' Sid." Some of the first steps of that journey carried him through the front door of Melton's Barbershop.

Sid Harkreader's timing was exquisite, because fiddle music had once again become the rage of the day. The fiddle had been the main instrument of frontier and mountain music, well before the widespread introduction of the banjo and guitar. During the last two decades of the nineteenth century, fiddle music was wildly popular, especially in the South. Fiddle tunes captured the exploits of revered American heroes, such as Davy Crockett and Andrew Jackson. Governor Bob Taylor, who served as Tennessee's chief executive for two terms, was known as the "fiddling governor." A respected fiddler in his own right, Taylor had incorporated fiddle contests and expositions into his election campaigns.

Rapid changes in technology and progressive social movements in the early 1920s created a desire in some quarters for the revival of older traditions as a counterbalance. On top of that, Americans were still reeling from the horrendous effects of the Spanish flu pandemic, World War I, and the economic recession that had followed the war, and they were simply ready for some fun. In terms of musical expression, the desire for a form of traditional entertainment meant listening to rollicking fiddle music. Often strange and eccentric fiddle players strutted their stuff at local, state, and regional fiddle contests, which sometimes lasted for days. In local communities, top fiddlers were respected artists who plied their artistry at hoedowns and barn dances. When record labels made their first recordings of old-time music in the early 1920s, fiddlers were the featured artists.

From Uncle Dave's perspective, gaining a musical partner who was good on the fiddle had several advantages. The addition of a fiddle would not only expand the repertoire of songs he could offer but would meet the popular demand for fiddle music. Sid could act as a straight man during comedic routines and allow other humorous, back-and-forth banter. A good vocalist, Sid's ability to sing harmony would add a new musical dimension to shows. Perhaps just as important, Sid already owned a Ford Model T, the possible solution to Uncle Dave's transportation problems. Within hours of first meeting, Uncle Dave and Fiddlin' Sid agreed to join together as a new duo act, sealing their oral agreement with a handshake.

The meeting the following afternoon with Ediston Vinson resulted in a significant career boost. The theater manager offered a three-week contract for the two to perform at the Loew's Vendomme, including a salary of $50 per week. Uncle Dave and Fiddlin' Sid readily agreed to the terms, and Vinson explained that the show would debut after some necessary advertising had taken place. The duo provided biographical information for press releases and posed for pictures for posters and newspaper advertising. A contract was soon executed, and the act was set to begin in the last weeks of the year.

When the duo debuted, they were a big hit. The show's opening was designed for dramatic effect. As the curtain rose, Uncle Dave rode to center stage in a small farm wagon pulled by two small mules. He sat in the wagon astride a log sawhorse wearing overalls, a red shirt with a matching bandana handkerchief, and a big, broad-brimmed straw hat. Dave played and sang as he rode, perhaps mimicking the rolling performances he had once conducted from a freight wagon. At the close of the opening number, Dave dismounted while Fiddlin' Sid joined him at center stage, and then the performance began in earnest. The thirty-minute show, which was called "Whoa Mule!" was cut from pure vaudeville cloth. At age fifty-one, Dave achieved the fulfillment of a dream that had first taken root when he was a teenager in Nashville in the 1880s.

The act ran for three weeks, and its success led immediately to other bookings. The Princess Theater in Springfield, Tennessee, about twenty miles north of Nashville, signed the duo and attracted large crowds. Word of mouth carried news of the act's success far and wide, and Uncle Dave and Fiddlin' Sid were soon on the road, appearing at venues all throughout Tennessee and southern Kentucky. Concert locations were as diverse as the types of songs they delivered. They began to play at banquets, business conventions, reunions, and regular meetings of civic groups. Small, rural shows at schools and churches remained a core segment of their touring schedule. In many respects, they provided a stark, visual contrast. Sid was young, tall, and slender while Dave was older, shorter, and rotund. The fiddler seldom smiled and was more intense with his music, while Dave was jocular and less concerned about hitting each note with perfection.

They traveled together in Sid's Model T. The agreement was for Sid to provide the car and do the driving while Uncle Dave paid for gasoline, oil, tires, and any necessary repairs. On the road, Sid observed some of the amusing and eccentric behavior that eventually became part of the Uncle Dave Macon legend. Concerned that he might not find his favorite food on the road, Uncle Dave always took along a thick cut of salt-cured country ham wrapped in wax paper or newspaper. He carried the wrapped meat into restaurants, asking the waitress to slice off a few pieces and have it cooked and served along with other side dishes. His favorite condiment was strawberry preserves, and he regularly carried a jar in one of his pockets, smearing the jam on pancakes. Whenever a curious waiter approached to see what he was doing, Uncle Dave would lean back, nod at the pancakes, and with a big grin exclaim, "You don't have anything like this, do you?" He also had the ability to sleep almost anywhere, an important advantage for one constantly traveling. He packed a thick blanket in the car, and when time allowed, would wrap himself in the covering and curl up on the back seat for a nap.

Safely crossing train tracks was a big concern. As a wagoner, Uncle Dave knew that mules and horses were always alert for locomotives, but he feared that the whirl of an automobile engine and the noise of other nearby trucks and cars might prevent drivers and passengers from clearly hearing an approaching train. At his partner's insistence, Sid stopped the Model T at every train crossing. Uncle Dave would dismount, peer intently in both directions, and after he was convinced that all was safe, he waved the car across the tracks using exaggerated hand gestures. Sometimes other people rode along, and whenever they expressed displeasure at the odd behavior, Dave would simply smile and murmur, "Better safe than sorry." The safety practice eventually paid off. A few years later, Uncle Dave and Sam McGee were nearly killed one dark, stormy night at a train crossing near Louisville, Kentucky, and only Uncle Dave's caution saved their lives.

If Uncle Dave sometimes exhibited eccentric behavior, Sid Harkreader had an obsession with money management. No money issue could be ignored or overlooked, even down to the management of the last penny, or even half-penny. Respectful of his partner's desires, Uncle Dave patiently endured Sid's financial micromanagement. Despite some personal differences, Uncle Dave and Sid had a very important and special bond: their respect for religion and love for the Bible. Both believed that their abilities to play, sing, and perform were God-given talents. They spent long hours in the car and at hotels discussing their religious beliefs and the Bible's historical narratives. More than likely, they learned from each other and even prayed together. Their faith cemented a personal bond that endured for decades.

When not traveling by car, the duo went by train, employing a touring method they called "bustin'." The two would rendezvous at Union Station in Nashville on a Monday morning and hop aboard a departing train, with the route to Chattanooga being one of their favorites. The train made frequent stops at small communities. Uncle Dave would pick a stop where he introduced himself to a storekeeper, played a tune, and told some funny stories. At length, he popped the key question: "Reckon we could get a few people around here tonight and put on a show for them?" Storekeepers nearly always favored the idea, and that night locals showed up to watch Uncle Dave and Sid perform from a storefront porch or the bed of an empty wagon. Sid recalled that several of these relaxed shows went on for nearly two hours, becoming "real old-fashioned hoedowns." They passed a hat for tips and routinely made as much as $25 per show. The next morning, they were back on the train and looking for their next stop. By week's end, the duo would return to Nashville.

At another show in Walter Hill, Tennessee, Uncle Dave and Sid were robbed. Promoters were collecting admissions at the front door and, lacking a suitable container to hold the money, Sid loaned them his hat. As the show started, the organizers passed the hat with the money inside to the fiddler who unknowingly placed it on a table near an open window. Sometime during the evening performance, a thief reached in through the window, purloining the money as well as the hat. Afterward, Uncle Dave and Sid were disappointed that their money was gone, but most of all, Sid was furious that someone actually had the gall to steal another man's hat and that he had to go home that night bareheaded.

Uncle Dave always desired great relations with his fans, but frequent shows sometimes resulted in oddball encounters. One night, as he and Sid greeted fans following a show, an elderly man charged up and exclaimed, "Uncle Dave, I want you to go home with me! My wife was unable to attend tonight, and she needs to see you." Uncle Dave studied the man with a puzzled look before replying. "Why should I go home with you?" he retorted. "I don't know you or your wife, and I've already made arrangements to stay at a hotel tonight." Not deterred, the man fired back: "She thinks she's married to the ugliest man in the world, and I want her to see you so she can see it isn't so." Uncle Dave and Sid slowly backed away to turn and talk to other guests.

At one show, the crowd was especially animated, stomping their feet and clapping throughout the performance. As one number came to a close, an excited young man staring at Uncle Dave from the front row suddenly jumped forward and screamed: "Where in the hell are you from?" Not startled one bit, Uncle Dave flashed the fellow a wild-eyed look, jutted out his chin, and shouted back: "And what part of hell are you from?" Without missing a beat, Uncle Dave instantly jumped into the next number to keep the high spirits rolling. He was always ready with punchlines and one-liners certain to make audiences laugh. Whenever Uncle Dave related an incident in which he had encountered an unusual or peculiar person, the story ended with: "Folks, when Columbus discovered America the land was filled with nuts and berries, and now the berries are just about all gone!"

On one occasion, Uncle Dave simply lost his cool. While busking on the sidewalk of the courthouse lawn in Shelbyville, Tennessee, a dusty car with Michigan plates pulled over suddenly, stopping at the curb. The driver called out from a lowered window with a northern accent, explaining that he was lost and looking for the best road to Chattanooga. Uncle Dave paused for a moment, eyeing the car's license plate as he gathered his thoughts. Perhaps he was reacting to the heat or just having a bad day, but Uncle Dave fired back. "Sir, I'm not going to tell you how to get to Chattanooga. Your ancestors had no trouble finding Chattanooga in 1863, so you shouldn't either. Now you go on and get outta here!"

For nearly three years, Uncle Dave and Fiddlin' Sid traversed the countryside, playing wherever they were welcomed. Their second big break came in the fall of 1924. A furniture retailer in Murfreesboro was Uncle Dave's good friend, and one day he called the house in Kittrell with an offer. A group of Southern furniture retailers were having a convention in Chattanooga soon, and the man was helping to organize the event, including the entertainment. Would Uncle Dave and Fiddlin' Sid consider performing at the convention during the main evening banquet? Arrangements were completed, and the duo were soon off to Chattanooga.

Before the age of music shops, electronics stores, and big-box retailers, phonographs and records were sold in furniture stores. Early phonographs came dressed in elaborate, shiny wooden cabinets, making them just as decorative as they were functional. Retailers often promoted them as furniture accessory items, in addition to their functionality as a record player. Mounting phonograph sales prompted furniture retailers to begin offering records as yet another way to promote sales in their showrooms.

In the early 1920s, Sterchi Brothers Furniture Company was the largest furniture retailer in the Southeast with eighteen stores. Its new, ten-story headquarters building in downtown Knoxville dominated that city's skyline. Sterchi's aggressively sponsored regional musicians on radio programs and at store locations in order to boost phonograph and record sales. As a result, the furniture chain had become a major distributor for Vocalion Records, a subsidiary of the Aeolian Piano Company, both based in New York City.

When Uncle Dave and Sid arrived in Chattanooga, they made their way to the massive Read House, one of the city's landmark hotels in downtown and the site of the furniture convention. It's hard to imagine Uncle Dave going to his room and passively awaiting show time. More than likely, he put on an impromptu, charismatic performance in the hotel lobby—as was his custom—in order to meet guests, build hype for the pending performance, and solicit invites to play elsewhere.

The evening's show, done under the sparkling lights of the Waterford Crystal chandeliers that decorated the Read House's banquet room, must have been especially memorable. The performers were probably unaware that in the audience were Sterchi executives who were specifically looking for new talent to make records to sell in their stores. Immediately following the performance, Charles C. Rutherford, one of those very men, approached Uncle Dave and Fiddlin' Sid. A man apparently used to deal making, Rutherford came right to the point.

"How would you boys like to go to New York City and record records for Sterchi Brothers?" the executive asked. "We sell a lot of records, and we'd like for you to go up there and represent the state of Tennessee. You'll make some money, and it would be an honor for you to go." Uncle Dave and Sid probably stared at the executive in disbelief at such a golden opportunity. The two performers shared a quick glance, and without a second thought, Uncle Dave turned back to Rutherford and exclaimed: "OK, we'll go!"

At the start of the 1920s, the American recording industry was in a state of transition. Thomas Edison had invented the phonograph in 1877, but the inventor perceived his recording and playback device as a tool for legal, business, and educational matters rather than entertainment. Another inventor, Emile Berliner, understood the potential for mass-producing recording for entertainment. Berliner made his vision a reality with the invention of a phonograph that could play flat disc records. Before World War I, record players were largely a plaything of the rich, and recordings reflected the tastes of affluent and educated city dwellers. Among the most popular early records were John Philip Sousa marches, Al Jolson show tunes, and a host of jazz and classical orchestral offerings. A number of record companies became big business, including such names as Victor, OKeh, and others. By 1914, annual, national record sales had reached over half a million, and within five years, sales had ballooned to two million units. Record sales peaked in 1921 at $105 million, a sum that would not again be surpassed until after World War II.

The dawn of commercial radio put a dent in record sales; the slowdown was simple economics. Working-class people were more inclined to invest discretionary income in a rudimentary radio set and listen to free broadcasting rather than continue to pay higher prices for phonographs and records. Hoping to revive sales, record company executives went searching for new markets and talents. One musical genre with possible sales potential was easy to recognize by sound, but hard to label with a single word; it was known variously as *old-time, mountain music, barn-dance,* and even *hillbilly.*

The very first recording of such music came in New York City in June 1922. Fiddler A. C. "Eck" Robertson, accompanied by fellow fiddler Henry Gilliland, recorded their version of "Arkansas Traveler" on the Victor label. At the same session, Robertson delivered a remarkable rendition of "Sally Gooden." Victor finally released the two cuts in April 1923. Over the next year, the label released two more records from the same session, which enjoyed respectable sales.

Meanwhile, other record companies were looking for Southern, old-time musicians to record. The OKeh Record Company found their man in the form of "Fiddlin' John" Carson, who had already distinguished himself as the seven-time Georgia state fiddling champion. In June 1923, Carson recorded "Little Old Log Cabin in the Lane" and "Old Hen Cackled" during an OKeh field recording session in Atlanta. Not overly impressed with the recordings, OKeh executives—including the legendary Ralph Peer who was OKeh's general recording manager at the time—at first approved the record for only limited release and sale in the Atlanta area. But Southern listeners thought otherwise; the record quickly sold nearly 20,000 copies and ultimately went on to garner sales of nearly half a million nationwide.

Fiddlin' John Carson's success taught record companies that Southern, old-time music was an untapped market, and they quickly sought new artists. It was natural then for Sterchi's to invite Uncle Dave and Fiddlin' Sid to New York City for a recording session. Uncle Dave had heard his first old-time music recording at a small town in Kentucky during one of his earliest tours. The incident made such an impression that Uncle Dave left his own account:

> On the way to the depot, I passed a large crowd in front of a music store. Thinking some accident had occurred, I stopped to inquire, but they were listening to records made by a Kentucky man, George Reneau, playing and singing on his guitar. They asked me how I liked it. I replied "very good for a guitar, but I believe I can beat it with my banjo."

A trip to New York City to make records presented Uncle Dave with an opportunity to strut his stuff before a national audience and convince listeners that he was indeed "the world's most outstanding banjoist."

The trip north began with a stop in Knoxville. Uncle Dave and Fiddlin' Sid made their way to Sterchi's tall office building downtown to meet executives, learn the details of travel and recording arrangements, and pick up necessary paperwork. Sterchi's agreed to pay all travel expenses, which the two were to record dutifully in a small notebook. In addition, they were to stop in Knoxville on their way back to render a report on the recording session and to turn in their travel records for reimbursement. Having run his own small business for twenty years, Uncle Dave was comfortable with all the arrangements and the requirement to keep good travel and pay records.

The duo were soon on the train to New York City, arriving there probably on the afternoon of Monday, July 7, 1924. The physical and cultural shock Uncle Dave and Fiddlin' Sid experienced as they arrived must have been jarring. As they strode beneath the high, vaulted arches of Grand Central Station's main lobby, no one could have blamed them for thinking they had just landed on another planet. The towering skyscrapers, crowded streets, and constant hustle and bustle of midtown Manhattan were at the extreme opposite end of the spectrum for two men used to the slower-paced, rural farm life of Middle Tennessee. To overcome the challenges of recording in New York City, Uncle Dave relied upon a tried and true philosophy, which he used in any new situation: remain supremely confident, do your best, and never let them see you sweat!

Uncle Dave's first recording session was a landmark moment in his career and merits a detailed recounting of events. Sterchi's had booked the duo into the Hotel Times Square on 43rd Street in midtown Manhattan for a stay of nearly a week. Vocalion's recording facility was located within the Aeolian Hall building, which stood at 33 West 42nd Street, easy walking distance from the hotel. Uncle Dave and Fiddlin' Sid first stepped into a recording studio on Tuesday, July 8. There they encountered the acoustic horn, an older recording device that captured the sounds of vocals and instruments, channeling the vibrations to a wooden stylus that cut wax master cylinders. The acoustic horn recording method, which had been around since the late 1870s, produced scratchy recordings dogged with echoes. Furthermore, the device had difficulty picking up weak vocals and instruments with less volume. But with his booming voice and loud banjo projections, Uncle Dave Macon was just the type of performer best suited for acoustic horn recordings.

Vocalion put Uncle Dave hard to work on the very first day. He performed a total of thirteen cuts on five separate tunes, resulting in ten different master recordings. Compared to future recording sessions, the work of July 8 was rather sedate with straightforward renditions. Uncle Dave recorded five songs in all—"Keep My Skillet Good and Greasy," "Hill Billie Blues," "Old Maid's Last Hope," "All I've Got's Gone," and "The Fox Chase"—with several of them becoming career songs he often played and would rerecord in coming years. As always, Uncle Dave sang about common themes, both uplifting and perverse, which appealed to basic human instincts and the personal experiences of his listeners. The subjects included love and romance, faith and salvation, money, food, the beautiful countryside, and horses and mules as well as whiskey, moonshine, and automobiles. The banjo came off sharp and clear, including several frantic runs of varied notes that reflected the strength and intricacy of his picking. Uncle Dave's high-pitched voice had adequate range and terrific volume, but he was not the best singer, often straining to hit high notes.

By the end of the session, Uncle Dave was warmed up and full of vigor. Vocalion wanted to record a "descriptive novelty," a song that painted a vivid picture of one aspect of life in the rural South, and Uncle Dave cut loose with "The Fox Chase." He sang of Pilot Knob, the high, bald hill near his own home in Kittrell, describing the actions of his own dog, "Rockwood," while on the hunt. Filled with whoops and shouts, the song certainly captures the spirit and sound of Uncle Dave's live performances.

The second day was just as prolific, but with poor technical results. Uncle Dave and Fiddlin' Sid crowded together before the acoustic horn, performing ten cuts of five additional songs. Uncle Dave had a personal motto— "It ain't what you got, it's what you can put out, and I can deliver!"—and his high-spirited enthusiasm in the recording studio made for trouble. The steady, rhythmic thumping of Uncle Dave's left foot on the floor as he kept time while picking the banjo came through on recordings and even jostled the recording needle. When engineers asked Uncle Dave to play without stomping his foot so hard, he replied that he simply couldn't. They finally came up with a novel solution: someone found a small pillow and tied it to his left foot with a belt to muffle the racket. It would not be the last time Uncle Dave caused a ruckus in the recording studio. In the end, Vocalion decided that only one recording from the day's session, "Papa's Billy Goat," was acceptable for release. The other four songs—"Muskrat Medley," "Old Ship of Zion," "Just from Tennessee," and "That High Born Gal of Mine"— would be rerecorded in following years.

At nearly the same time, another type of jarring event took place that was more psychological and financial than physical. During a session break, a Vocalion executive explained the process of royalty payments from record sales. To ease the administrative burden of distributing royalties, Vocalion's policy was to pay only the primary artist rather than all participating musicians. Fiddlin' Sid was understandably taken aback at the news, but Uncle Dave quickly assured him that the two would draw up a fair and equitable written contract as soon as they returned home. Uncle Dave was entitled to only a 2 percent royalty on each record sold, the standard mechanical royalty rate of the day mandated by law. At the going sales price of 75 cents per record, the royalty payment due was 1.5 cents per record. A second financial issue soon arose. Even though Sterchi's had agreed to reimburse all trip expenses, Sid had woefully underestimated the costs of staying, eating, and working in The Big Apple and had not brought enough cash with him. Not long into their stay, Sid was broke. Uncle Dave patiently loaned his junior partner $37 to cover his expenses until they returned to Tennessee.

Trips back and forth between the recording studio and the hotel resulted in encounters with locals, which became part of the Macon legend. The sight of the dapper Tennessean strolling down the sidewalks of Manhattan in full suit and tie, wearing a black fedora hat, carrying a banjo case with his name on it, and grinning all the while, certainly piqued the interests of native New Yorkers. One exchange went something like this:

NEW YORKER: You're not from around here are you, old man?

UNCLE DAVE: No, sir, I'm surely not.

NEW YORKER: Have you ever been to New York City before?

UNCLE DAVE: No, sir, I haven't.

NEW YORKER: I'll bet you've never seen anything as big as New York City then, have you?

UNCLE DAVE: Yes, sir, I have. I was born and raised in the hills of Tennessee, and they are a lot bigger than New York City!

Another marathon recording session ensued on Thursday, July 11, which included thirteen takes of five different tunes. The session began with Sid centering himself on the acoustic horn to deliver the main vocals for "The Little Old Log Cabin in the Lane." Uncle Dave backed his partner on the banjo and joined in the chorus. The next song, "Chewing Gum," became an Uncle Dave classic, even though a later arrangement became the more favored version. For the first time on a recording, Uncle Dave introduced the main tune with a banjo prelude, a brief rendition of "Shortenin' Bread," a technique he surely used in his live performances.

The third recording was "Jonah and the Whale," a popular hymn in Southern Methodist churches at the time. It recounts the rigors the reluctant prophet Jonah experienced in carrying out his God-given assignment to preach repentance in ancient Nineveh, "a city that was steeped in awful sin." At first refusing his divine mission, Jonah boarded a ship and sailed in the opposite direction, until a storm swept him overboard and a whale swallowed him whole, finally depositing him safely back on land and toward Nineveh. Going beyond the biblical narrative, Uncle Dave presented listeners with a moral lesson in song:

> Some people don't believe that a whale could him receive,
> But that does not make my song at all untrue.
> There are whales on every side,
> With their big mouths open wide,
> Just take care, my friend, or one might swaller you!

By now comfortable in the recording studio, Uncle Dave next let loose with "I'm Going Away to Love You, Love." Music historian Charles Wolfe best described the recording as "a high-spirited collection of free-floating lyrics." Uncle Dave smacks his lips to mimic kissing sounds and then delivers a series of hollers and owl-like hoots. The tune reflects the tradition in old-time music that raw enthusiasm and energy are more important than perfectly rhymed lyrics. That day's session ended with Sid Harkreader recording two classic fiddle tunes, "Love Somebody" and "Soldier's Joy." The first song, a quick-paced banjo and fiddle duet, is a lasting example of Uncle Dave and Fiddlin' Sid at work, demonstrating a format that was very popular in the day.

Sometime during the visit, an unexpected call came for Uncle Dave at his hotel. An old friend was on the line, a banker Uncle Dave had known in Murfreesboro years earlier. The man had done well for himself, eventually moving to New York City to take a position with a prominent bank and becoming a leader in the Southern Bankers' Society. The society was having a big meeting at the Hotel Astor on Times Square that very week, and the banker asked if Uncle Dave could perform at their evening banquet. Not the least intimidated to play on such short notice before a prominent group at a celebrated hotel, Uncle Dave gladly accepted. Other entertainers performed that night, but Uncle Dave and Fiddlin' Sid, now newly minted recording artists, were introduced as the stars of the show. Playing under the high, arched ivory and gold ceilings of the Hotel Astor's renowned banquet hall, which often served as a meeting place for New York's political bosses, Wall Street tycoons, and industrial barons, the two Tennesseans were about as far removed as possible from their normal performance venue at small schools and churches in the rural South. Undaunted by their surroundings, the duo delivered a rousing performance. As Uncle Dave and Fiddlin' Sid left the Hotel Astor, members of the Southern Bankers' Society showed their appreciation by paying them $50 apiece in gold coins.

At one point, Vocalion's studio had already booked a recording session with a band, so the Tennesseans had several hours free to see more of New York City. Uncle Dave decided he needed a haircut and proceeded to a nearby salon. At age fifty-three, he was already bald, but his long sideburns, chin whiskers, and goatee needed a trim. After the barber finished, Uncle Dave decided a shave and shoeshine were in order; after all he was traveling on Sterchi's dime. When the services were complete, Uncle Dave stood up, posing the same question he always used in restaurants and stores: "How much do I owe you?" He must have nearly keeled over when the barber quoted the exorbitant price of $8.50. Never allowing himself to appear flustered or surprised in unexpected situations, he grinned and declared, "That's cheap! I figured it would be a lot more than that." However, an entry in Uncle Dave's travel expense book revealed his true reaction: "Robbed in the barber shop of $8.50." A week later, that notation prompted a ripple of laughter among the clerks in Sterchi's accounting department.

Uncle Dave returned to his hotel following the salon robbery, and with extra time on his hands, he decided to play for a while in the lobby. As always, he enjoyed entertaining other guests and passersby. New Yorkers seemed to love his music and antics just as much as Southerners. Time got away from him, and he soon realized that he was late for his recording session. Uncle Dave and Sid dashed to the studio, profusely apologizing for their tardiness. Vocalion's engineers took it all in stride and the recording session was soon underway. By this last session on July 11, Uncle Dave was relaxed and hitting his stride. There were two takes of "Bile Them Cabbage Down," which also would become a big hit. New York City's subways, elevated trains, and crowded streets must have made a big impression, but Uncle Dave by now was ready to head home. He performed a prelude on the banjo and then offered a spoken introduction:

Now, I'm a way up here where these cars run under the ground and over my head bothered with side cars and folks, and I'm like the poor, lonesome nigger who got lost one night, praying to the Lord. He began to sing, "Lord, I wonder when will I ever get back home, get back home."

Between verses Uncle Dave added spoken tidbits about life "back home," including topics as diverse as riding mules, eating "slapjacks and molasses," and dealing with misbehaving dogs. "Down by the River" completed the four-day recording session. Uncle Dave and Fiddlin' Sid had recorded a total of eighteen songs in forty takes, and Vocalion would go on to release fourteen of them. The 1924 New York City recording session established Uncle Dave and Fiddlin' Sid as recording stars and propelled them to new highs as professional entertainers.

A close listen to these very first recordings reveals that Uncle Dave already possessed a unique and complex picking style. His favorite method was a repetitive, three-finger roll that was more intricate than clawhammer style, a rudimentary playing technique from Appalachia that most banjo players employed in the 1920s. Among the three-finger rolls are interspersed strumming, clawhammer and other individual fingerpicking. One can also hear arpeggio, a classical construct of cascading notes, which was much more sophisticated than common mountain playing styles. More than likely, Uncle Dave learned these more intricate playing techniques while observing vaudeville and semiprofessional artists in Nashville in the late 1880s. In all, Uncle Dave had a unique picking style, which no one was able to imitate at the time or ever afterward.

Uncle Dave was singular as an old-time vocalist in the early 1920s—fiddlers and string bands predominated at the time—and he skillfully used the banjo to further accentuate his vocals. Instead of his voice following the musical lead of his instrument, Uncle Dave used the banjo to support and reinforce his singing. One of his favorite playing techniques was unison notes, in which the notes plucked on the banjo strings perfectly matched his voice. By using the same, precise melody on vocals and instrument, the banjo literally sang along with him. While G is the standard key for a five-string banjo, Uncle Dave often dropped the key from G to F in order to match his singing voice. In all, Uncle Dave used spoken introductions, instrumental preludes, and unique singing and picking methods to generate a style and sound in his recordings and appearances that no one had ever heard.

On Saturday, July 12, the duo from Tennessee were back on the train and headed home. The trip south resulted in one of the most unusual occurrences in Uncle Dave's public career. Prohibition was in full enforcement, but the railroads had devised a way to get around restrictions on serving alcohol. On long trips, passengers could pay a ticket surcharge, which gave them access to a private club car, a type of rolling speakeasy, where liquor flowed freely. When patrons in the private car realized that Uncle Dave Macon was on board, they invited him to come and play for them. Perhaps flushed with success in the aftermath of his great recording session and relieved to be headed home, Uncle Dave put on an animated performance, no doubt fueled by alcohol.

Sometime during the carousing, Uncle Dave suggested that Fiddlin' Sid should join them; together they could make even better music for the revelers. A porter soon found Sid and escorted him to the private car, but he didn't stay very long. After a few duets, Sid decided that things were getting too boisterous for his tastes and excused himself, returning to his coach. Late that evening, the train made a brief stop in Richmond and then headed west on an overnight run across the Appalachians with only a few stops.

The next morning, the train arrived at its final destination in Knoxville. Sid got off and waited on the platform for his partner. A few minutes later, the train pulled out with no sign of Uncle Dave. Not sure what else to do, Sid proceeded to Sterchi's corporate headquarters alone to turn in his travel vouchers and render a report on the recording session. At one point, Sterchi executives naturally asked about Uncle Dave's whereabouts. Sid replied that they had left New York together but that his partner had taken up with others en route and was now simply missing.

The next morning Uncle Dave arrived in Knoxville, making his way to Sterchi's headquarters to report that the recording session had been splendid and to turn in his travel voucher. While there, Uncle Dave and Sid drew up a simple, one-page written contract to specify the distribution of record royalties from Vocalion. At some point, Uncle Dave pulled Sid aside for a private consultation. At the invitation of some of those who had partied with him on the train, he had gotten off during a stop in Lynchburg, Virginia, to spend the night.

"I'm worried to death about what happened," Uncle Dave confided. "I'm afraid that I might have said something to offend them, especially some of the wives." Sid told him to forget about the whole incident; if something truly egregious had occurred, Uncle Dave would have been arrested or "beaten up." But Uncle Dave continued to fret about the episode and finally decided he would return to Lynchburg in an attempt to locate his hosts and render apologies. The next morning, Sid boarded a train heading west to Nashville, while Uncle Dave climbed onto a train headed back east. It is unknown what transpired when Uncle Dave arrived in Lynchburg; no one even mentioned the incident again until decades later. Whatever happened in Lynchburg stayed in Lynchburg, but true to his character, Uncle Dave had tried to make amends.

Vocalion immediately released their new Uncle Dave Macon recordings. The first record came out in September 1924 with "Keep My Skillet Good and Greasy" on one side and "Papa's Billie Goat" on the reverse. The following month, Vocalion released two more records. To draw attention to Uncle Dave as a new recording artist, Vocalion pressed the original 78 rpm issues in red shellac instead of the standard black color. Those first releases included an important milestone for the fledgling country music recording industry. "Hill Billie Blues" was the first recorded song to have some form of the term *hillbilly* in its title, and when Vocalion issued the record, it was the first time the term ever appeared on a record label. Uncle Dave first saw one of his own records when an advance copy arrived in the mail from New York shortly before its national release. He was thrilled to see his name in print on that very first recording.

A short time later, Uncle Dave ventured to a furniture store in Murfreesboro that regularly stocked and sold records. There, for the first time, he saw his records available for sale to the public. That surely made a large, lasting impression. He took a seat, and for the longest time, just sat there, staring at the record in his hand and lost in his own thoughts. His energy, good business sense, and innate talents as a songster and banjoist had enabled him to become a successful entertainer who had already procured a recording contract with a national label and was wildly popular on tour. Even more would come soon.

If things were rapidly changing in Uncle Dave's music career, a similar transformation was taking place at home. During Dave's frequent absences, Miss Tildy captained the ship. The amount of farm cultivation had declined greatly because of Dave's travels, but there were still so many things to tend to on the homestead. Despite her great devotion to her family and the farm, and her tremendous capacity for hard, physical work, Tildy soon needed relief.

A middle-aged black couple in Kittrell, Houston and Myrtle Jones, soon came on the scene as hired help. Houston was short, the same height as Uncle Dave, and everyone called him "Stump." He acted as the groundskeeper and general maintenance man for the house and farm. Myrtle, whom the Macon's called "Aunt Myrt," was tall and slender like Miss Tildy and walked with quick, long strides. Aunt Myrt was an excellent cook who seemed to glide effortlessly about the kitchen as she prepared meals. Everyone agreed that she was one of the best cooks ever. Aunt Myrt would feed the family and a wide range of visitors to the home, from well-heeled Hollywood film executives to downtrodden, Depression-era drifters. Stump and Aunt Myrt became a near-constant presence at the Macon household for the next twenty years.

When Uncle Dave came home after several days on the road, he had a habit of staying in close proximity to Tildy. She had an abiding interest in his travels, and the two would sit together on the front porch or in chairs pulled close together before the fireplace while Dave described the people and sights he had encountered. In return, Tildy would bring her husband up to speed on family matters and local news. She was always aware of his business dealings, including the percentages paid to promoters and record companies, even though she never took an active role in managing his career. One time Dave told her that a promoter for an upcoming show had reduced the performance percentage already promised due to higher, unexpected costs at that particular venue. Tildy frowned, declaring that the promoter was probably just trying to rob Dave outright. Always protective of her husband, Tildy suggested that Dave call the promoter in order to demand his original, promised pay. When Dave balked at the suggestion, Tildy declared that if he didn't do it, she would.

Dave continued his habit of regular attendance at Haynes Chapel whenever he was home. One Sunday in 1922, he noticed that the church's original wooden shingles, which had been installed in 1887, had greatly deteriorated. Following the service, Dave pulled the preacher aside to point out the problem. The man replied that he was aware of the situation but that the church lacked funds for the repairs. Dave told the minister to have the entire roof replaced and to send him the bill.

With his music career in full swing, Dave dedicated much of his time at home to further practice on the banjo, learning new songs, and original songwriting. The first step in songwriting was sole, solitary concentration. Dave would pace back and forth inside the house or on the front porch, or walk alone through the fields. He pondered the melody and lyrics as a whole, working out all the details in his mind, even before he touched an instrument. When he was comfortable enough with his work, Dave would play a verse or two, or perhaps the chorus, to family members, friends, and other local musicians and then ask their opinion. Once he was satisfied with the composition and had mastered the song on the banjo, it would be introduced at shows and the crowd reaction gauged. In addition to writing songs with traditional themes, Dave began to compose new comedic and protest tunes, especially within the social context of Prohibition, women's suffrage and the new teaching of evolution in public schools.

Annie Macon became a driving force in her brother's songwriting efforts. On days when Annie's kids were at school, Dave rode in a horse and buggy to her house in Readyville for a day of practice and composition. As Dave picked his banjo, Annie played along on her piano, helping her brother to choose the best melodies and lyrics for new songs. Knowing Tildy's relative indifference to Dave's music, Annie kept most of the sheet music and composition notes at her house. At other times, Annie came to the house in Kittrell, where she played the same family piano she and Dave had relished as children at Macon Manor in Warren County. Brother and sister thoroughly enjoyed themselves during sessions marked with frequent outbursts of fun and laughter. Occasional passersby on the Woodbury Road heard piano and banjo music emanating from the house, interspersed with loud merriment and hilarity, as Dave and Annie held their practice and composition sessions.

A second musical partner in the local community was Uncle Dave's long-time chum, Mazy Todd. Mazy had abandoned his Readyville blacksmith shop in 1917 to move to Kittrell. There he operated a sawmill on a parcel of commercial land just across the road from the Macon home. In addition to working and raising four daughters, he regularly played the banjo and fiddle, mastering a fluid playing style on the fiddle that most people had never heard. Mazy was a frequent guest in the Macon household, playing sets with Uncle Dave before the fireplace or outside on the long, open porch.

The Macon family was undergoing its own changes as well. The boys were growing up, discovering their own interests and desires. In 1922, Archie left home to strike out on his own. It was a particularly emotional moment for

Dave. He told his oldest son that he had been the best of hands and that he hated to see him leave. Standing on the front porch, Dave broke down crying. Archie told his father not to give him so much credit and that he still had six other sons to rely upon. As a parting gift, Dave handed his son $25, nearly a full month's wage at the time for manual laborers. Archie and a friend traveled to Nashville "seeking fame and fortune," but all they found was "a pick and shovel." A month later Archie was back home. Suspecting that his son was unable to find good work, Dave arranged a driving job for him with one of the rival trucking companies that had prompted the closure of his own freight business. Dave encouraged his son to work for himself rather than others, advice that Archie took a few years later when he opened his own blacksmith shop.

While basking in the glow from his first recording session and record releases, Dave Macon once again had to deal with a sudden family loss. Archie had married a local girl, Melissa Weeks, in October 1923, and she was soon pregnant. The child was due in August 1924, the month following Dave's first recording session. Dave and Tildy were surely happy, expectant grandparents, but when the delivery date came, the infant was stillborn. A day or so later, the Macons gathered for the burial at Coleman Cemetery, where Dave had purchased two long rows of grave plots eight years earlier. Sadly, the first ground broken there was to bury Dave and Tildy's first grandchild.

Dave's success seemed to dampen the frequency and intensity of his bouts with alcoholism and depression, but both occasionally reared their ugly heads. The anecdotal evidence seems to suggest that he became more of a maintenance drinker, even though it was still within him to indulge in a bedridden, drunken bender. Planning and coordinating his music career kept his mind free of the distortions of depression, but those moments still cropped up. One time Archie stopped by the house to talk to his father, and he found him out in the fields resting under a shade tree while sitting on the tongue of a plow behind a mule. Dave sat morose and silent, a far cry from his normal demeanor. When he finally spoke, Dave indicated that he was still fretting over the money owed to the Bowling family from the dispute over Tildy's dowry. On this rare occasion, Archie had had enough of his father's fretting. Archie turned on his heels and walked away, but not before telling his father that he should pay off his debts just like everyone else and then forget about the whole situation.

Dave's travels greatly curtailed routine farming activities, but from time to time he still undertook special chores. One day he decided to clear a parcel of land using dynamite to remove stubborn stumps and rocks. A work gang was assembled, with Dave in charge and Archie assisting. Dave directed the clearing work and the placement of explosives, relishing his role as the head boss. After lighting the fuses, he would hurriedly scamper away a safe distance to escape harm from the violent explosions and flying debris. Suddenly, Dave stopped dead in his tracks, standing with hands on hips and staring across the fields lost in his own thoughts. Moments later, he abruptly turned toward the house and strode away. Archie thought little of the incident, assuming that his father was returning to the house to tend to a forgotten chore or to use the outhouse. Fifteen minutes passed, and then a half hour. Becoming concerned, Archie told the crew to take a break and then left to check on his father. He soon reached the house, and stepping into the main room, found his father sitting in his favorite chair near the fireplace and reading a newspaper.

"Pap, is everything all right?" Archie asked with concern. At the sound of his son's voice, Dave lowered the paper and looked up.

"Sure," Dave replied without concern.

"Are you coming back out to help us?"

"Nope," Dave answered as he took off his reading glasses. Archie paused a moment, puzzled by his father's behavior.

"If you don't mind," Archie finally responded, "can you say why you're not coming back out to help us?"

"Arch, something dawned on me all of a sudden when I was out there." The newspaper fell into his lap as Dave raised his hands before him with the palms facing outward. The long fingers which allowed him to pick the banjo with such acumen stretched upward toward the ceiling. "I've got money in my fingers! All I've got to do is pick it out on the banjo. And I can't do that if I blow 'em up handling that dynamite. So from now on, you and the other boys will be takin' care of all the dynamitin'." And with that pronouncement, Dave picked up his newspaper, replaced his glasses and went back to reading. Archie left the house with a chuckle, amused at his father's eccentric behavior but fully appreciating the wisdom of his words.

Sam Fleming McGee stood completely mesmerized on the lawn of the Williamson County Courthouse on the public square in Franklin, Tennessee. He had come to town one morning in the late summer of 1924 from his farm in nearby Peytonsville to purchase materials for his blacksmith shop. An unexpected commotion on the courthouse lawn caught his attention, and when he joined a gathering crowd, Sam observed a man in a fancy suit and hat playing the banjo and singing with tremendous energy and charisma. The entertainer was continuous action and motion, telling stories and jokes and spitting out hilarious one-liners between songs. A musician himself, Sam fully appreciated the banjoist's playing abilities. When Sam returned home, he told his wife that he had just witnessed "the funniest man I had ever seen." Such was the first encounter between Sam McGee and Uncle Dave Macon.

Sam McGee had been born into a family of amateur musicians in 1894. His father was a fiddle player, as was his younger brother, Kirk. Realizing that his family did not need another fiddler, Sam decided to try a less popular instrument. At a young age, he picked up the acoustic guitar. He developed a fresh, innovative playing style that incorporated blues styles into old-time music and made his guitar produce sound patterns normally heard only on the piano and harmonica. For years, Sam practiced in solitude, playing only in public at family and local events.

Several weeks after seeing Uncle Dave in downtown Franklin, Sam noticed a handbill posted in a store announcing a performance by Uncle Dave and Fiddlin' Sid at a local school. On the night of the show, Sam sat near the very front, enjoying every single moment. When the event ended, Sam stepped forward to tell the duo how much he enjoyed their performance. A conversation ensued, and before it was over, Sam invited Uncle Dave and Sid to stay at his house overnight. Apparently the hour was late, and facing a very long drive back to their homes in Kittrell and Lebanon, the two were glad to spend the night locally.

When they all arrived at Sam's home, Uncle Dave and Sid were still feeling the energy from their performance. They broke out their instruments and continued playing. A humble man who was a bit intimidated by Uncle Dave's already established reputation, Sam was reluctant to join the jam session. During a pause, Uncle Dave noticed Sam's Martin guitar standing in the corner of the room and asked if he played. When Sam replied that he did, Uncle Dave invited him to play a song.

Sam took up his guitar and performed "Missouri Waltz." What Uncle Dave saw and heard that evening impressed him a great deal. Sam's guitar work made it sound as though his instrument was producing both rhythm and melody at the same time. Uncle Dave realized that Sam McGee was an exceptional guitarist with the potential to perform on stage. He had a pleasant disposition to boot, with qualities that appealed to Uncle Dave: an unassuming humility, a ready laugh, and a willingness to work. By the time Sam finished the number, Uncle Dave was a believer. "Would you like to come with me if I could book us a few dates?" the elder musician asked. Without hesitation, Sam replied that he would be honored to perform with Uncle Dave.

Uncle Dave and Fiddlin' Sid continued to entertain at various locations throughout the fall of 1924, until one day Sid received an unexpected call at his home in Mt. Juliet. On the line was Ediston Vinson, the same theater manager who had first booked the duo at the Loew's Vendomme in Nashville. Vinson had since moved to Birmingham, Alabama, where he now managed the Loew's Bijou. He posed the same question from nearly three years earlier: would Uncle Dave and Fiddlin' Sid be interested in playing a three-week stint?

Uncle Dave and Fiddlin' Sid arrived in Birmingham just after Christmas Day 1924. They were set to debut at the Bijou's "New Year's Eve Midnight Frolic," and rehearsals and promotional events were necessary. Vinson had asked the duo to include other performers in their act. Uncle Dave enlisted a popular dancer, "Dancin' Bob" Bradford, who has been described as "a tap dancer and old-time flat foot buck dancer." In an effort to elicit the same response Uncle Dave and Fiddlin' Sid had enjoyed years earlier in Nashville, manager Vinson planned for the show to start with Uncle Dave riding to center stage in a wagon pulled by a team of mules, playing all the time while dressed in a big straw hat, a red shirt, and overalls. As testimony to his growing popularity, Uncle Dave garnered pay of $100 per week, double the salary he had earned from Loew's three years earlier.

The show debuted just after New Year's Day 1925 and was a colossal hit. During the main act Uncle Dave performed a battery of his favorite tunes, including "Keep My Skillet Good and Greasy," "Chewing Gum," "Jonah and the Whale," "Arkansas Traveler," and "I Might Be Ugly, but Not Lonesome." Three daily performances occurred: an afternoon matinee and two evening shows. To round out the two-hour routine, five other acts appeared, including a comedian, two musical duets, a Broadway singer and a musical troupe described as a "Gypsy-Spanish Review." At one point, a live dancing bear even appeared on stage. At the end of the first week, Vinson was thrilled with ticket sales and asked if the trio might add another musician. Sid Harkreader fired off a telegram to Franklin, Tennessee, and the next evening Sam McGee arrived in Birmingham by train carrying his Martin guitar. Sam was just as natural as a stage performer as he was on the guitar. He played an original guitar solo while Dancin' Bob Bradford strutted his stuff, a song that became known as "Buck Dancer's Choice." Sam was especially effective as a comedian, giving animated responses to one-liners and acting as a foil for other comedy lines.

By the second week, Birmingham and central Alabama were in the grip of Uncle Dave Macon mania. Uncle Dave's previous successes on tour and increased popularity from record releases helped to pull in large audiences. Local railroads added cars to trains to allow more people from outside the city to attend. Theater attendance went from a full to a jam-packed house; then people had to be turned away. The huge crowds drew the attention of the Birmingham fire marshal who first cited the Loew's Bijou for overcrowding and then threatened to shut down the whole spectacle. When Uncle Dave wasn't busy at the theater, he performed at other venues, including Kiwanis and Shriners Club meetings. He finally had to refuse new invites in order to meet previous commitments. When a Birmingham newspaper opined that Uncle Dave had played his way into the ranks of vaudeville stars, the banjoist admitted that he had not yet "gotten quite used" to all the attention and fanfare.

An initial stint of three weeks was extended to five due to high public demand. Loew's advertising for the extended engagement was pure hype. Given top billing, Uncle Dave was described as the "Struttinest Strutter That Ever Strutted a Strut!" who presided over a program of "mountain humor" and dances and songs fresh from "Moonshineville." Another poster identified him as the South's "peerless banjo picker" and "world famous phonograph artist." Fiddlin' Sid pulled a "soothing bow over a hot fiddle" while Sam McGee "climbed all over a wicked guitar." A show poster warned fans not to miss Dancin' Bob, "the stepper who just can't control his feet." Taken together, the four were billed as the "Billy Goat Hill Quartet."

During his weeks in Birmingham, Uncle Dave sat down with a newspaper reporter for a rare interview. After the preliminary introductions, Uncle Dave offered that he was not quite sure what to say because he had never had anyone "think me good enough to want to print things about." The reporter put him at ease by asking Dave to expand on his personal philosophy of life. Dave lit his pipe while formulating his thoughts and then began:

> Life is like this old banjo of mine. If you know how to pick it you can get right
> pert music from it, and if you hit the wrong string you don't get nothing but

discord. Then there's lots of folks who don't know how to tune the banjo of life. They depend on themselves too much. Think the other feller don't know nothin' and wouldn't ask him if he did. I always tune my banjo with the feller at the pianny 'cause he knows how to help tune it.

Use your fellerman and let your fellerman use you. That's my way of gettin' along. Now and then a feller will bust a banjo string, just like a feller will bust a string of life. Some of 'em get disgusted and jest quit trying to make more music, but the feller with any horse sense will go out and get a new string and start all over again. Now ain't I right?

The blowout in Birmingham convinced the Loew's theater chain to offer Uncle Dave a contract for a nationwide tour. Sid Harkreader was ecstatic at the prospect, convinced that he was on the threshold of achieving national stardom and the money that went with it. Uncle Dave was not so sure. He missed Tildy and the boys and realized that playing on a national circuit would keep him away from home for even longer periods. A second concern was religious. Some of the vaudeville acts included language and presentations that were too over the top for even Uncle Dave's morality, and while he could justify playing in city theaters occasionally, a complete commitment to the theater circuit was just too much. When Uncle Dave finally turned the offer down, Sid was "very much disappointed," believing that he had been deprived of an opportunity to make "quite a sum of money" and perhaps even gain his own contract with Loew's.

Loew's quickly countered Uncle Dave's rejection with a second, more modest offer: would the duo undertake a tour of theaters in major Southern cities? Uncle Dave and Sid quickly signed a new contract to appear in Memphis, Dallas, New Orleans, and Atlanta. For ten weeks in the spring and early summer they were on the road, ending the excursion in Atlanta. It was during this tour that Uncle Dave was first given the nickname the "Dixie Dewdrop," with Uncle Dave crediting the title's inception to Ediston Vinson. Despite the excursion's great results, Uncle Dave's refusal of a national contract created a fissure in the foundation of the business relations between him and Sid, and the fiddler soon began to seek solo appearances and other business opportunities for himself.

With the success in Birmingham and good record sales, Sterchi's soon sent Uncle Dave back to New York City for another recording session. Sid accompanied him, and the duo once again stepped before Vocalion's acoustic horn on April 13, 1925. In four days, they performed thirty-eight takes of eighteen separate songs. Among these were a number of Uncle Dave's biggest hits, including "Old Dan Tucker," "All Go-Hungry Hash House," and "From Jerusalem to Jericho."

Compared to his first recording session, Uncle Dave was even more confident and energetic. The Dixie Dewdrop stomped, kicked, laughed, and shouted his way through the four-day session, and it's easy to envision him swaying and swinging his whole body like a human metronome to help keep time. He introduced a number of techniques that became hallmarks of his recordings, including longer spoken and musical preludes, laughing choruses, and outbursts of loud, cackling laughter at his own jokes. Another routine was to address listeners using a professorial tone while delivering a cascade of tongue-twisting, frenetic phonics, such as: "I'm gonna give you a little of 'Old Dan Tucker,' containing more heterogeneous, constapolicies, double flavor and unknown quality than usual." The 1925 session definitely gives the listener a better sense of what one of Uncle Dave's live shows must have been like.

The outing reflected Uncle Dave and Fiddlin' Sid's increased musical artistry and expanded repertoire. Most songs were either minstrel favorites or popular old-time tunes other artists were also recording at the time. One of these was "Run, Nigger, Run," an African American folksong from around 1851, which in its original format, told the story of a black slave attempting to avoid capture by white slave patrols, thereby gaining his freedom. While the original melody and chorus were retained, other new lyrics addressed mostly Southern foods and living. Uncle Dave recorded a few original compositions as well, including "All Go-Hungry Hash House," "I Tickled Nancy," and "I Don't Reckon It'll Happen Again." There was more intricate harmony as well, with Sid taking the lead vocals on a number of songs. On several takes, Uncle Dave displays his talents as a square dance caller. "The Girl I Left behind Me" is a unique moment in Uncle Dave's discography; it's the only known recording in which he plays the guitar rather than the banjo. Confident in Uncle Dave's continued success, Vocalion released two records from the session in August 1925. The first double-sided vinyl included "Run, Nigger, Run," and "I Don't Reckon"; the second contained "Old Dan Tucker" and "Old Ship of Zion."

In only five short years, Uncle Dave Macon had made the transition from an amateur to a professional entertainer, an accomplishment that many musicians attempt but seldom achieve. He had gained regional fame as a dynamic entertainer and procured a recording contract with a major label.

A number of personal traits had allowed such success. In addition to his natural abilities as a banjoist and songster, Uncle Dave had displayed good business acumen and maintained amicable relations with promoters and fellow musicians. He had a nearly insatiable need to play, please and entertain, a desire fed by a hearty physical constitution and seemingly inexhaustible amounts of nervous energy that helped to propel him from one engagement to another. Against all odds—including discouraging advice from some family members—Uncle Dave had achieved his first goals as a professional musician. On a personal level, he was probably most gratified with his ability to bring in enough income to maintain his family's comfortable lifestyle and to keep their skillets "good and greasy." The Dixie Dewdrop's next major career advancement would not come at local venues, city theaters, or in a recording studio, but over the airwaves.

CHAPTER 4

"Take It Away, Uncle Dave!"

AT THE START OF THE ROARING TWENTIES, radio reception throughout Tennessee was erratic and unpredictable. Huddled by battery-powered crystal sets while listening on primitive, metal headphones, rural folk strained to tune in the signals of distant radio powerhouses broadcasting from New York City, Pittsburgh, and Atlanta. To hear the live sound of an announcer or music coming from a broadcast station hundreds of miles away was at first considered a mysterious, almost mystical experience. Of the over 500 radio stations nationwide at the end of 1922, less than 20 percent were located in the South, but as the 1920s progressed, the reach of commercial radio expanded across the entire country. Radio advocates argued that the quick transmission of news, entertainment, and advertising would change the social and economic fabric of American society. Many others insisted that radio was a passing fad that would quickly disperse like clouds on the wind.

Driven by southern pride and increasingly frustrated with their distant and limited listening choices, Tennesseans desired their own local radio stations. The first station licensed in the Volunteer State was a byproduct of religious zeal and economic opportunity. James D. Vaughn, a nationally known publisher and distributor of gospel hymnbooks, organized WOAN, which went on the air in January 1923. Located in Lawrenceburg, not far from the Alabama line in south-central Middle Tennessee, WOAN's mission was to preach the gospel and sell hymnals, even though the station transmitted with only 150 watts of power. A second station, also motivated by the Christian desire to evangelize nonbelievers, popped up in Nashville. WCBQ—We

Can't Be Quiet—was wholly owned and operated by First Baptist Church in downtown Nashville and went on the air in April 1924.

For someone who routinely eschewed new, emerging technology, Uncle Dave fell in love with radio. From the beginning, he seemed to grasp the entertainment, marketing, and advertising power of the medium. If Tennesseans listening on a good night could hear announcers and music from as far away as Chicago, Atlanta, and even New York City, the opposite had to be true as well. Surely, listeners in those distant cities could hear someone from Tennessee broadcasting over the airwaves while playing the banjo, singing, telling jokes, and dispensing earthy, country philosophy. Compared to other younger musicians who were struggling to become professional entertainers, Uncle Dave seemed more attuned to radio's potential to develop a nationwide fanbase. People listening to him for the first time over radio might be prompted to buy his records. In turn, radio programs and record sales constituted a powerful advertising and marketing combination with the potential to draw even larger crowds at new venues in major cities throughout the South, Midwest, and Northeast. He had jumped at the first opportunity to record, knowing that record sales would expose him to a new national audience, and now radio offered a second similar prospect.

A broadcasting breakthrough occurred in Nashville in the late summer of 1925 with the activation of WDAD. The station was in a very real sense Nashville's first commercial radio enterprise. The owner was Fred "Pop" Exum, who ran Dad's Auto Accessories, a popular Nashville store that also offered radios and radio parts for purchase. Exum fully realized radio's potential as a purveyor of musical entertainment and an advertising platform. Listeners tuning in to WDAD heard an eclectic array of musical offerings, from classical to black blues and old-time.

Uncle Dave's first radio appearance was on WDAD, which from the start featured a number of local, old-time musicians. It was there that Uncle Dave first met Dr. Humphrey Bate, who, on September 18, 1925, became the very first to play country music over a Nashville radio station. A rural family doctor from Castalian Springs, Tennessee, Bate had earned his medical degree at Vanderbilt University. When he wasn't treating patients, he loved to play a variety of music genres, including old-time. He eventually formed his own band, "Dr. Humphrey Bate's Augmented String Orchestra," which developed a reputation of its own throughout Middle Tennessee. As a musician, Humphrey Bate preferred the harmonica and the guitar; as a bandleader, he excelled at promoting and scheduling the act while developing a wide repertoire of popular songs. Another musician Uncle Dave met at WDAD was DeFord Bailey, a young black artist who was a virtuoso on the harmonica. All three men would help to shape the sound of music and radio in Nashville in the coming years.

At WDAD, Uncle Dave first encountered a hindrance that would dog him for decades: the microphone. On stage, Uncle Dave's unrestricted, freewheeling style seemed beyond restraint, but in radio and recording studios, it was imperative that he should speak, sing, and play directly into a microphone using moderate sound levels. However, loud playing, singing, and shouting were integral to his performance style, and Uncle Dave never seemed to understand proper electronic sound levels. At first, his seated position while playing kept a proper distance between himself and the microphone, but Uncle Dave got excited as he performed, inching his chair forward and closer to the microphone with each exaggerated motion of his body. Sound engineers tried to explain that boisterous singing and playing distorted their radio signals and recording devices, but to no avail. Station managers surrendered in their efforts at harnessing Uncle Dave's performing style to the microphone. Handed a lemon, they decided to make lemonade. In advertising, promoters and radio stations began to bill Uncle Dave as "the loudest voice on radio." For Uncle Dave, microphones were an unnecessary albatross that cramped his style, and for his entire career, he believed he was better off without them.

One of the greatest milestones in American broadcasting took place on the evening of October 5, 1925, when Nashville's WSM took to the airwaves. Sponsored by the National Life and Accident Insurance Company, WSM's intent was to provide listeners with news and entertainment while supporting National Life's insurance sales agents, especially those operating in more remote, rural areas. The call letters WSM—We Shield Millions—was clear testimony to the integral, corporate relationship between the station and National Life.

Standing among the many officials and dignitaries who had assembled for WSM's first broadcast was an outsider. George Dewey Hay had been born in Attica, Indiana, in November 1895. After a short stint in the army, he moved to Memphis and worked as a reporter for the *Commercial Appeal*. From the earliest moments of his public career, Hay demonstrated a flair for the dramatic and embraced unabashed romanticism. Assigned to cover the city court's deliberations, Hay churned out a series of articles entitled "Howdy, Judge," using humor to inform and entertain readers about often complex judicial proceedings and unsavory, criminal activity. The popularity of these articles gained Hay the nickname "Solemn Old Judge," which he embraced and cultivated.

In January 1923, the *Commercial Appeal* formed its own radio station, WMC, and transferred Hay from print to broadcasting. When Hay stepped before WMC's microphone, the man had met his moment. A soothing, mellow voice delivered news and commentary in a deliberate, rhythmic cadence that was easy on the ears. He brought a unique sense of style and even showmanship to broadcasting. Hay chanted the station's call letters and blew an imitation steamboat whistle at the start of each day's broadcast. At the same time, he had a tendency toward organization and preparations. He sketched out scripts for each program and then let his natural flair for innovation and romanticism add unique on-air elements.

A seminal event in Hay's life had occurred a few months before he debuted on radio. The *Commercial Appeal* dispatched him to Mammoth Spring, Arkansas, in the Ozarks, to cover the funeral of a World War I marine veteran. The solemn ceremony impressed Hay, who decided to loiter in Mammoth Spring for a day of rest and reflection. That afternoon he encountered a local farmer who lived on the edge of town in an abandoned railroad freight car with his wife and eight children. The man's only respite from backbreaking toil was music, and before long he was showing his fiddle and bow to the Memphis reporter. Before their conversation ended, the farmer invited Hay to attend a local hoedown.

That night, George D. Hay, a three-man string band, and about twenty other residents crowded into a small cabin on the edge of Mammoth Spring. In the glow of oil lamps, people laughed and danced for endless hours. Hay observed that "no one in the world has ever had more fun than those Ozark mountaineers did that night." Their music had an "earthy rhythm" and its essence was as "fundamental as sunshine and rain, snow and wind and the light of the moon peeping through the trees." The power of music exhibited during one remarkable night in Mammoth Spring, Arkansas, would shape the remainder of Hay's life.

With his rising notoriety at WMC in Memphis, it was not long before Hay received better offers for employment. In May 1924, he moved to Chicago, becoming an announcer on WLS. Eighteen months earlier, WBAP in Fort Worth, Texas, had organized a live "barn dance" show that featured hoedown bands playing old-time and barn-dance tunes. A month prior to Hay's arrival in the Windy City, WLS had organized the "National Barn Dance," featuring down-home music and dance tunes by fiddlers and string bands. Hay was a true natural as an announcer on the WLS Barn Dance and other station programming. Only six months after arriving in Chicago, he won the *Radio Digest* poll as the most popular announcer in the country.

By inviting Hay to its debut broadcast in October 1925, WSM not only intended to recognize his status as a rising radio man and announcer but to make a serious effort to steal him away from WLS. Their plan worked. Edwin Craig, the National Life senior executive who had been the driving force in WSM's creation, approached Hay at a broadcasting convention in Texas two weeks after the Nashville gala to offer him the job as WSM's station manager. Hay accepted, and on November 2, drove his family from Chicago to Nashville.

Within days of George D. Hay's arrival in Nashville, Uncle Dave played on WSM for the first time on the evening of November 5, 1925. The Nashville Policeman's Benefit Association hosted its major fund-raising effort that year as an evening concert at Ryman Auditorium. To promote the event further, WSM agreed to broadcast it live. When showtime came, an estimated 6,000 people crowded the auditorium's upper and lower galleries, with another 2,000 turned away at the door. Typical of the period, the range of music offerings was eclectic, from instrumentals, solos, and comedy to Hawaiian, jazz, and classical. As the evening progressed, the music became more spirited and local. Dr. Bate finally directed his "orchestra" on stage as he played the harmonica. The band rendered several numbers of popular and old-time tunes, and the audience "never got enough."

To close out the evening's entertainment, Uncle Dave and Fiddlin' Sid took center stage. Uncle Dave opened the show by telling the audience that he felt a bit awkward standing on the large, formal stage at the Ryman; there was no big, wood fireplace for him to spit into between numbers! As the crowd roared with laughter, the experienced duo ripped into a set of their most popular offerings: "Turkey in the Straw," "Sugar Walks Down the Street," "Ain't Goin' to Rain No More," "Don't Reckon T'will Happen Again," and "Go Away Mule."

Four days following the Ryman Auditorium broadcast, George Hay took over as WSM's station manager. With him came the name, "Solemn Old Judge," which had first taken root in Memphis. But WSM soon learned that Hay was not solemn, old, or a judge. In reality, he was a promoter extraordinaire with a knack for advertising and a terrific announcing voice. Hay moved immediately to replicate the success of the WLS Barn Dance on WSM.

The story of the launch and earliest stages of the Grand Ole Opry has been well-documented in other places and need not be retold at length here. Needless to say, Hay organized the first program of old-time music on WSM from Studio A at 8:00 p.m. on Saturday, November 28, 1925. The featured performer was "Uncle Jimmy" Thompson, an award-winning but cantankerous old fiddler, who played for a solid hour accompanied by his niece on the piano. While serving as the program's announcer, Judge Hay invited listeners to send in requests for old-time fiddle tunes, and almost immediately, telegrams started to pour into WSM. Letters and telegrams continued to arrive afterward, and for the next few weeks, Judge Hay, Uncle Jimmy, and his niece held down the fort, naming the show "WSM Barn Dance." Not for another two years would the program become known as the "Grand Ole Opry."

Uncle Dave seems to have started playing on WSM in early December 1925, though his relationship was strictly informal. His first documented appearance was on December 17. Large sums of favorable fan mail poured in, and a week later, the WSM Barn Dance program featured both Uncle Dave and Uncle Jimmy Thompson, who played requests from callers. While the two appeared on the show together, they did not perform as a duet, an indication that Uncle Dave was increasingly unwilling to share the limelight with other performers. Following the December 26 Barn Dance performance, Uncle Dave would not play on WSM again for a number of months.

At the end of 1925, Judge Hay was hard at work canvassing the Middle Tennessee area to create an established roster of talent for WSM's newest program. At the top of the list was Humphrey Bate's band, but only after Judge Hay had changed its name to the "Possum Hunters." By Hay's own recollection, the Possum Hunters was the first old-time band to play on the Opry. At least three other string bands were qualified and available: Paul Warnack's "Gully Jumpers," George Wilkerson's "Fruit Jar Drinkers," and the "Crook Brothers." At the top of the roster of solo performers were DeFord Bailey and Sid Harkreader. Meanwhile, WSM was besieged with fiddlers, banjoists, guitar players, and even a female zither player, all seeking auditions toward appearing on the Saturday night program. It was during this frenetic talent search that Judge Hay declared that "WSM had a good natured riot on its hands."

The Grand Ole Opry talent roster by early 1926 numbered twenty-five musicians. Judge Hay had a habit of thinking big, and while he was pleased with the quality of the talent pool, he wanted more. Hay desired an already established, experienced entertainer whose name recognition and popularity would boost both WSM and the Opry. In terms of actual experience and fan recognition, no other talent on the early Opry could even come close to Uncle Dave Macon. His fame and recognition had spread from Middle Tennessee to other parts of the South. Uncle Dave had been a huge success on the Loew's theater circuit, and his own bookings had added to his reputation and popularity. Perhaps what most set him apart from other regional musicians is that he had already cut thirty-six commercial records. In many ways, the early Opry needed Uncle Dave Macon much more than he needed it.

The specific details of the initial meeting between Uncle Dave and Judge Hay are unknown, but what is known is that their relationship developed into a deep, abiding friendship that endured for more than twenty-five years. On a professional level, Hay respected Uncle Dave's abilities as a showman, musician, and leader among other musicians. Conversely, Uncle Dave revered Hay's abilities as an announcer, master of ceremonies, and organizer. Hammering out the details of fair business arrangements came naturally for both, a rarity in the entertainment world. Judge Hay considered Uncle Dave a rugged individualist with a "cheerful, very quick witted and God-fearing" spirit who recognized the rights of others, never said an unkind word to anyone, and possessed more drive and energy than most men half his age.

Uncle Dave Macon's first appearance on WSM as a formal member of the Grand Ole Opry cast came on April 17, 1926. The first song he played on the Opry was his big hit, "Keep My Skillet Good and Greasy." Newspapers had announced Uncle Dave's formal debut on the program and, in local communities throughout Middle Tennessee, people gathered around their radios for the performance. The situation in Lascassas, Tennessee, where Uncle Dave had performed early and often, was probably typical. The Jarman family had one of only two radios in the village, and a large number of friends and neighbors from that part of Rutherford County swarmed into the house to listen to their local legend.

At WSM's Studio A, Uncle Dave's broadcast performance exhibited all of the traits of his stage shows. The Solemn Old Judge recalled they had to move Uncle Dave back from the microphone so that he would have "plenty of room to kick as he played." Even at WSM, Uncle Dave considered microphones a nuisance, and Hay observed that it took "a long time to 'hitch' him to it." Judge Hay eventually developed a standard series of phrases to introduce the Dixie Dewdrop on air by describing his physical appearance. The typical introduction had Uncle Dave wearing a "plug hat, gates-ajar collar, gold teeth, and his great big, Tennessee smile!" The punch line that transferred the action from announcer to performer became an Opry byword: "Take it away, Uncle Dave!"

During April–July 1926, Uncle Dave was an Opry mainstay along with Uncle Jimmy Thompson and Dr. Humphrey Bate. For the remainder of the year, he performed there less frequently, but his appearances still kept Uncle Dave in touch with the radio audience and further established his identity with WSM and the Opry. In coming years, those ties would strengthen until Uncle Dave became known far and wide as "The Grand Ole Man of the Grand Ole Opry."

If Uncle Dave's Opry appearances waned as 1926 progressed, it was only because the year was one of his busiest. The long, strong fingers, which he preserved from the damaging effects of a possible dynamite blast, served him well throughout the year and for the remainder of the decade. At the top of his game, Uncle Dave was constantly on the move for several years, cutting records, playing on radio broadcasts, and appearing at large and small venues too numerous to count. At the same time, he balanced the needs of home life and his touring schedule, with significant changes occurring in both areas.

The reason Uncle Dave did not appear on WSM at the start of 1926 was because he and Fiddlin' Sid had returned to the Loew's Bijou theater in Birmingham for a second extended engagement. This time, things did not turn out so well. A critic from a local newspaper was in the audience during a show when Uncle Dave let loose with several inappropriate comments. A negative review appeared in the next day's newspaper, which managed to make it all the way to Loew's corporate headquarters in New York City. When asked decades later about the exact nature of those remarks, Sid could not recall the specifics but speculated that the words had been "either too raunchy or too religious." Determined to defend the integrity of its brand, Loew's immediately dispatched a popular singer to Birmingham to act as a headliner while demoting the Tennesseans to the status of a warmup act until their contract expired.

On the first night of the new arrangement, the Dixie Dewdrop and Fiddlin' Sid performed as usual to an enthusiastic audience. When their performance ended, encore calls went on for another twenty minutes before the duo finally withdrew. When the headliner singer appeared on stage, things got ugly. He paused momentarily to let things calm down, but cries for Uncle Dave's return only got louder. Finally, the singer began his opening number, but the crowd became even more boisterous. Halfway through the song, the performer abruptly stopped and sat down at center stage. He announced that his allotted time was thirty minutes, and that he was determined to remain on stage whether the crowd let him sing or not. The Southerners took up the challenge, becoming ever more unruly. Moments later, the angry, frustrated singer stalked off the stage and located Ediston Vinson, who still served as theater manager. The singer launched into a tirade against the uncouth audience, finally breaking down in a crying fit.

Vinson realized he had a problem and conferred with the Tennesseans and the singer over lunch the next day. Unable to cancel either performance, Vinson came up with one of the most novel solutions in the history of vaudeville acts. The singer would still be advertised and perform as the headlining act per instructions from corporate headquarters, with Uncle Dave and Sid as the warmup act. However, during the actual performance, the headliner would perform first with the warmup act coming last. In this way, Uncle Dave and Sid could play as long as they desired, which is exactly what the crowd wanted.

In April 1926, Uncle Dave returned to New York City for his third recording session, but with a number of differences from his previous trips. Sid Harkreader declined to accompany his mentor, convinced he could make better money with continued personal appearances compared to the stingy royalties received from record sales. In Sid's mind, trips to New York drained him of precious time and money better spent on continued personal appearances, and the decision put further space between the two. Needing a backup musician, Uncle Dave invited Sam McGee to go along, a decision that benefited both.

Another difference was that Vocalion had been sold to an early version of the Brunswick Company, though the Vocalion label was retained for a time. Brunswick had upgraded its recording technology to electronic equipment and microphones, compared to Vocalion's acoustic horns. The microphone rendered recordings with crisper tones and better definition and clarity, all without the hollow background noise that plagued acoustic recordings.

When Uncle Dave reported to Brunswick's facility in Manhattan, he faced a recording studio microphone for the first time. Completely ignoring any technical considerations, Uncle Dave dove into the session with full gusto, including loud singing, laughing, and shouting, which caused distortions in the early takes. Brunswick's engineers dutifully reminded him to stay back a distance from the microphone. Uncle Dave willingly obliged by scooting his chair back some distance at the start of each new cut, but within only a few bars, he had once again inched forward in excitement, drawing too close. Finally, a sound engineer took a piece of chalk and drew a line on the floor an appropriate distance from the microphone, telling the banjoist in the strictest terms that he was never to cross that line while recording. The sound engineer who coached Uncle Dave that day was Jack Kapp, a twenty-five-year-old Chicago native who got his start with Columbia Records. Kapp would later become a cofounder of Decca Records.

Over three days, Uncle Dave recorded twenty-six takes of thirteen songs, including some of his most renowned hits. Foremost among these was: "Way Down the Old Plank Road," "Whoop 'Em Up Cindy," "Late Last Night When My Willie Came Home," and "Poor Sinners, Fare Thee Well." He also recorded one of his personal favorites, "Death of John Henry." As always, Uncle Dave's recording sessions produced an eclectic mix of comedy, romance, ballad, worship, and social commentary. One of the most original songs was "On the Dixie Bee Line," a tribute to the Ford motor car and the network of paved highways appearing across the country. Uncle Dave eventually mailed a copy of the record to Henry Ford.

One of the most remarkable recordings was "The Bible's True," the Dixie Dewdrop's unabashed defense of biblical truth and creationism. The song was timely because the Scopes Monkey Trial, one of the most sensational court cases of the twentieth century, had just transpired the previous summer in Dayton, Tennessee. A Tennessee statute had made it unlawful to teach any theory that "denies the story of divine creation as taught by the Bible" in favor of the narrative "that man was descended from a lower order of animals." At its heart, the trial focused on the right to teach evolution in the public schools but, in reality, the proceedings became a nationwide showdown between Bible-based traditionalists and modernist progressives. Despite the trial's outcome favoring the teaching of evolution, Uncle Dave considered the entire matter far from settled. Scorning the decisions of jurisprudence, he opined in a spoken introduction that he "did not believe in evolution nor revolution" and then sang:

Evolution teaches man came from a monkey,
I don't believe no such a thing in the days of
a week of Sundays.

God made the world and everything that's in it,
He made man perfect and the monkey wasn't in it.

And the chorus declared:

For the Bible's true, oh yes, I believe it!
I've seen enough and I can prove it.
It's what you say, what you say,
It's bound to be that way!

The tune remains a comedic classic and a prime example of Uncle Dave's gift for using humor to address thorny social issues.

Compared to his previous recordings, the April 1926 session was the most intricate in terms of composition and presentation. Instead of straightforward arrangements of single songs, the cuts are slices of vaudeville-style stage performances. Complex recording structures emerge including curtain calls, elaborate spoken and musical preludes, and various whoops and shouts between verses. Uncle Dave was never repetitious, always offering new jokes and fresh witticisms. His spoken preludes included topics as diverse as the hazards of riding New York's subways, a humorous incident at a black church, and a secret formula for concocting a potent whiskey cocktail despite the constraints of Prohibition. To all of this, Sam McGee added slapping and banging on the back and flat top of his Martin guitar.

In September 1926, Uncle Dave returned to New York City for another recording session. It was the first time he conducted two recording sessions in a single year, clear evidence of his immense, growing popularity. Unlike previous sessions, he traveled and played solo. The session was testimony to his remarkable energy; in two days he performed fifty-six takes of twenty-eight songs. Over time, Brunswick released all of the tunes save one. The most popular releases included: "We Are Up Against It Now," "Sourwood Mountain Medley," "Kissin' on the Sly," and "Never Make Love No More."

Their foray to New York had further cemented the relationship between Uncle Dave and Sam McGee, and they began touring together, especially on longer trips or whenever Fiddlin' Sid was unavailable. Sam's musical abilities, good nature, and folksy stage presence endeared him to audiences everywhere. During performances, he was much more than a backup musician.

At the simplest level, he was a foil for jokes and a partner for back-and-forth banter. Sam even went so far as to wear a wig sometimes while portraying a country bumpkin character named "Toby." But his real contribution was with the guitar. Part of his musical genius was to adopt a wide range of styles—from blues to gospel and even ragtime—and to introduce the guitar as a new solo instrument. Uncle Dave readily appreciated his abilities, even allowing Sam to play a few solos during their performances. Listeners in the crowd, especially at small venues where they could see his intricate picking up close, often would call for Sam to play solo again after he and Uncle Dave had done a few numbers together. But Uncle Dave was not always so willing to share the attention with other musicians and, on occasion, he announced that the show was almost out of time rather than letting his partner perform additional guitar solos.

When traveling by car, Sam drove his automobile with Uncle Dave picking up most expenses. As the Dixie Dewdrop booked longer tours farther from home, the duo traveled more and more by train. With Uncle Dave's rising popularity, greater numbers of people recognized him in train stations and coaches. During rail trips, he moved about frequently while visiting with people on the train, never staying in the same seat for more than ten minutes. Passengers would discover with delight that Uncle Dave was in their car, and on long trips, he would move to the front of the coach and put on a show as they all rode the rails. One night in Atlanta, Uncle Dave and Sam went to an upscale restaurant following a show downtown. During the meal, people recognized and conversed with Uncle Dave, and before it was all over, he put on a show in the establishment, passing his big black hat around for tips while joking that once before his hat had failed to come back to him, a possible, oblique reference to the heist at Walter Hill.

During a return to Birmingham, the duo were booked to entertain at a regional fiddle contest. To build more excitement for the event, organizers sponsored an open invitation banjo picking contest with a top cash prize of $25. Billed as the "Championship of the South" for banjo, it was a blind competition with a dense, fabric curtain separating the panel of judges from the contestants. Uncle Dave and Sam both entered. Confident one of them would win the cash prize, Uncle Dave pulled his partner aside to propose that they agree to split the money after one of them won first place. They both agreed on a handshake, self-assured that the money was theirs. Both played to the best of their ability, and when the votes were tallied, Sam won the top prize; Uncle Dave was off his game and didn't even place.

Afterward, Uncle Dave pulled Sam aside again, but this time his concern was over something more valuable than cash. Uncle Dave congratulated the younger musician on his win but then explained that it would "hurt him" if anyone in Tennessee ever learned that the Dixie Dewdrop had been bested in a banjo picking contest. Sam understood the elder musician's concern, keeping the contest's outcome a secret until after Uncle Dave's death more than twenty-five years later.

One of the most unnerving events of Uncle Dave's career occurred one night in East Tennessee. He and Sam had a dual booking at a town in coal country. The region had seen extreme labor strife, exploding into violence between miners and management. The first appearance was a routine affair at a schoolhouse, and when it was over, the two transferred venues to a large building on the edge of town where a square dance was scheduled. As Uncle Dave and Sam tuned up for the dance, dozens of couples gathered inside.

Just as the hoedown was about to begin, a sheriff in a big hat barged in, displaying a shiny badge on a long, dark duster jacket and brandishing a long rifle in his hands. The lawman assured everyone that he wanted them to have a good time, but reminded the revelers that violence had occurred all too recently. To insure that there would be no trouble during the dance, he ordered everyone to disarm and to stack their weapons on a table at the head of the hall. To Uncle Dave and Sam's astonishment, handguns started to appear from hidden shoulder holsters, inside coat pockets, the front and rear pockets of mens' trousers, ankle holsters, and even ladies' purses and clutches. Before long, a large number of pistols of all sizes and calibers lay stacked on the table. The musicians warily studied the weapons, realizing that several gun barrels were pointed directly at them from the table only a few feet away. Uncle Dave called to the sheriff, asking that those guns be turned in the opposite direction before he played. The sheriff agreed, quickly fixed the problem, and soon the fun started.

Sam witnessed Uncle Dave's sincerity and generosity during a performance at an open-air political rally. A storm brewed up during the show, with lightning striking a house some distance away and setting it afire. The music came to a halt as the performers and audience alike stared in disbelief at the ghastly sight of the house burning to the ground. Uncle Dave suddenly whipped off his hat and announced that he was going to pass it around so the crowd could make a contribution to the family that had just lost its home. "Folks, you can see this; you don't have to take anyone's word for it," he announced. "These people will need help!" With that, he reached for his wallet, pulled out a bill and placed it in his hat before passing it into the audience. When it came back at the end of the show, the hat held a collection of $140.

Uncle Dave continued to tour with Fiddlin' Sid on a regular basis, with one of their most challenging trips occurring in the last half of 1926. When Sid arrived in Kittrell to pick up his partner, Uncle Dave was usually packed and ready to go, but on this occasion, Miss Tildy emerged from the front of the house to talk privately. Sid had gotten to know her over the years and greatly admired her. Tildy was stressed, explaining that Dave had inexplicably fallen into a deep depression, but that he had not yet taken to drinking. "He takes these spells," she explained somberly, "and there's nothing else I can do for him. If you get him out of the house and playing somewhere, it will probably make him feel better."

Sid exited his Model T to help Uncle Dave finish packing and to get everything loaded into the car. They soon departed for Horse Cave, a town in south-central Kentucky, where several bookings had been scheduled in the town and surrounding area. During the long trip, Dave sat silent and morose, staring aimlessly at the countryside. Whenever showtime came, the fog seemed to lift, and during performances Uncle Dave was his usual self. When they returned to the hotel at night, Dave's world went black again. The morning they left Horse Cave to return to Tennessee, Dave was his usual, chipper self, but the bout with depression had made the trip especially trying.

Dorris Macon hated farm work. His favorite chores included all types of housework, and it was not unusual to find Dave and Tildy's fifth son in the kitchen helping his mother and Aunt Myrt prepare meals or working in the family garden. Still, he realized fieldwork had to be done, and he did it without complaining. On one particular day in late 1926, Dorris was in the fields with another brother plowing with a mule. His father had come home from a tour the previous day, and something was amiss. Uncle Dave and Miss Tildy had talked privately, and Dorris and the other sons still living at home weren't sure what was wrong. Sometime late that afternoon, Uncle Dave emerged from the back of the house. Going to the fence that bordered the field where the two Macon sons were working, Uncle Dave motioned for Dorris to join him. Dorris approached his father, casually asking him what he wanted to talk about.

"Dorris, I had to let Sid go," Uncle Dave announced without fanfare. After nearly five years of touring and recording together, Uncle Dave and Sid Harkreader had decided to part regular company. The breakup was for the most part mutual, even amicable. The main catalyst was Sid's desire to seek his own, more lucrative and creative opportunities. He was planning to get married as well and seeking to find his own way. Beneath the surface, Sid still harbored resentment of the lost opportunity of a national contract with Loew's theaters. Still, the two had agreed to perform together whenever appropriate opportunities arose. The news set Dorris back, but Uncle Dave continued before he could react: "I ain't gonna be playing with Sid anymore, so I want to make a deal with you to go with me."

"Pap, I ain't good enough yet to go with you!" the sixteen-year-old blurted in reply.

"Why, I'll get you by," Uncle Dave said with fatherly assurance. "You're a good car driver. Tell you what I'll do. I'll give you five dollars a day, and I'll furnish the car."

"When do you want to leave?"

"In the morning!" Uncle Dave replied without batting an eye.

"Well, get out of the way then, and let me get this plow and mule into the barn!" was Dorris's enthusiastic reply.

Even at the tender age of sixteen, Dorris Macon had become a good guitarist. Mazy Todd had four daughters who had all learned to play the guitar, an obvious hereditary endowment from their musically inclined father. Dorris was considered the most handsome of the Macon brothers, and the Todd sisters spent time with him, teaching him how to play the guitar. Still, his experience at performing in public was limited. Most of his playing had occurred around the house with his father and older brother, Glen, who formed a family string band to play for visitors. His main performance setting was with a local, amateur string band that provided music for community gatherings. One of their favorite venues was strictly private. A small, secluded glade along the banks of Cripple Creek, not far from the Macon home, became a favorite getaway for dating couples. On Saturday nights, they would gather there, utilizing the headlights of their Ford cars to provide lighting. Dorris and the band made music as the couples socialized. The haven at Cripple Creek allowed the young to dance, smoke, drink, and smooch, all free from prying eyes and the intense scrutiny of local church-lady gossips.

Dorris may not have known it at the time, but Glen had been his father's first choice for a new musical partner. Glen was a truly gifted musician, perhaps even a prodigy. The most casual visitors to the Macon house could see and hear that Glen was much better than his father on the banjo and guitar, and he would go on to master the mandolin. A voracious reader, the steady habit had earned him the nickname "Book." While still living at home, he made a modest income as a house painter. Glen was completely ambidextrous, capable of playing an instrument or working a paint brush left- or right-handed. He became a local sports legend as a pitcher in a Murfreesboro baseball league. Glen once pitched and won the opening game of a doubleheader throwing right-handed. When the team's assigned pitcher for the second game failed to show, Glen took to the mound again, pitching the second game left-handed.

Unfortunately, Glen was an extreme introvert. Although he was at ease among his family and a close circle of friends, the outside world posed a real challenge. Uncle Dave realized and cherished his son's musical talents, believing that Glen would still make an ideal touring and recording partner, despite his need for privacy. Three times, Uncle Dave tried to convince Glen to go on tour, but he adamantly refused. On another occasion, his father asked Glen to accompany him only as far as Nashville to play on the Opry but, once again, Glen declined.

During his first trips with his father, Dorris probably performed only as driver, valet, and flunky, but one Saturday afternoon not long after that conversation along the fence line, he accompanied Uncle Dave to Nashville to play on the Opry. Dorris's first public performance before an audience occurred at WSM's Studio A during a live broadcast of the Grand Ole Opry. The challenge of beginning his public music career at such a prominent venue must have been daunting. Once asked if he had experienced any stage fright during that first performance, Dorris thought for a moment, smiled a bit, and then humbly replied: "Well, if I did, I guess I got over it real quick." Other performers, WSM management, and Opry staff warmly welcomed the young performer into their inner circle. Judge Hay modified the standard introduction he used for the Dixie Dewdrop to include the closing phrase, "Uncle Dave Macon and his son, Dorris."

When the early Opry cast members posed for their first group photo in 1927, Dorris appears sitting beside his father on the front row. All dressed in dark suits, the musicians appear more like glum jurors impaneled for a serious murder trial than fun-loving entertainers. In fact, a study of the Opry's annual cast shots reveals a number of important characteristics about the organization. Judge Hay understood the power of imagery, and in annual photographs for subsequent years, Opry members donned hillbilly and farm costumes, which reinforced the mountain and rural roots of their music. In each of these images, the Dixie Dewdrop sits at center stage, acknowledging his status as the Opry's main headliner and its most recognized, revered personality. Gathered around Uncle Dave are Dorris, Judge Hay, and the other most popular performers for that particular year. True to form, Uncle Dave appears to be playing, singing, and stomping in the photos. In contrast, the other musicians struck more subdued poses while holding their instruments. It was an apt metaphor for Uncle Dave's performance style; while younger entertainers often needed more time to get their acts rolling onstage, the Dixie Dewdrop always hit the ground running in full force, grabbing the crowd's attention with shouts and loud raps on the banjo from the very start.

One of the most iconic images of Uncle Dave's career is an official Opry photograph of him and Dorris sitting on either side of a WSM microphone with instruments in hand. The Opry printed the 8-by-10-inch image on heavy gauge paper to be used as an outreach in fan correspondence. On the front was the image of the popular father-son team, and on the reverse appeared a heartfelt, spiritual essay entitled "Reminiscences of Early Life," which Uncle Dave had penned. He counseled youth about the vagaries and brevity of life, encouraging them to "learn the beautiful things of life in your early years." When they received fan mail, it was typical for the Dixie Dewdrop and Dorris to sign one of the photographs, sometimes with a brief, inscribed message. They then folded the photo and essay into a business-sized envelope and mailed it back to the admirer. By responding in such a manner, Dave Macon did more than merely answer fan mail; he left a lasting impression.

It was about this time when Uncle Dave received one of his most amusing fan letters. A woman in Arkansas had heard his music over a Dallas, Texas, radio station and was so enthralled that she decided to write:

Uncle Dave Makins:
We certainly did enjoy you over our Radiator last night, and from the way you talk, laugh and sing, you must be one of the most wonderful old negroes in the South . . .

Uncle Dave certainly got a good chuckle from the letter, commenting later that "the good old sister just could not see me over the air."

The highlight of 1927 was a return trip to New York City by Uncle Dave and an ad hoc string band. Old-time bands were immensely popular at the time, with several making their own records. One of the most well-liked was the "Skillet Lickers" who recorded on Columbia, usually featuring two or three fiddlers. In an effort to best their competition, Brunswick asked Uncle Dave to assemble a string band of his own and to bring the group to New York City posthaste for a recording session.

While putting the ensemble together, Uncle Dave relied on one of his tried and trusted methods: count upon close friends or family and their demonstrated talents. For the lead fiddler, he chose his close friend and neighbor, Mazy Todd. During Judge Hay's early Opry talent search, Uncle Dave had recommended Mazy to play on WSM. Apparently, the Solemn Old Judge also recognized Mazy's fiddling talents and allowed him to play several times on the WSM Barn Dance. For second fiddle, Uncle Dave turned to another trusted associate, Kirk McGee. Uncle Dave had gotten to know Kirk through his older brother Sam, and the three had even appeared together at a few local venues. Kirk was eager to play and confident in his abilities. As the youngest member of the forming band, Kirk was most attuned to contemporary music tastes and those songs that fans loved the most. To round out the group, Uncle Dave naturally selected Sam McGee to play guitar. Uncle Dave's choice of musicians indicated that he had determined that young Dorris was not yet ready for a major recording session.

The Dixie Dewdrop had never before recorded with a band—in fact, he may have never before even played professionally in a four-man band—so things were a lot more complicated than all of them just hopping on a train and heading to New York. Wanting to muster the best performance possible, Uncle Dave called the band to Kittrell for a marathon practice session—and for good reason. His own sense of musical timing was freewheeling rather than regular. As a result, Uncle Dave couldn't follow other musicians and always had to play lead. "You had to play with him," Kirk McGee observed, "he couldn't play with you." Over a two-week period, the Macon house more resembled a recording studio than a family home. The four musicians drew up a list of songs, developed spoken and instrumental preludes, composed jokes, and practiced their numbers. Mazy Todd was a great fiddler, but he did not know that many of the more popular, contemporary fiddle tunes. Kirk McGee stepped up and was invaluable in teaching Mazy those numbers.

On the morning of Saturday, May 7, 1927, the newly assembled band arrived at Brunswick's recording studio in Midtown Manhattan. The quartet crowded close around a single microphone. When a light bulb flashed on indicating the start of the recording session, the group exploded like a tight, coiled spring suddenly unleashed, delivering a spectacular rendition of "Bake That Chicken Pie." With Uncle Dave on vocals and playing lead on banjo while Sam McGee followed on guitar, Mazy Todd and Kirk McGee made their fiddles whine and squall throughout. The extended rehearsal session in Kittrell had paid off; that day's rendition of "Bake That Chicken Pie" remains one of the most remarkable specimens of old-time band music ever recorded.

The energy on that first cut extended throughout the entire day's session. They recorded seven songs, including the Uncle Dave classics "Rock About My Sara Jane," "Hold That Woodpile Down," "Carve That Possum," and "Sail Away Ladies." The vocals and instruments on the fourteenth take were just as dynamic as they had been on the very first. Caught up in the excitement of the moment, Uncle Dave unexpectedly shouts "Whoo! Kill Yo'self!" right in the middle of the final cut of "Sail Away Ladies." Brunswick knew they had a series of new hits on their hands and soon released every record from that first day's session on the Vocalion label.

After listening to those seven recordings, one might conclude all the performers needed rest the next day. Indeed, the following day was a Sunday, but instead of relaxing at their hotel, Sam and Kirk McGee were anxious to tour the city and asked Uncle Dave if he wanted to go along. By the time of his fifth visit to New York City, the Dixie Dewdrop realized that the safest thing was not to wander the streets but to stay close to the hotel, especially at night. In the end, the trio agreed to venture to the Bronx Zoo.

When they arrived, Sam and Kirk headed off to view the animal cages and displays while Uncle Dave wandered off on his own. Not long afterward, Uncle Dave encountered an animal he had never before seen, an Australian kangaroo standing erect on its hindlegs. Curious as to whether or not a kangaroo would respond to voice commands just like a mule or a horse, he reared back and shouted "Gee!" At the sound, the kangaroo unexpectedly sat down on its rear haunches. Captivated by the animal's response, Uncle Dave shouted "Haw!" and, when he did, the kangaroo bolted fully upright. The Dixie Dewdrop delivered a series of "Gee!" and "Haw!" commands as the kangaroo bobbed up and down with each alternate shout. A crowd of onlookers soon gathered to observe the zany spectacle. Sam and Kirk heard the commotion and immediately dashed in that direction. When they arrived, the Tennesseans were just as amazed as the New Yorkers. But what the brothers noticed most was while half of the crowd was eyeing the spastic kangaroo, the other half gawked at the antics and excited demeanor of the eccentric, old gentleman from Tennessee.

The next day, the band was back in the studio, picking up where they had left off without missing a beat. They recorded eleven songs in twenty-two takes, including "The Gray Cat on the Tennessee Farm," "I'se Gwine Back to Dixie," "Go Along Mule," and "Tom and Jerry." The last song is unique in all of Uncle Dave's recorded repertoire. In the spoken introduction, he deliberately dedicates only the first half of the song to Henry Huddleston, a Murfreesboro banker, indicating there might have been some bad blood between the two. Again, Brunswick realized they had big hits on their hands and quickly released the records for sale.

Sometime during the two days of recording, Uncle Dave committed one of the few business missteps of his career. A Brunswick manager asked him the band's name, which was to appear with Uncle Dave's name on the actual record labels. Without much thought, he blurted out the name the "Fruit Jar Drinkers." He may not have fully realized it at the time, but another band of the very same name was becoming prominent on the Opry.

On Tuesday, May 10, the quartet was back in the studio to cut a number of worship songs. The religious classics recorded included "Walking in Sunlight," "Shall We Gather at the River," and "In the Sweet Bye and Bye." For those recordings, Uncle Dave designated the band as the "Dixie Sacred Singers." Brunswick was less enthusiastic over some of the numbers, but still released eight of the ten hymns. Uncle Dave stayed that afternoon to record another six solo numbers. Among them was "When Reuben Comes to Town," which some musicians believe includes the most intricate and accomplished banjo picking of Uncle Dave's career. The outing ended on May 11, when Uncle Dave returned to the studio with Sam and Kirk to record four more songs. In all, thirty-eight songs were recorded in four days during eighty-six separate takes. Brunswick ultimately released all of them, except two, on the Vocalion label. The highlight of the entire session was clearly the first two days of band recordings, which survive today as perhaps the best old-time string band music ever recorded.

On June 4, Uncle Dave made his way to WSM's offices in downtown Nashville. George D. Hay was hard at work there, and soon motioned the Dixie Dewdrop into his office. The door clicked shut and before long a shouting match ensued. Hay was incensed that Uncle Dave had selected the *Fruit Jar Drinkers* name for his ad hoc band, the same name Hay was using for one of the Opry's mainstay hoedown bands. Whether Uncle Dave had used the name on purpose or by honest mistake is unknown, but Judge Hay's concern was with the potential for confusion among fans, promoters, and the payment of record royalties. Hay fired off a letter to Brunswick asking them to stop the release of records labeled with the *Fruit Jar Drinker* name, but the request came too late, as pressing and advance distribution were already underway. The personal aspects of the dispute soon blew over, as Uncle Dave and Judge Hay were both inclined to forgive and forget, and Hay was sensible enough to realize that he did not want to alienate the Opry's main headliner. While some confusion over the double naming did occur, problems over record royalties never materialized; the Opry's Fruit Jar Drinkers never had an opportunity to record.

Uncle Dave's four-year contract to record on the Vocalion label expired in May 1928, prompting him to sign a new agreement directly with Brunswick. Soon afterward, the Dixie Dewdrop and Sam McGee were on their way to Chicago to record at Brunswick's studio on Wabash Avenue. The July 25–26 session was shorter than previous ones, resulting in fewer cuts and releases. The first recording was "From Earth to Heaven," an autobiographical rendering of the days when "Mr. Dave" had run the Macon Midway Mule & Mitchell Wagon Transportation Company. Other notable songs were the frenzied "Worthy of Estimation," the political piece "Governor Al Smith," and "The New Ford Car," a waxing tribute to the Ford Model A sedan, which had just been released. The engineers in Chicago may have been less particular than those in New York. All of the thirteen songs recorded were accepted on the very first take. Still, Brunswick was careful in what it authorized for release. The company rejected two medleys—one of love songs, the other of hymns—and an Uncle Dave solo entitled "The Dying Thief."

The Dixie Dewdrop had a reputation for never being at a loss for words and always ready with a reply. However, two persons managed to get the best of him in public during his life, and both were women. Sometime during his Chicago visit, Uncle Dave was standing on a sidewalk waiting for a streetcar at a busy downtown intersection. A group of pedestrians crossed the wide boulevard walking in his direction, including an attractive lady sporting a fancy, wide-brimmed straw hat. Suddenly, a forceful gust of wind off Lake Michigan whipped down the boulevard, lashing the pedestrians. The woman firmly grasped the brim of her hat with both hands to prevent it from flying away. At the same time, a blast of air got underneath her skirt, lifting the hem well above her waistline and exposing all of her concealed finery. Uncle

Dave was taken aback, and he could not help but make a comment as the woman passed by seconds later.

"Lady, that was a mighty embarrassing situation you were caught in out there on the street," Uncle Dave observed. "Why don't you hold your hat with one hand and your skirt with the other, and you won't get caught like that again?" She stopped suddenly, giving him an evil eye.

"I'll have you know," she replied, "this hat is new. I bought it yesterday. I've got to take care of it. What you saw has been around here for thirty years. It's old enough to take care of itself!" With that, she abruptly wheeled about and stalked off, leaving Uncle Dave on the sidewalk at a complete loss for words.

While in Illinois, he completed arrangements for a tour throughout the greater Chicago area and the upper Midwest, with Sam accompanying him throughout. Their final appearance came in Madison, Wisconsin, where the duo packed the house. The midwesterners were fascinated just as much as they were entertained; while they had heard banjo playing on WSM and WLS, most had actually never seen a banjo firsthand. Following the performance, fans crowded backstage to get a closer look at the instrument, and Uncle Dave was glad to explain and demonstrate at length the banjo's construction, characteristics, and workings.

By 1928, Uncle Dave's immense popularity and name recognition led to the first of a series of nationwide product endorsements. The Gibson Mandolin-Guitar Manufacturing Company of Kalamazoo, Michigan, approached the Dixie Dewdrop for an endorsement of their lines of quality banjos and guitars. Uncle Dave and Sam McGee both agreed to participate in Gibson advertising. The company arranged a professional photo shoot with Wagner Studios of Cullman, Alabama, which resulted in several handsome images of the two performers clasping Gibson instruments. The photos became part of Gibson's sales catalog. (In 1928, a Gibson Model RB-1 banjo with case sold for $26.) A national advertising campaign featured Uncle Dave sitting and grinning with a Gibson banjo resting in his lap with this cutline: "Only a Gibson is good enough." As part of his compensation, Gibson agreed to supply Uncle Dave with their RB-1. They even went so far as to make Uncle Dave one or two open-backed instruments without resonators; their lighter weight made them easier to spin, flip, and twirl during shows. Over time, Uncle Dave put aside the banjos from the first decade of his career and came to rely exclusively on his quality Gibsons.

When Sid Harkreader departed, his Model T went with him and, at age fifty-eight, Uncle Dave decided it was finally time to buy his first car. In his usual manner, Uncle Dave went big on the purchase, buying a new Ford Model A sedan. In almost all respects, the Model A was a quantum leap in technology over the Model T. The Tin Lizzy had been a 30 mph car, but the sleek Model A, given a good, paved road, could easily cruise at 50 mph. Uncle Dave would be able to ride to his appearances with more speed, power, comfort, and reliability than ever before. Kirk McGee knew some friends at a Ford dealership in Franklin, Tennessee, so Uncle Dave went there to purchase his car. Looking over the impressive sedan, he posed a key business question to the sales representative.

"How much will it cost per hour to operate this car?" the Dixie Dewdrop asked. After some grimacing, chin scratching, and ciphering with pen and paper, the salesman finally generated a number. With all factors considered, it cost about $1 per hour to run the Model A, Uncle Dave was told.

"Well, that's not too bad," the Dixie Dewdrop grinned. "Especially considering they pay me about fifty dollars an hour to play that old banjo of mine!" With that, the deal was closed, and Uncle Dave headed back to Rutherford County riding in a shiny, new 1929 Ford Model A sedan. Still, to keep expenses down around the farm, Uncle Dave for many years kept a horse and buggy readily available at home for him and his sons to use on local errands.

By the end of the 1920s, Uncle Dave Macon was riding high. He was the undisputed headliner of the Grand Ole Opry, and WSM's broadcasts had further expanded the geographic reach of his popularity. The Dixie Dewdrop had accomplished a trifecta no one before had ever achieved; he was a Grand Ole Opry superstar with substantial recording contracts who was also successful on tour. His music continued to entertain and inspire wherever he appeared. Folks wanting a good time laughed and danced the night away while listening to his energetic, high-spirited tunes. Conversely, the less fortunate and downtrodden drew strength and inspiration from his earnest hymns and ballads, which inspired and encouraged them forward against life's challenges. During any given live performance, audiences both laughed and cried, always wanting more.

Uncle Dave's last recording session of the decade came in June 1929. He had signed a one-year contract with Brunswick, and the company wanted a second recording session under the original terms. Apparently, Uncle Dave was still reluctant to place Dorris in a recording studio, and Sam McGee was unavailable. The McGee Brothers had started to team up with the brilliant fiddler and composer Arthur Smith, and the three would soon debut as the remarkable string band, the "Dixieliners." Uncle Dave contacted Sid Harkreader, who agreed to record once more with his mentor.

The reunited duo sat down before a Brunswick microphone in Chicago on June 20, 1929. As always, the session produced several classics: "Man that Rode the Mule around the World," "Over the Mountain," "Traveling Down the Road," and "Railroadin' and Gamblin'." In his personal life, Uncle Dave was a thoughtful, respectful person, but his music and lyrics often projected the image of the rebel and nonconformist. Perhaps no song better captures this spirit than "Tennessee Jubilee," with its repeated refrain of "It's nobody's business, nobody's business, nobody's business what I do!" During a spoken interlude in the middle of the tune, Sid Harkreader suddenly blurts out: "Uncle Dave, you're an awful old man to be a-cuttin' up that way!" To which the Dixie Dewdrop cries in response: "Yes, but listen bud, it's nobody's business what I do!" In two days of recording, they churned out thirty songs in as many takes. Uncle Dave had been a moneymaker on the Vocalion and Brunswick labels, but for some reason, Brunswick decided to reject twelve numbers. Uncle Dave later recorded some of these in other sessions, but just as many others were forever lost.

Uncle Dave and Fiddlin' Sid reunited for another tour near the end of 1929. A talent agent had organized a series of shows around Bristol, Tennessee. During their time together, Uncle Dave asked the agent if he happened to know the popular, rising musical trio from nearby, the Carter Family. When the agent replied that he did know the Carters, Uncle Dave indicated that he would love to meet them. Phone calls were made, and one afternoon Uncle Dave and Sid drove the twenty miles to Maces Spring, Virginia, negotiating the high ridges and narrow, deep hollows that defined the countryside.

When the two arrived at the Carter house, A. P. and Sara welcomed them into their home. One can only speculate as to how the gregarious, comical Uncle Dave got along with the taciturn, aloof A. P. Carter. Not long afterward, a car drove up, and a young Maybelle Carter strolled into the house carrying her guitar. The conversation continued for a while longer until someone finally suggested they play a few songs together. For the next several minutes, the house filled with the sounds of Sara strumming her autoharp, Uncle Dave picking his banjo, Sid bowing his fiddle, and Maybelle fingering the "Carter scratch" on her guitar. They all joined in the singing and harmonizing, with

A. P. occasionally dropping his bass tones. What a jam session that must have been!

It was well that the entertainers lost themselves for a time in their music and camaraderie, for their lives were about to change drastically. For all Americans, and especially the entertainment industry, the entire bottom was about to drop out.

CHAPTER 5

"Eleven-cent Cotton, Forty-cent Meat"

RAY SMITH WAS A MAN at the end of his rope. Riding alone on a mule across the open spaces of eastern Rutherford County gave him time to reflect on all that had transpired the past few weeks. His father had just died, and desiring to be fair to all of his children, the older man had willed equal parcels of the family farm to each of them. Ray, with his own wife and children, had always lived on the farm to help his father work the land. By a great dint of effort, Ray had somehow managed to scrape together the money necessary to buy out his siblings and to take sole possession of the property.

Then things got really bad. After settling his father's affairs, a banker from Murfreesboro had arrived at the farm with unexpected, startling news. Out of the kindness of his heart, Ray's father had cosigned a loan earlier on another farm in the community, putting up his own acreage as collateral. When the Great Depression hit, the owner had been unable to make the payments. The banker informed Ray that he was now responsible for the loan, and that if a payment was not made forthwith, the bank intended to foreclose on the Smith farm. On the verge of losing everything he had ever worked for, Ray had saddled one of his work mules just after completing the morning chores and was making the four-mile ride to the home of the only man he believed could save the day: Uncle Dave Macon.

As Ray Smith rode along, the fields, hills, and cedar glades of Rutherford County seemed to groan under the weight of the Great Depression. The calamity that had struck the stock market in October 1929 had spread quickly, adversely affecting the entire country. With unemployment nearing 30 percent, the lack of money had become a national epidemic. Businesses and families that had accumulated debts during the Roaring Twenties were unable to pay their bills. Those who had once lived securely in their own houses or on farms found themselves huddled around campfires in shanty towns comprised of plywood and paper shacks. Their confidence shaken, Americans began to fear the country would never recover from the widespread economic devastation and that their lives might never again return to normal.

Middle Tennessee shared in the hardships. With agriculture prices plunging, rural farms were hit especially hard. Local newspapers were filled with entire pages of ads announcing foreclosures, auctions, and the sale of livestock. A major bank in Nashville had collapsed, wiping out millions of dollars in state tax revenues. A bank in Murfreesboro had gone under as well, taking with it the jobs of management and employees and all of the depositors' savings. When a second bank there approached dissolution, a group of nearly thirty local businessmen had teamed up to rescue it with a fresh infusion of cash and new management.

By midmorning, Ray had reached Kittrell. Instead of going straight to the Macon home, on a hunch he rode to the local country store nearby. Uncle Dave was inside with an unlit pipe clenched between his gold-capped teeth, "cutting up and having a great time" with some neighbors. The entertainer's face broke into a big grin when he recognized Ray Smith. Ray's father had been one of Uncle Dave's best friends. The two had met more than forty years earlier, when a young Dave Macon had worked as a liveryman at his mother's boarding house in Readyville. During a break in their back-and-forth conversations, Ray pulled Uncle Dave aside to tell him that he would like to discuss "a little business." The two soon withdrew to the Macon home across the road for more privacy.

While Ray tied up his mule and seated himself in one of the wooden Adirondack chairs on the front porch, Uncle Dave went inside and soon returned with a bottle of Jack Daniels and two glasses. He poured a few ounces into each glass, and as the two sipped their whiskey, Ray explained his predicament and that he needed to borrow $300 to pay off the loan his father had cosigned. Uncle Dave listened patiently throughout.

"Ray, it's too early in the morning to discuss money," the Dixie Dewdrop declared. "Let's have some music and relax for a while." Uncle Dave went inside and soon reappeared carrying one of his cherished Gibson banjos. Seating himself on the porch, the Dixie Dewdrop launched into a set of songs, as if he were performing before an entire audience. Between tunes, he hit Ray with pithy one-liners and funny jokes and spoke of the people and personalities he had encountered while playing on the Grand Ole Opry and during his recent travels. The session went on for two hours, and as noon approached, Ray mustered the courage to ask once again about the loan.

Uncle Dave replied that they would discuss the matter after lunch and then invited Ray inside for the noon meal. Afterward, they again returned to the front porch for more socializing. Finally, Ray told his elderly neighbor that he would soon have to head back to his farm for the evening chores. Uncle Dave excused himself, returning a few minutes later with a large wad of money in hand, more cash than Ray Smith had ever before seen. The farmer extended the palm of his hand as the Dixie Dewdrop counted out $300.

"Uncle Dave, we need to get some paper and draw up a proper written agreement," Ray volunteered.

"We don't need to sign anything," Uncle Dave replied, "because a hand-shake between neighbors is all that is needed." The older man paused a moment, studying Ray before continuing. "Ray, if for some reason circumstances keep you from paying me back, I want you to know that I understand that your wife and children need that money a lot more than I do." Ray thanked Uncle Dave profusely, said good-bye, and mounted his mule for the long ride home, greatly relieved to have the money needed to save his farm. Ray kept his nose to the grindstone throughout the Great Depression, and true to his word, was eventually able to repay his neighbor every penny owed.

Uncle Dave also kept his nose to the grindstone throughout the 1930s, always seeking ways to stay in touch with his audience and to maintain his popularity. Economic challenges fostered new venues, with Uncle Dave performing on Grand Ole Opry road shows and at new summer music festivals where he debuted fresh protest and religious songs. Whether spinning records at home, listening over the radio, or attending a live show, the Dixie Dewdrop's fans could forget about their cares and economic hardships for an hour or two while enjoying his performances. On a personal level, Uncle Dave was generous with his time and money toward other entertainers, neighbors, and even strangers, as they all coped with loss and adversity. At the same time, Uncle Dave dealt with his own hardships, including the greatest personal crisis of his life, which would come in 1939.

If the start of the 1930s was a troubling time for the country, the same could be said for Uncle Dave's career. His first big outing of 1930 was a trip to Knoxville, Tennessee, for a field recording session. What transpired there remains one of the most ambiguous and unproductive episodes of his entire career.

In the aftermath of Ralph Peer's famous 1927 field recording sessions in Bristol, Tennessee, other record companies began to view the East Tennessee region as a hotbed of old-time and mountain music. Peer himself had returned to Bristol in 1928, hoping to uncover additional, new songs and acts. Determined not to be outdone in the search for new talent in East Tennessee, Columbia Records sent a recording team to Johnson City in 1928 and 1929. For the same reasons, Brunswick sent technicians to Knoxville in August 1929. Sterchi Brothers Furniture, with its interest in promoting and selling old-time music records, had already marked Knoxville as a regional music center. Furthermore, Sterchi's had established WNOX, the city's first radio station.

Of the sixty-seven sides first recorded in Knoxville in 1929, Brunswick released nearly two-thirds and considered the outing a success. Planning soon began for a second Knoxville session. About this time, the company wrote Uncle Dave asking if he would care to participate. It appears as though Brunswick was hedging its bets; in the event no real talent surfaced, the company would at least have several new selections from the Dixie Dewdrop for release. Never one to turn down an opportunity, Uncle Dave agreed to record, and the session was scheduled for Monday, March 31, 1930.

The Dixie Dewdrop set about immediately to prepare for the trip. By this time, Dorris was good enough to record, and the father-son team worked up a number of songs. Wanting to exhibit a bit more musical variety, Uncle Dave once again turned to a trusted friend. Sid Harkreader was available and agreed to accompany the Macons. In the last week of March 1930, the trio jammed all their luggage and instruments into Uncle Dave's Model A Ford, and with Dorris at the wheel, set out on the 175-mile trek to Knoxville.

Brunswick's second field recording session began on Saturday, March 29. The location was the St. James Hotel, which also housed the broadcast studios for WNOX. The act from Middle Tennessee probably arrived that weekend, and an enterprising reporter from the *Knoxville News-Sentinel* managed to collar Uncle Dave for a rare interview. The economic decline was obviously on everyone's mind. When the reporter asked about it, Uncle Dave replied, "Of course, things are getting worse—things and old people and young." Then he launched into a discourse on the decline of music, morals, and religion:

A man who can't enjoy music has no heart and very little soul. People today are drifting away from the old tunes, the real music. And at the same time they are drifting away from morals—one is the cause of the other. When I was young you never saw more than the toe of a woman's shoe. No respectable girl would ever dream of allowing a boy to hug her—then. I never saw a drunk man when I was a boy. A man doesn't care for liquor when he can get all he wants and when he is not breaking a law when he drinks it.

Religion is not the same way anymore. Nowadays a preacher gets up in the pulpit and he doesn't preach; he says what the congregation wants him to say because they pay him to say it. There were always more people saved by the music than by the preachin'. No, I don't believe in a preacher makin' his congregation profess religion by gettin' them afraid of hell, either. If you make a man join a church by makin' him afraid of hell, you've got to keep him afraid of it to keep him a member.

If Uncle Dave seemed uncharacteristically down and dour during the interview, what happened during the recording session on Monday, March 31, didn't help. Uncle Dave, Sid, and Dorris recorded as many as ten songs; ten Brunswick sequence numbers were reserved for the session, but the titles of only eight songs survive. The exact arrangements for each tune remain uncertain as well. The Dixie Dewdrop may have done a few solos, but Dorris and Sid certainly accompanied him on other songs. Sid specifically recalled fiddling alongside Uncle Dave that day but never performing a solo himself. One summation of the session suggests that Uncle Dave and Dorris performed as many as five duets.

From the outset, the session was fraught with problems. The engineers informed the musicians that something was wrong and that the audio had gone bad. Still, efforts at recording went on for about an hour. At one point, Uncle Dave had a discussion with a Brunswick representative about that session's contract. A disagreement had arisen, and Uncle Dave refused to sign it. Not long afterward, the trio packed up their instruments, checked out of the hotel, and headed home. According to Sid Harkreader, the usually unflappable Uncle Dave "was kind of disgusted about the whole thing." They were out all of the expenses of the trip, did not make a penny from the outing, and had even turned down another engagement to go to Knoxville. While all of this was certainly disappointing in the short term, the far more significant result of the failed session was that as many as ten Uncle Dave songs were forever lost to music posterity.

The Knoxville session marked the conclusion of Uncle Dave's six-year relationship with Brunswick-Vocalion. There was a certain poetry to the ending, which took place only a short distance from where it had all begun. In spring 1924, Uncle Dave had stopped in Knoxville at Sterchi's headquarters building to pick up necessary paperwork before continuing to New York City for his first recording session. Six years later, his last recording session with Brunswick-Vocalion took place at the St. James Hotel in downtown Knoxville, less than a city block from the same Sterchi building where he had first embarked upon his recording career.

The abortive Knoxville outing was perhaps indicative of the fact that the whole recording industry was in the middle of a major crackup. In 1929 total, national record sales stood at $74 million. A year later, the same sales took in only $46 million, stark evidence of the economic collapse engulfing the nation. And things got progressively worse. By 1933, annual record sales plummeted to only $5.5 million, a decline of nearly 93 percent from peak sales levels just four years earlier. National record sales would not recover fully until after World War II, despite a slight uptick in the late 1930s. Recordings and sales of old-time and mountain music were not immune from the downturn. For example, there would not be another field recording session in East Tennessee until after World War II.

Undaunted by mounting evidence that the recording industry was falling on hard times, Uncle Dave still sought new opportunities to record. He eventually contacted H. C. Spier, a Jackson, Mississippi, business man and talent scout for OKeh Records. Arrangements were soon set, and Uncle Dave traveled to Jackson with Sam McGee for his only recording session with OKeh. On December 17, 1930, the duo cut ten sides on fourteen takes, comprising some of the best banjo-guitar and banjo playing they ever recorded. OKeh released six of the ten tunes, and because of the struggling economy, they sold poorly. Fortunately, the master pressings of three of the rejected songs—"Oh Lovin' Babe," "Come On Buddie, Don't You Want to Go," and "Go On, Nora Lee"—were discovered in the Macon family's possession in the late 1970s and subsequently released on modern albums.

During the session, Uncle Dave once again demonstrated his genius at capturing in song the contemporary, human experiences and emotions of his fans. "The Wreck of the Tennessee Gravy Train" graphically depicted the public's outrage with the corruption, cronyism, and failed leadership too often manifested among elected officials. At the onset of the Great Depression, Governor Henry Horton of Tennessee hoped to boost economic activity and combat unemployment with a road-building program. The state raised $5 million with the sale of bonds, and Governor Horton appointed a highway commission to allocate the monies and oversee the work. Unfortunately, most of the funds went out on noncompetitive bid contracts to a large road-building company owned by a Horton crony. Other funds went into the coffers of banks owned and managed by Horton operatives, who used the money to recoup losses incurred in the stock market crash. In the end, the money disappeared with hardly a mile of new pavement laid or any jobs created. The song's opening verses explained Tennesseans' dismay and disgust with the scandal:

> The people of Tennessee want to know
> who wrecked our gravy train.
> The one we thought was run so well
> and now who can we blame.
> They want to know who greased the track
> and started them down the road.
> The same old train contained our money
> to build our highway road.

The chorus captured the fear and frustration people felt during the Great Depression, even suggesting that relief from life's troubles would be found only in the hereafter:

> But now we're up against it
> and no use to raise a row.
> But of all the times I've ever seen,
> we're sure up against it now.
> The only thing that we can do
> is do the best we can.
> Foller me, good people,
> I'm bound for the Promised Land.

Pain and suffering in the lives of musicians often generate their most sublime work. In Uncle Dave's case, the distress of the Great Depression produced perhaps his most renowned protest song, "Eleven-cent Cotton, Forty-cent Meat." Based on an original composition and recording of the same title by producer, songwriter, and performer Bob Miller in the late

1920s, Uncle Dave's arrangement employed mostly new lyrics. Though the Dixie Dewdrop never recorded it commercially, his ode to the quiet desperation of farmers and the rural poor became a standard performance staple. Its simple words and stark images of poverty struck a chord with audiences. The first verse declared:

> 11-cent cotton, 40-cent meat
> How in the world can a poor man eat?
> Mules up high; cotton down low,
> How in the world I'm gonna raise the dough?

Uncle Dave apparently felt that he had so much to say in one song that there was no room for a chorus, and the lack of a chorus is nearly unique among his repertoire. Another verse opined:

> 11-cent cotton, 10-dollar pants,
> Who in the world has got a chance?
> Can't buy clothes; ya can't buy meat,
> Got too much cotton; not enough to eat.

A lifelong Democrat, Uncle Dave encouraged listeners to place hope in the many federal, work, and financial programs that comprised President Franklin D. Roosevelt's New Deal:

> Say there Uncle Sam, so what will they do?
> Can't solve the problem, so it's up to you.
> 11-cent cotton and 2-dollar hose,
> Guess we'll have to go without clothes.

The protest song would one day achieve a singular distinction in the Dixie Dewdrop's career by becoming the final number he ever performed.

Another expansion of Uncle Dave's performance repertoire occurred in the early 1930s when he added gospel songs to his national broadcasts. While he had always included sacred hymns as part of his shows and recording sessions, he had shied away from performing them on the Opry. Uncle Dave's oldest son, Archie, noticed that even though his father strove to be a good Christian in his private life and had recorded sacred songs, he never mentioned God during public performances on WSM. One day, Archie cornered his father with a straightforward question: "Why can't you play something for the Lord in your programs?" Uncle Dave responded that he was uncertain how the managers at WSM and the Grand Ole Opry or other performers would react, let alone the listening audience. Uncle Dave finally concluded: "You have to either be for the barn dance, or against it."

But Uncle Dave must have given the whole matter a second thought, for a few weeks later, he closed his set on the Saturday night Opry with "Shall We Gather at the River." The live audience response was enthusiastic, and letters and telegrams from listeners across the nation flooded WSM, conveying their thanks and asking that more sacred music be performed. From that time forward, Uncle Dave closed each of his Opry broadcasts with a religious song.

Over the years, "How Beautiful Heaven Must Be" became his signature sacred song. The hymn first caught his attention during a graveside funeral service near Kingsport, Tennessee. He had put on a show there, and during the visit, a close friend of the promoter had died unexpectedly. Deeply shaken by the sudden loss, the promoter asked if Uncle Dave would shore him up by staying at his side throughout the funeral, and he was glad to oblige. Kirk McGee had traveled there too, attending the funeral as well. At the graveside service a local Methodist church choir performed "How Beautiful Heaven Must Be." Struck by the hymn's lilting melody and hopeful words, Uncle Dave leaned over to Kirk and whispered for him to get the name of the song so that he "could work it up." Work it up he did, and the hymn and Uncle Dave became forever linked.

If Uncle Dave's music career was undergoing change in the first half of the 1930s, the same could be said of WSM and the Grand Ole Opry. Perhaps the most important developments in WSM's history came in 1931. In one fell swoop, federal communications regulators boosted the station's power from 5,000 to 50,000 watts and assigned it a clear channel frequency on the radio dial at 650 AM. The clear channel designation meant that no other radio station in the nation was allowed to broadcast on WSM's frequency at night, giving listeners unimpeded, nighttime access to the "Air Castle of the South." With the tremendous boost in power and clear channel status, WSM could now be heard at night in all of the thirty-five states east of the Rocky Mountains. To transmit its powerful signal, WSM needed a new antenna. The towering, iron spire, standing nearly nine hundred feet tall and located eight miles south of downtown Nashville, went fully operational in October 1932. If Ralph Peer's 1927 Bristol recording session had been the "big bang"

of the country music recording industry, WSM's boost in power and clear channel status on the radio dial was the "big bang" of the country music broadcast industry.

WSM's new reach as a radio powerhouse introduced Opry stars to legions of new fans. In northwestern Illinois, some 500 miles from Nashville, William Doubler took a weekly respite from the backbreaking, incessant labor of running a large farm, operating a local tavern, and raising a family by tuning into the Opry every Saturday night. Those hours were sacrosanct; work never interfered and quiet was demanded throughout the whole house during the broadcast. Uncle Dave was his favorite performer. Whenever the Dixie Dewdrop closed his last set for that night's performance, William Doubler would lean forward in his chair, slap his knee in excitement and gleefully declare: "By God, I'd sure like to meet that ol' codger!" Though William would never meet the Dixie Dewdrop, his youngest son did. Alvin Doubler would enlist in the army in 1940, survive the fighting in Europe during World War II, return to Illinois for a time, and finally move to Tennessee where he married Uncle Dave's granddaughter, Mary Victoria Macon, and became a favored son-in-law to the Macons.

On another occasion, a resident of Woodbury had to make a trip out West and decided to drive. A low gas tank necessitated a stop at a filling station in Arizona. When the attendant saw the car's Tennessee plates, he asked the traveler where he was from. "Oh, it's a little hill county you never heard of called Cannon," the Tennessean replied. "Oh, yes," responded the attendant, "that's Dave Macon's county. I listen to him every Saturday night."

In addition to technical advances, new types of performers and entertainment styles were joining the Opry. One of these was the "Vagabonds," a trio of vocalists from the Midwest who had made a name on WLS and at KMOX in St. Louis. Though Uncle Dave remained the Opry's most celebrated performer and predominant vocalist in the first half of the 1930s, the Vagabonds marked the beginning of a transition to more vocal acts. Comedians became more prominent as well, especially the female duo "Sarie and Sally" and a blackface comedian, Leroy "Lasses" White, who, with his partner, "Honey" Wilds, formed the hit team "Lasses and Honey."

The increasing crowds that showed up for the live Opry broadcasts resulted in a continuous quest for a suitable performance venue. By 1934, the WSM studios in the National Life building could no longer handle the acute overcrowding and, in October of that year, the Opry moved to a new home at the Hillsboro Theater, which seated 2,400. Two years later, the show moved once again to the Dixie Tabernacle in East Nashville, a larger but more Spartan facility. Meanwhile, a ticketing system emerged primarily as a means of crowd control, but a show admission would not be charged for another five years.

The Opry also settled on a new format, making the transition from the "good natured riot" it had been in early 1926 to a more professional and polished act. The driving force behind the transformation was Vito Pellettieri. An earlier illness had ended his career as a musician, and Pellettieri had worked for a while as WSM's music librarian before becoming the Opry's stage manager. Perhaps his most significant reform was to divide the program into discrete, fifteen-minute segments. The measure assigned performers to specific time slots, allowed for better transitions between acts, and yielded a more polished on-air presentation. At the same time, WSM sought sponsors for both the entire Opry broadcast as well as individual segments. The new show format endures to the present day largely unchanged.

Realizing that most families were strapped for cash and unable to travel long distances to Nashville for live shows, and that others were too poor to attend even small, local performances, the Opry decided to do a better job of taking its wares to the people. In a shrewd business move, it organized groups of performers into traveling shows, booking them on circuits throughout certain geographic regions with an emphasis on performances in larger cities. A big contract with the RKO theater chain, which owned nearly 140 locations in the Northeast and Midwest, sent Opry members to new locales, thereby introducing tens of thousands of Americans to country music.

The Opry's "Unit #1" included its biggest stars. Uncle Dave was the headliner, accompanied by Dorris, Sam and Kirk McGee, and Humphrey Bate along with his son Buster, daughter Alcyone, and Alcyone's aunt, Lou Hesson. As a group, the performers were billed as "Uncle Dave Macon and His Moonshiners." They never performed together onstage as a single act, but conducted a vaudeville-style show by offering Humphrey Bate and his band as an opener, followed by Sam and Kirk, with Uncle Dave and Dorris appearing on stage last as the final crescendo.

DeFord Bailey's masterful harmonica playing made him one of the Opry's most renowned performers, and it was during travels in the 1930s that he struck up a sincere friendship with Uncle Dave. Their relationship included a truly unique dimension. As a product of the Old South, Dave Macon grew up in an age of blatant discrimination and segregation against blacks. While he largely accepted these social and legal norms, Uncle Dave bristled whenever blacks in his direct company faced discrimination or unfair treatment.

DeFord was often refused basic services while touring in the South, and Uncle Dave frequently took action to right the wrongs. In hotels where blacks were not allowed, the Dixie Dewdrop routinely told desk clerks that DeFord was his personal valet and that a room was needed with an extra bed or a couch where he could sleep. Most hoteliers were glad to oblige, while just as many others completely looked the other way, welcoming the music stars with no qualms. One hotel manager declared that while DeFord was welcome to stay, a bed was just not available. Uncle Dave solved the problem by asking others to remove the lower, back seat from his Ford sedan and lug it into Uncle Dave's room as a sleeping pallet for DeFord. Restaurants, too, posed a problem. Most establishments would not allow DeFord to eat at a table or a counter, but did permit him to take meals in the kitchen. Whenever all service was refused, Uncle Dave carried meals to DeFord who remained outside in the car. One time Uncle Dave delivered him a sandwich, and DeFord thanked the elder man profusely. "Poor old black man. I was aiming to charge him," the Dixie Dewdrop replied with a big laugh, "but I can't charge him now. He's done thanked me for it." The friendship stuck; when DeFord Bailey passed away in 1982 one of Uncle Dave's grandsons, David Ramsey Macon, acted as a pallbearer.

Back in Nashville it wasn't all fun and music; there was a growing unease between Opry stars and management. The requirement for performers to return to Nashville each Saturday night put a damper on touring schedules, especially when show admissions were a primary source of income in the face of paltry record sales. To placate cast members, the Opry began to pay musicians a fee of $5 for each performance. To counter the charge that weekly returns to Nashville restricted booking opportunities, the WSM Artists Service was formed in 1933. Its role was to book appearances and perform promotional work for entertainers in exchange for a 15 percent management fee.

George D. Hay's influence at the Opry was already on the wane due to management conflicts. With the debut of new acts and styles, the Solemn Old Judge was concerned the Opry was too soon drifting from its original, "down to earth" music roots, a factor less concerning to WSM management. Long work absences due to stints of poor health further reduced Hay's influence. In an effort to restore his prestige, WSM appointed Hay the additional duty of heading the Artists Service. Its first major booking at a large, black church in downtown Nashville was a flop. Despite a respectable slate of performers, attendance was so poor and the gate so small that Hay decided to donate it all to the church.

Promoter and entrepreneur C. Reid Dowland provided the Artists Service with its next big opportunity. Originally from Skullbone, Tennessee, Dowland was a federal employee in Nashville who had developed a reputation as a businessman and entrepreneur. A true music lover whose ancestors came from the Celtic Highlands, Dowland concocted a moneymaking scheme with plans to bring the Opry's stars to rural fans in a big way. Renting farm acreage for a major outdoor gathering was cheaper than leasing a large theater in a city center, and Dowland soon secured suitable land near Backusburg, Kentucky. He then contracted with the WSM Artists Service for a day of country music entertainment, with Uncle Dave Macon as the main headliner.

Dowland organized the Backusburg, Kentucky, site with the precision and functionality of a military encampment. A stage decorated with American flags and red, white, and blue bunting and equipped with a sound system was strategically positioned under trees. Rows of benches for attendees neatly lined the fields and other shaded areas. Paths were designated for foot traffic and automobile access. Around the seating areas stood long tables and booths from which vendors would sell soft drinks, sandwiches, breads, and other snacks. Dowland advertised the "musicale" far and wide with posters, newspaper ads, and radio spots. The event's main poster featured a picture of Uncle Dave, promoting him as the "Funniest Man in the World."

America's first major outdoor music festival commenced on July 4, 1934. Within two hours after sunup, as many as 8,000 people were already on hand. Uncle Dave was already there, warming up for the day's performance. At midmorning a caravan of other Grand Ole Opry stars arrived. Judge Hay was in the vanguard, hoping that his personal supervision would help to insure the day's success. The convoy of entertainers included DeFord Bailey, Paul Warnack's Gully Jumpers, and the Fruit Jar Drinkers. When the show was delayed due to pedestrian and traffic congestion, the crowd grew restless. At one point, people noticed Dowland striding along the event's perimeter with a sack of money and an escort of deputies. While the promoter was actually removing the money to a more secure location, word spread that he was taking flight with the early ticket proceeds without actually putting on a show. A considerable surge of anger and disgust swept rapidly through the audience.

Uncle Dave saw what was happening, jumped onto the stage, and immediately grabbed the microphone. He calmed the entire crowd with his commanding presence and reassuring words:

> Folks, you think this whole woods full of people is a big crowd, and it is, but you ain't seen nothin' yet. The roads are jammed for miles, and we had to walk through the corn fields to get here and all. But we are here, so simmer down and let's have some fun! Mr. Dowland is not to blame.

The Dixie Dewdrop then took up his banjo, delivering a set of songs and jokes that turned the crowd's anxiety into sheer delight. Writing nearly thirty years later, Dowland declared that Uncle Dave had "saved the day, if not my life!"

The turnout for the Backusburg festival exceeded 20,000 fans. The immense numbers of wagons, buggies, and cars kicked up a dust cloud that was visible miles away. Ticket attendants collected money as fast as their hands would allow: admission was 25 cents. With the temperature at 105 degrees, festivalgoers turned to food and drink for refreshment. Vendors sold 19,200 bottled sodas, countless tubs of lemonade, the butchered pork of 35 hogs, and 8,000 hamburgers.

At the end of a long day, Dowland and Judge Hay huddled in a secure tent, and with the help of trusted individuals, sorted and counted the piles of quarters and paper bills that had been collected. The money was separated into empty cigar boxes, and at the end of the process, Dowland handed Hay a high stack of boxes, which represented the Artists Service's payment. The event's great success insured that others like it soon followed. The Backusburg Musicale of 1934 established one of America's favorite entertainment venues: the outdoor summer music festival.

The Delmore Brothers needed help; such was the stark conclusion of WSM's senior management. Indeed, from the very start, Alton and Rabon Delmore had a rocky relationship with WSM. The brothers had grown up near Athens, Alabama, as part of a musically inclined family. Their mother had composed songs, a gift that she passed in spades to her son Alton. Both brothers loved to perform, and after good success with appearances at regional shows and fiddle contests, they had recorded for the first time in

Atlanta on the Columbia label in 1931. Among their prominent performance traits were soft harmonies, original and well-crafted songs, and exceptional guitar work. Despite their early accomplishments, the brothers yearned to make it to WSM and the Opry. Alton launched a regular letter-writing campaign, asking for an audition. Rejection letters came back just as regularly, explaining that the Opry's slate of performers was full. Alton came to believe that WSM hired only Tennesseans, but one day a letter of acceptance arrived from Harry Stone, WSM's station manager. The siblings were invited to an audition at WSM's studios on a Monday in early April 1933.

The Delmore Brothers were elated at the new opportunity, but euphoria soon turned to anxiety when they realized their old car could probably not make the long trip to Nashville without breaking down. A cousin volunteered to drive them in his car but he was unavailable on the scheduled day. Alton and Rabon decided they would simply go to Nashville the following day when their ride was available, but they failed to grasp the need to get Harry Stone's approval for the schedule change. "We didn't think one day would make much difference," Alton declared, "so we headed for Nashville without giving it much thought."

Their lapse in judgment resulted in an icy reception. Upon arriving in downtown Nashville, they made it to WSM's offices and asked for the station manager. He was not in at the moment, and a receptionist invited them to tour the studios and offices while they waited. Dressed in drab, rough-hewn work clothes and carrying their guitars in cases made from cotton pick-sacks, the regal appearances of WSM's facilities awed the brothers. A testy Harry Stone soon arrived, wanting to know why the Delmores had not shown up the previous day. A tense conversation ensued, with Alton not being able to grasp Stone's reaction to a "trivial thing like not being there on the day he stated." Setting aside his disappointment, the station manager finally asked the brothers to audition on the spot. Alton and Rabon launched into a series of original songs for Stone and a number of other executives. Their performance won the day. When it was all over, the Delmore Brothers were hired, appearing on the Opry for the first time on April 29, 1933.

While the Delmore Brothers' superb musical and performance talents were never questioned—Alton would eventually compose approximately one thousand songs—they struggled to manage their business affairs effectively. Like many aspiring artists, they made the profound mistake of placing inordinate emphasis on the music while all but ignoring the routine but necessary administrative and financial aspects of the entertainment business. "We were just two country boys, very young and green and timid," Alton confessed, "and never coped with the cruel world of reality. And the cruel world took advantage of it." Still, WSM realized their long-term potential and decided to assist the brothers by teaming them up with the Opry's most experienced and successful performer.

In the spring of 1933, Uncle Dave needed the Delmore Brothers just as much as they needed him. Dorris had decided to get married, and Uncle Dave was on the brink of losing his musical accompanist and chauffeur. In fact, one reason Dorris was getting married was because his father had played matchmaker. Dorris had taken a liking to a Woodbury woman, Tina Mae LeFevers, though she was his senior by a few years. From a wealthy family, the sudden death of an older sister had put Tina Mae in a position to inherit all of her parents' lands and money. Always conscious of the worth of money, Uncle Dave strongly encouraged the union, and the couple wed in March 1933. To begin their new life together, Tina Mae insisted that Dorris come off the road and find local work. The marriage's first few years were stormy, with Dorris often returning home to Kittrell for extended stays or holding up in a local hotel until the two reconciled.

Uncle Dave and the Delmore Brothers began touring together in earnest in the latter half of 1933. The Dixie Dewdrop implemented similar travel arrangements he had previously made with others; the brothers were to provide the car with Alton doing the driving, while Rabon and Uncle Dave covered all of the expenses of gas, oil, and repairs. The siblings couldn't help but notice Uncle Dave's honesty and fastidiousness in financial matters. The elder musician kept track of earnings and expenses in a small notebook he carried in his black grip. Show earnings were split between the three down to the last penny. Uncle Dave taught the younger men good techniques for negotiating contracts and placing effective advertising. By watching the Dixie Dewdrop in action, Alton and Rabon learned that tending to business matters was just as important to a professional musician as continuous practice and the learning of new songs.

One of their earliest and greatest lessons in deal-making unfolded at a Chevrolet car dealership in Athens, Alabama. The car they toured in initially burned an inordinate amount of oil, and Uncle Dave finally declared that maintaining the contraption would "break up a millionaire." It was time to find another automobile. They soon made it to the dealership, with the brothers heading to the used car lot while Uncle Dave sought out the establishment's proprietor. The owner was a friendly, gregarious fellow, and the two swapped stories, jokes, and much laughter.

The Delmores came inside shortly to inform Uncle Dave they had found a suitable used car. Uncle Dave took advantage of the interlude to spring his real plan. "Cap," he said to the owner, "let's see what you have in a new car you can sell the boys." While Alton and Rabon soon left to look at new cars, Uncle Dave closed the deal; the owner agreed to give the brothers a good value on their trade-in with Uncle Dave writing a check for the balance of the new car. Before he made a final commitment, Uncle Dave checked with his companions. While the Delmores had no money at all to purchase the car, Uncle Dave agreed to write the check, with them making periodic payments to him out of their future show earnings. Before long, the three rode off the lot, the first time the Delmores had ever ridden in a new car. The siblings were awed by the smooth, confident manner in which Uncle Dave had proposed and closed the deal. As the brothers drove away from the dealership in their new car with their renowned passenger, they were convinced beyond all doubt that the Dixie Dewdrop was "strictly big time."

An unexpected recording opportunity surfaced in the late summer of 1934. A few years earlier, Kirk McGee had recorded with Gennett Records, a subsidiary of the Starr Piano Company in Richmond, Indiana. Early that summer, Kirk wrote Gennett to ask if the label would be interested in a recording session featuring Uncle Dave and the McGees. When Gennett agreed, the trio headed to Indiana. The Gennett session took place over two days, August 14–15. In all, Uncle Dave recorded eleven songs in as many takes, with Sam and Kirk accompanying him at various times on fiddle, banjo, and banjo-guitar. The McGees also recorded three songs separately, including a Sam McGee guitar solo masterpiece, "Railroad Blues." Of the eleven Uncle Dave tunes, Gennett accepted only four for release. The most popular of these was "When the Train Comes Along," a great gospel song from the black tradition, which likens the gathering and departure of passengers from a train station to the blessings and release from earthly trials believers will experience the day they pass from this life to the next. The four Gennett recordings were subsequently rereleased on the Champion, Montgomery Ward, and Decca labels.

Uncle Dave and the Delmore Brothers toured together regularly for three years, performing onstage as both a trio and as separate acts. At the same time, Alton had struck up a relationship with Eli Oberstein, the talent scout who had taken Ralph Peer's place at RCA Victor. As a result, the Delmore Brothers recorded several times on the Bluebird label, RCA's budget record line. In late 1934, Alton and Oberstein made arrangements for another recording session which was to include the Delmore Brothers, the Dixie Dewdrop, and Opry fiddler Arthur Smith.

The session was set for New Orleans, Louisiana, and Uncle Dave and the Delmores arrived there by car on the afternoon of January 21, 1935. The next morning they awoke to a big surprise; a freakish winter storm had covered New Orleans with a heavy dusting of snow and cold temperatures. RCA had rented an old warehouse, which had no heat, for the field recording session. Eli Oberstein had procured a coal oil heater, but the unit seemed to give off more smoke than warmth. The warehouse was right on a busy back alley that delivery trucks used frequently, and their rumblings would cause background noise issues throughout the day.

A marathon recording session began on the morning of January 22, which lasted far into the night. Alton and Rabon recorded first, producing sixteen sides in six hours. The cold made the brothers' fingers go numb, and between numbers they vigorously rubbed them to restore feeling. Arthur Smith then recorded eight instrumentals, accompanied by the Delmores. Throughout the day, Uncle Dave waited patiently in the cold warehouse. A black group, the Southern University Quartet, was there as well waiting to record. True to form, Uncle Dave struck up a conversation with the young blacks, and before long, they were cracking up with his jokes and tall tales. Finally, it was the Dixie Dewdrop's turn. During the first take, he turned away from the microphone several times to grin at the black quartet, resulting in sound distortions. A buzzer sounded indicating that the recording was no good, and everyone stopped playing. Seconds later, Eli Oberstein emerged from the sound booth. He had seen Uncle Dave joking with the quartet earlier and knew exactly what had happened.

"Now, Uncle Dave," the talent scout began, "you are not here to sing for those boys back there, so come on now, and let's get something going." Uncle Dave had endured a long day in the cold waiting patiently to record, only to be cut short in the middle of his first take. While Oberstein was no doubt correct about the sound problem, he had made the mistake of admonishing the Grand Ole Opry's most esteemed entertainer in front of younger, less experienced musicians. Uncle Dave felt the need to defend himself, and he did:

Now, Cap, I can sing anyway I want to, and still be heard. I've got a lot of gitup and go. And I've got a smokehouse full of country hams and all kinds of meat to eat up there in Readyville. I've got plenty of wood hauled up, and I don't have to be bossed around by some New York sharpshooter just to make a few records, 'cause I've done done my part of the record making anyway.

A break ensued in which everyone regrouped, and before long, the session resumed. The Delmore Brothers recorded four songs with Uncle Dave—"Over the Mountain," "When the Harvest Days Are Gone," "One More River to Cross," and "Just One Way to the Pearly Gates,"—which prominently featured their delicate, involved harmonies. The Dixie Dewdrop rerecorded a solo comedic song, "I'll Tickle Nancy," a number filled with sexual innuendo. The last title was a slower paced version of his first big hit, "Keep My Skillet Good and Greasy." Bluebird accepted every song for release and subsequently contracted with Uncle Dave for two more recording sessions.

If the Delmore Brothers learned and grew during their time with the Dixie Dewdrop, the relationship was not a one-way street, especially considering Alton's songwriting abilities. Dorris went along once when Uncle Dave and the Delmores had a show in Birmingham. An unexpected change in their schedule freed up several hours, and the four crowded into a hotel room for a jam session. Uncle Dave asked Alton to critique a new song he had been writing. As Uncle Dave began the number, Alton pulled out a blank piece of sheet music, and with rapid, computerlike precision, jotted down the notes and recorded the lyrics in shorthand. When the tune ended, Alton reviewed his work and then asked Uncle Dave to perform it again. As the song was repeated, Alton reconsidered the notes and words, making minor alterations. Finally, Alton picked up his guitar, saying "this is the way the song should sound" when it was recorded and then played the improved version all the way through.

By 1936, the Delmore Brothers had become a big act in their own right, and the Opry was no longer willing for them and Uncle Dave to tour as a single unit. The Delmores now had to swim on their own, and Uncle Dave would have to find a new accompanist and traveling partner. Alton and Rabon stayed at the Opry for two more years until differences over bookings finally prompted them to depart. The brothers never forgot the kindness and professionalism Uncle Dave had shown toward them, and neither did the entire Delmore family. Alton's daughter, Norma, summed up the family's sentiments: "The Delmore Brothers would simply not have gotten started if it hadn't been for Uncle Dave."

If Uncle Dave's career continued to thrive throughout the Great Depression, there was a bad moon rising in Kittrell in several respects. Even though the Macons' home and lands remained secure throughout the crisis, their finances had been hit hard. It is not known how much money they lost due to bank closures, but the amount was enough to cause considerable anxiety. Dave had long forgotten his grievance over paying other family members for a house and lands that had been gifted; his new financial angst centered on bankers. On those occasions when he drank too much, or when a mild resurgence of melancholy occurred, he would sit near the fireplace and cuss the banks while wiping away tears. His most severe declarations were reserved for bank robbers. Anyone depraved and brazen enough to charge into a bank with a loaded tommy gun and make off with the life savings of depositors in the midst of the financial crisis was the lowest of the low, and Dave believed that convicted bank robbers should suffer the death penalty.

While her husband fumed and wept, Miss Tildy took action. She, too, had lost confidence in the banks but was determined to find ways to protect her family's financial security. The Macons acquired a sizable, heavy safe to store important papers and money. At the same time, Tildy began to squirrel away cash in an old suitcase, which she hid on the property. To make sure the money was neither disturbed nor stolen, Tildy never disclosed the bag's location to anyone.

Dave always relied upon his faith to sustain and comfort him. Whenever home, he regularly attended Haynes Chapel. The church's most celebrated member routinely occupied the same position at services: the right front pew in the seat closest to the center aisle. Despite the hard financial times, Dave maintained a set schedule of tithing. An usher at Haynes Chapel never forgot an incident one Sunday morning. When the offering plate came to Uncle Dave, he dutifully contributed. The usher was shocked when he saw the $5 bill the Opry star had deposited, a significant amount of money in that day. Once the collection was completed, Dave discreetly motioned for the usher to return up front. Going forward, the man assumed that Uncle Dave wanted to make change for the large bill he had given. Instead, he slipped another $5 bill into the plate. Looking up at the usher with an uncharacteristic, sheepish expression, Dave quietly whispered: "I didn't give enough the first time."

Wanting to make sure that his name stayed in the public limelight throughout the economic downturn, Uncle Dave took the unusual step of displaying conspicuous signage on his property. In one of his most eccentric moments, he hammered a line of large, block letters nearly two feet high that spelled out his name across the entire front of the house facing the Woodbury Road: *UNCLE DAVE MACON.* Anyone passing by could not help but notice where the Dixie Dewdrop lived. When he realized that the slanted roof above the front porch obscured the top portion of the letters as viewed from the highway, Dave nailed a second set of smaller but more visible letters just below the first to prevent any possible confusion. The most garish signage was a billboard on stilts in the front yard. A theater in Rockingham, North Carolina, had created an attractive, mounted image of the Dixie Dewdrop measuring about ten feet high and five feet wide to promote an appearance there. Uncle Dave was so impressed with the sign that he asked for it, and the theater obliged. Somehow, it got back home to Tennessee and went up on a pair of stilts in the front yard. Finally, when the supports gave out, Uncle Dave propped the huge sign upright on the front porch where it remained on display for nearly a decade.

While the signage invited fans to stop at the house, it also attracted the attention of down-and-out drifters. An irregular stream of hobos and tramps came onto the property, begging for clothing, money, and food. While he always tried to be generous to those less fortunate, one day Dave reached his limit. When a wanderer approached to ask if they could spare a meal, Dave ordered the man to get off his property. Overhearing the exchange from inside, Tildy emerged onto the front porch. When the visitor assured her he was hungry and only craving something to eat, Tildy overruled her husband, instructing the man to circle around to the rear of the house and enter through the kitchen door. A meal was served and afterward, the visitor expressed his thanks and quietly departed. Dave was miffed over the incident, and Tildy finally had to explain herself. "As long as a person comes here only wanting something to eat while we have enough for ourselves," she offered, "my Christian faith won't allow me to turn him away."

Dave and Tildy began hosting big Sunday dinners at their house whenever he was home. While the dinners were meant to strengthen family ties, the gatherings also ensured that all extended family members were getting enough to eat during the Great Depression. The family's cook, Aunt Myrt, put on huge meals with all the trimmings. Annie's daughter, Ruth, recalled that even at a time when many people were suffering from hunger, the Macon table was "always fully loaded." Dave entertained his family with songs and stories of his travels. Following dinner, Dave would sit under a big shade tree in the front yard, perusing the fan mail he had picked up the previous night at the Opry, having toted the mail home in his banjo case. With age creeping up on him, Dave was not bashful about asking others to wait on him. He regularly requested family members to fetch his shoes, pipe, a drink, reading glasses, or whatever else he might need. Sunday afternoons would sometimes see him taking a nap on a chaise lounge on the front porch, and it fell to the grandkids to fan him and shoo flies away as he slept. "Pap didn't host Sunday dinners," Robert Macon, the oldest grandson, observed later with a chuckle, "he held court."

While visiting America's larger cities, Uncle Dave was introduced to a new, modern convenience: indoor plumbing. On one occasion, Dave talked to Tildy about the possibilities of installing plumbing and an inside bathroom. Comfortable with using an outhouse all of her life, Tildy couldn't imagine anyone relieving themselves indoors. When her husband persisted, she finally put her foot down. There was no way she was going to allow "that stink" inside her home, and there the matter ended. For as long as the Macons owned the Kittrell house, neither indoor plumbing nor an interior bathroom were ever installed.

Dorris always remembered a humorous incident about Uncle Dave and an outhouse. One cold, winter night, they stayed at a remote, rural hotel that had an outside bathroom behind the building. Dorris used the facility before bedtime while feeling the full effects of a cold, cutting north wind. Minutes after returning to his room, Uncle Dave asked him if he had found the outhouse. Dorris gave the directions, warning his father to brace himself against the icy blast. When Uncle Dave reappeared a few minutes later, Dorris asked how he had fared, especially against the frigid wind. "I didn't notice it going out," Uncle Dave replied, "but it sure was cold coming back!"

At the start of 1935, Dave suffered an acute loss when neighbor, close friend, and music partner, Mazy Todd, passed away. He had been severely injured in an accident at his sawmill sometime earlier and never fully recovered. After an extended illness, Mazy died at his home in Kittrell on January 11, 1935, at age fifty-three. Survived by his wife and four daughters, one of the most remarkable, amateur fiddle players of all time was laid to rest in Evergreen Cemetery in Murfreesboro.

A major reconciliation between siblings occurred later that same year. Uncle Dave often confided to Judge Hay on personal matters, including Dave's uneasy relationship with his oldest brother regarding his entertainment career. Fifteen years earlier, Van Macon had discouraged his younger brother's dream of becoming a professional entertainer. Judge Hay recalled that even after Dave's success, Van "looked down his nose at Uncle Dave's proclivities in the field of entertainment." A Macon through and through, Van at one time used humor in an attempt to acknowledge Dave's accomplishments. At his home on the western outskirts of Woodbury, Van affixed a large sign high above the double doors of a garage which faced the Woodbury Road. The first line of signage read "Brother of Uncle Dave Macon," and just below was a bold, black arrow pointing west toward Kittrell. A final line underneath read "Ten and three-quarters miles west," a direct quote from Dave's autobiographical song, "From Earth to Heaven."

On the afternoon of July 4, 1935, Dave put on a show at a school in Woodbury. It was so hot that organizers scrapped plans for an indoor program; Dave played on the school's front porch while fans lounged on the open lawn. Seeking to avoid the blazing heat, the crowd of nearly 400 clustered in the shade of several large trees. The show soon began, and as Uncle Dave strutted his stuff, the laughter and applause grew with each passing number.

Van Macon sat among one group of listeners some distance back in the crowd, not too closely identifying himself with his brother. Though he had often heard Dave play at the Macon homes in Kittrell, Readyville, and Woodbury, and in other private settings, Van had never before attended an Uncle Dave Macon performance. For the first time, Van himself saw his younger brother's musical talents and performance genius on public display, and he was profoundly moved. In the middle of one song, Van suddenly rose to his feet, and with a measured, steady gait, headed straight for the porch. Everyone watched with curiosity as Van climbed the stairs, took a position behind his brother and placed a hand on Dave's left shoulder. When the song ended, an awkward pause ensued, with Dave staring up at Van. Other than the debacle at Liberty, Tennessee, in 1919, it was the only time an Uncle Dave Macon public performance had ever been interrupted. Van finally looked out at the audience, and in a strong but emotional voice proudly declared: "This is my brother, Dave!"

The public reconciliation between siblings came at an opportune time. Shortly thereafter, Van Macon fell ill, and for the next three years, was in and out of hospitals. He finally passed away in a Nashville hospital on April 25,

1938, at age eighty-one. Van was buried at Riverside Cemetery just west of Woodbury, and when his will was finally read, Dave received an inheritance of $4,000 from his oldest brother.

Dave's long absences from home while on tour were having a corrosive effect on the family, especially among his younger sons. The older boys, who had grown up during the freight-hauling years, had left home and were doing well on their own. The exception was John Macon, the second oldest son, whose life was being destroyed by alcoholism. Married and with two young sons, John confessed to Tildy that a divorce was brewing and asked if he could move back into the house with his children. His mother adamantly refused, demanding that John stop drinking and provide for his wife and kids. For the youngest sons, Dave was largely an absentee father. In light of his fame and income, they were content for the most part in remaining at home rather than developing their own careers, largely relying on their parents for lodging, meals, and other upkeep.

By far, the most significant development at home was Tildy's declining health. After fifty years of hard work and the raising of seven children, her body simply began to give out. Acute asthma set in, which curtailed her daily activities. Regular attendance at church waned as well as her presence at Richardson family gatherings. More and more she was confined to a large, white rocking chair in the house. She turned the rocker toward a large window at the front of the house, enabling her to observe passersby and anyone coming onto the property.

When her health continued to deteriorate, Dave did everything possible to care for her. On several occasions, she convalesced at sanitariums high atop the mountains surrounding Chattanooga. Fresh air, sunlight, mineral water, and good nutrition were considered the best treatments for asthma. When the regimens seemed to help, Dave took a bold step. He hired a construction crew to add a new bedroom to the east end of their home. Large windows lined the walls to let in maximum sunlight and fresh air. Tildy spent one night in the new addition and promptly abandoned it in favor of her regular bed. When her husband asked what was wrong, she said the big windows made her feel too exposed to the outside and gave no privacy. She never again slept in that new bedroom.

Finally, Dave sought out a doctor best qualified to treat asthma. The physician was most concerned with Tildy's periodic coughing spells and prescribed adrenaline to treat her condition. The doctor taught Esten, the second youngest son, to measure out the medicine dosages and to administer periodic shots to his mother. As Tildy weakened further, Dave hired a housekeeper to perform daily, routine chores, but the woman did not jibe with the family and soon left. By spring 1936, Dave was at his wit's end in the quest to provide for his wife's daily needs and to keep the house running smoothly.

The cavalry arrived in mid-March 1936 when Vesta Blair appeared riding on the front bench seat of a delivery truck. Originally from near Smartt Station, Vesta's life had fallen apart at an early age. Her mother had died unexpectedly, and when her father soon remarried, the young, new bride insisted that the man's children be ferreted out to relatives so the couple could begin their own life together unencumbered with another woman's children. Vesta parted ways with her siblings and went to live with an uncle on a nearby farm, where she labored like an indentured servant, performing strenuous chores better suited for grown men.

Near the end of the eighth grade, Vesta's uncle informed her that she could not attend high school because farm work was more important than education. In a private moment, Vesta shared with a favored teacher the conditions under which she had lived for the previous few years. That same night, the teacher, a social worker, and a Warren County sheriff's deputy showed up at the farm. Vesta was sent to her room, and a conversation ensued among the adults. A few minutes later, the deputy came into Vesta's room, ordering the teenager to pack her belongings and informing her that she would be leaving that very evening. The priority was to find her a new home and a job. The next morning, Vesta was on her way to Rutherford County with a vegetable farmer who operated a truck delivery route between McMinnville and Murfreesboro. Tildy Macon was one of his regular clients and had indicated during a previous delivery that she was seeking a housekeeper.

Tildy interviewed Vesta and liked her right away. Dave was tickled that she was from near Smartt Station, where he had grown up. Attractive, strong, and mature for her age, the Macons hired Vesta on the spot. In addition to her room and board, she would receive pay of $2.50 per week. Her new living quarters would be the same east bedroom with the big windows that Tildy had declined. Vesta Blair would remain a live-in housekeeper there for the next seven years, providing her with unique perspectives on Uncle Dave and the entire family.

The first, distinct insight came the very next morning, when she was up early to help serve breakfast. From a farming community, Vesta was used to menfolk being up before dawn and in the fields by daybreak. But the Macon boys were just the opposite. Rather than going to work, they sat about the house aimlessly, paging through newspapers and magazines, whittling, reading, or just staring into space as they waited for breakfast to be served.

Vesta was thrilled to be working for someone as famous as Uncle Dave, and as a Grand Ole Opry fan herself, she expected to meet other famous musicians at the house. After a few conversations with Tildy, Vesta realized not everyone was welcome there. Tildy's religious beliefs had convinced her that most entertainers, with their lifestyle of traveling from town to town, entertaining and cutting up for strangers at dubious venues, and playing gritty, old-time music, were lost souls. As such, those unrepentant sinners were not welcome at the house. They could come there to discuss business with Dave or even to conduct a practice session, during which she was glad to offer a comfortable place to sit and something to drink. But providing meals and overnight accommodations would be considered an absolute endorsement of their debauched lifestyle and was simply out of the question. However, Tildy had gotten to know Judge Hay, Sid Harkreader, and Sam and Kirk McGee and was personally convinced of their good moral standing, so she extended to them her full hospitality. The Delmore Brothers were especially favored, spending many nights there and frequently taking meals. At the same time, Tildy differentiated her own husband's faithfulness and integrity from the lost, sinful condition of other entertainers based on Dave's dedication to the Bible, his church, and his constant support of the family.

As late as 1936, Tildy had yet to attend one of her husband's public performances. Because she was burdened down by the labors of maintaining the homestead, raising the children, interactions with neighbors and the Richardson relatives, and church activities, taking the time to travel to attend a live show seemed a luxury she could not afford. In some ways, Tildy personally accepted Dave's career as a necessary cross she had to bear for the family's greater good. If she wanted to hear Dave play before an audience, she could tune into the Opry. In her mind, hearing Uncle Dave Macon play the banjo live was far from a novelty; Tildy had already listened to Dave's playing before the fireplace and all around the farm for the last thirty-five years.

In the 1930s, as her sons grew older, Tildy allowed herself the luxury of better enjoying the fruits of Dave's labors. She expanded her wardrobe, buying clothes and accessories at Murfreesboro's most exclusive department store, where she maintained a charge account. Tildy especially enjoyed large hats and also purchased gloves, shoes, and purses to match her new dresses. At Science Hill Church of Christ, the other ladies could not help but notice

Tildy's new wardrobe, and she developed a reputation for being the best-dressed woman in eastern Rutherford County.

A second opportunity for Uncle Dave to record on RCA's Bluebird label came in August 1937. It was very similar to the New Orleans session nearly three years earlier in that the Delmore Brothers and Arthur Smith also recorded, all for Eli Oberstein; however, this session took place in Charlotte, North Carolina. On August 3, the Dixie Dewdrop recorded seven songs, with three having been recorded previously. Perhaps the most significant tune recorded was "Travelin' Down the Road" which had been recorded previously during the Brunswick session in Chicago in June 1929, but not released. Fortunately, Bluebird liked it and released it; the song has become a favorite Uncle Dave performance number for countless old-time bands. Bluebird issued all seven songs, which were subsequently released on the Montgomery Ward label as well.

Perhaps the most unique song request in the history of the Grand Ole Opry occurred only a few days later on Saturday, August 7, 1937. Before the Opry broadcast that night, the telephone rang backstage at the Dixie Tabernacle. Judge Hay soon found himself speaking to Joe Pope, the warden of the Tennessee State Prison in Nashville. Warden Pope explained that inmate Fred Ritchie was on death row for the murder of his wife, and with his execution only days away, the penitentiary was making efforts to grant the prisoner's final requests. Ritchie was an Opry fan, and Uncle Dave his favorite performer. That Saturday night would be the inmate's last opportunity to listen to the Opry, and he had a dying request: could Uncle Dave perform the gospel tune "When I Take My Vacation in Heaven"? Judge Hay passed the special wish to the Dixie Dewdrop, and during a song set that night, Uncle Dave performed the hymn, which urged believers to anticipate the joy and rest they would finally achieve in the heavenly kingdom. A few miles away, Fred Ritchie sat listening on a radio prison guards had placed just outside his cell, no doubt pondering events soon to come and his own eternal fate. Three days later, on Tuesday, August 10, Warden Pope led the prisoner down a hallway to his doom. Fred Ritchie perished in the electric chair at age thirty-two, perhaps soothed in his spirit by the Dixie Dewdrop's performance days earlier.

The breakup with the Delmore Brothers prompted Uncle Dave to undergo a search for a new accompanist and touring partner. With his wife's blessing,

Dorris agreed to come back on the road and to travel with his father for a while. When Dorris was unavailable, Kirk McGee usually traveled with the Dixie Dewdrop. The arrangements worked well until a more permanent solution could be found.

From the start, Opry entertainers had tried to maximize the amount of money earned at shows by selling additional promotional items, including costume jewelry and candy. The Great Depression only intensified the desire for extra revenue. In 1938, Uncle Dave decided to publish his own songbook for sale at shows. "Songs and Stories of Uncle Dave Macon" was a 24-page pamphlet containing the notes and lyrics to twenty-four numbers, all Uncle Dave originals save one. Interspersed among the songs were several photos and personal vignettes. After its publication, Uncle Dave and Dorris always left on tour with the car trunk loaded with song-books. Dorris had the primary responsibility for promotion and sales. At each appearance, he plugged the books from the stage before the last number and then afterward walked through the crowd selling them as fast as he could for 25 cents apiece. In all, as many as 10,000 songbooks were sold.

Meanwhile, Uncle Dave sought a dedicated musician to accompany him on the road. Sid Harkreader suggested "Smoky Mountain" Glenn Stagner, a young backup musician on the Opry who played banjo, guitar, and mandolin and was a good singer. Uncle Dave invited the performer to his house for an audition. When Glenn arrived, Uncle Dave greeted him on the porch dressed as if he were ready to go on stage. In the South, socializing always comes before serious business, so Uncle Dave took Glenn on a tour of his house and outbuildings. In the smokehouse, he proudly showed off hanging hams, shoulders, and side meats and then offered Glenn a nip out of a little brown jug. They eventually sat down and went through three songs together. Uncle Dave hired him, and so began what Glenn Stagner considered "four happy and prosperous years with the King of the Hillbillies."

A variety of venues took the new duo from small schoolhouses to the Municipal Auditorium in St. Louis, which seated thousands. An episode that Smoky Mountain Glenn never forgot occurred one Sunday morning in a town in North Carolina. Uncle Dave woke up that morning in a local hotel wanting to go to church. Both musicians soon left for a nearby Methodist church, where they took a seat in the back unnoticed. A ripple of excitement surged through the congregation when families realized Uncle Dave Macon had arrived. Before long, several asked him to perform a few hymns, but Uncle Dave explained that he had left his banjo at the hotel. Not so easily deterred, the congregation begged for a performance until Glenn was sent scurrying back to the hotel to get the five-string.

When the banjo arrived, Uncle Dave took a seat at the head of the church and launched into a set of his greatest hymns. The congregation sat enraptured through a heartfelt rendition of "How Beautiful Heaven Must Be." When the hymns ended, Uncle Dave set aside his banjo, and without missing a beat, stepped to the pulpit and launched into a powerful, uplifting sermon. The Dixie Dewdrop's charisma and communication skills were so commanding that the starstruck pastor and congregation were glad to turn over the complete conduct of that morning's service to their unexpected guest.

Uncle Dave's fourteenth and final commercial recording session came in the last weeks of January 1938. Once more, he recorded in Charlotte on the Bluebird label. Glenn accompanied Uncle Dave, and the duo recorded a total of sixteen numbers, with Bluebird releasing them all. Some became Dixie Dewdrop classics: "He Won the Heart of My Sarah Jane," "She's Got the Money Too," "Give Me Back My Five Dollars," and "Railroadin' and Gamblin'." The last song Uncle Dave ever recorded was "The Gayest Old Dude That's Out," completed on January 20, 1938. While there would be recorded airshots as well as other personal and home recordings made in coming years, Uncle Dave's active career as a recording artist had come to a close.

Tuesday, February 14, 1939, started as a fairly routine day for the Macons. Uncle Dave was at home resting and preparing for his next tour. Dorris called that afternoon to remind his father they had a show scheduled in Montgomery, Alabama, two days hence and would be hitting the road early the next morning. Before they departed, Uncle Dave had some important business to tend to. He had purchased a Valentine Day's gift for Tildy, and when things settled down after supper that night, he planned to present it to his wife.

Tildy broke into an asthmatic coughing spell in late afternoon that failed to subside. As her hacking continued with little respite, Esten administered an adrenaline shot. The medicine seemed to help for a while, but before long, the coughing resumed. Uncle Dave became so concerned that he called the attending physician, who arrived in late afternoon. After an examination, the doctor expressed concern over Tildy's condition. He hoped the adrenaline would eventually ease the coughing, but in case it did not, he handed Uncle Dave a number of small, white pills. Should the coughing persist, Tildy was to take the pills over the course of the evening.

Tildy was too fatigued and distressed from the coughing fit to eat the evening meal. Between late afternoon and early evening, Vesta had given her one or two of the white pills on direct orders from Uncle Dave. They seemed to do the trick; by around eight o'clock in the evening, the coughing had subsided, and Tildy was able to rest easy in her rocking chair for the first time in several hours. Not long afterward, she complained of discomfort and tightness in the lower-back portion of her neck and across the top of her shoulders. When the tightness persisted, Tildy asked Vesta to stop her work and do her best at massaging the affected areas.

Vesta positioned herself behind the rocker and set about to ease Tildy's pain by rubbing the neck and shoulders. After several minutes, Tildy seemed to relax. Suddenly, her head slumped sharply to the right. Concerned that something was wrong, Vesta stepped from behind the rocker, and leaning forward, examined Tildy's face. The eyes were closed and the countenance blank, and then Vesta noticed a distinct, bluish hue all around the lips.

"Uncle Dave, come quick!" Vesta cried. He was sitting on the far side of the room reading a newspaper when Vesta cried out. Dave dropped the newspaper immediately, and when he observed his wife, he shouted, "Tildy! Tildy!" Dave jumped from the chair and bolted across the room to kneel right before her. At that very instant, Tildy's body slumped forward, and Dave caught her in his arms. While he had always possessed considerable physical strength, the shock of the moment surely imparted additional power. In one single, fluid motion, Dave swept his wife of thirty-nine years into his arms while at the same time rising to his feet. He carried his stricken wife to her bed and gingerly laid her down. Staring at Tildy's discolored face, Dave surely feared the worst.

The commotion had drawn Esten's attention from a far bedroom in the house, and he was immediately at his father's side. On Dave's orders, Esten phoned the doctor, asking him to come as quickly as possible. Vesta sat trembling in a chair, too rattled to move. The doctor soon arrived, performed a brief examination and called the time of death at 9:00 p.m. Tildy Macon was dead at age sixty-one; she passed away having never attended a single one of her husband's public performances.

After an extremely restless night, Uncle Dave was up early the next morning taking care of business. An undertaker soon arrived, and a discussion ensued that generated the details of Tildy's memorial services and burial. She would not be embalmed but soon buried, placed at the center of the plots Dave had purchased at Coleman Cemetery in 1916. The visitation would occur at the house that very afternoon with the funeral and internment the following day.

The undertaker soon departed to put the wheels in motion for the visitation and funeral. The next step was to go to town to order a headstone. Uncle Dave sat down at a table with pen and paper in hand. In that moment, his romantic bent, command of the English language, knowledge of Scripture, and considerable talents as a songwriter all joined to produce a truly uplifting passage. With his own hand, Dave Macon composed one of the most inspired epitaphs a husband ever bestowed upon a wife:

A Noble Woman. A Lovely Wife. A Devoted Mother.
No Purer Spirit Ever Entered the Kingdom of Heaven.

One of the boys soon drove Dave to a monument company in Murfreesboro where he placed an order for a large headstone and provided the stonecutter with the desired inscription.

Meanwhile, the undertaker had returned to the house to complete preparations for the visitation. Vesta vacated her bedroom at the east end of the house, and by rearranging some furniture and placing some flowers, the funeral director converted the room into a temporary memorial chapel. Tildy's body was dressed, prepared for presentation, and placed in a coffin in the east bedroom. On the afternoon of February 15, a continuous stream of family members and friends came to the house to console Dave and his sons and to pay their respects. By early evening, the visitation was over.

Dave and Vesta sat up together late that night sharing their grief and swapping their best memories of Miss Tildy. As the evening came to an end, Dave reached into the inside pocket of his suit coat and pulled out a small jewelry box. He told Vesta that he had purchased the item during a recent trip, and after dinner on Valentine's Day, had planned to present it to his wife, adding in a sad voice that he never had the opportunity to do so. Dave passed the box to Vesta, saying that he wanted her to have the gift. She clasped the item in her hands, too shocked and surprised to respond. Dave rose to his feet, bid Vesta good night, and went to bed.

Vesta sat alone before the hearth, lost in her own thoughts and overwhelmed with emotion. Her own mother had passed away when she was just a child, and Tildy Macon had become a second mother to her in so many ways. Vesta finally opened the jewelry box to admire a beautiful, silver bracelet. She was both dismayed and grateful that Uncle Dave had given it to her. Moments later, she had second thoughts; the present was rightly Tildy's, and she should have it. Vesta quietly slipped into the east bedroom, unlatched and raised the coffin lid, and gently placed the box and bracelet next to Tildy's body. After saying her final good-byes, she closed the coffin and turned away. The next day, the bracelet was buried along with Tildy's remains, an intimate secret that Vesta kept to herself for nearly seventy-five years.

Tildy's funeral occurred on the afternoon of February 16 at Science Hill Church of Christ at 1:30 p.m. In addition to the many family members, relatives, and friends in attendance, Judge Hay was there to lend support to Uncle Dave. The service was relatively simple and, at the close, the congregation filed past the casket to pay their last respects. Uncle Dave was the final one to approach. As he drew close, grief overcame him. "Thank God I was home when you died!" he suddenly wailed. A moment later he cried: "Thank God you died in my arms!"

With the service concluded, everyone moved to Coleman Cemetery for the interment. Tildy was laid to rest in a simple graveside service. Afterward, the family and close friends returned to Kittrell to spend additional time together. Judge Hay stayed for a while and attempted to console Dave with the hope he would one day see his wife again. Uncle Dave returned the sentiment with a deeply spiritual declaration: "I cannot bring her back from where she has gone, but I can go to the place where she is."

By early evening, the house was nearly empty, but one last matter required attention. Ever the introvert, Glen Macon had refused to attend his mother's funeral, remaining at home during the memorial service and burial. Dave was furious at his son for his lack of respect for his mother and his self-centered attitude. In a rare moment, a righteous anger welled up within him, and Dave delivered a loud, scathing rebuke. Glen sat quiet and chastened throughout, not responding. At his wit's end with exasperation, Dave finally admitted that he did not know what might have transpired between Glen and his mother because he was so often away on tour. "Whatever happened between you two, blame me and not her," Dave finally concluded, "because she's not here to defend herself!" With that, the family broke up and retired for the night.

Dave had been through three days of living hell, and it wasn't over. The next morning he awoke to discover a truck stacked high with furniture and household goods backing up to the front porch. John Macon came inside to explain to his father that he was getting a divorce and had to move back into the house with his belongings and two young sons. With his mother dead and buried, John had not wasted a single day in countermanding her wishes that he should not move back into the house. Dave was perhaps too weary and exasperated to rebuff his son, and John and his two boys took up residence there for a number of years. There were some benefits; John helped with house chores, and the two boys became good companions to Vesta. At the same time, the entire family witnessed firsthand the great extent to which chronic alcoholism had come to rule and ruin John Macon's life.

Tildy's sudden death still retains elements of controversy. Her obituary at the time raised a measurable degree of doubt: "Although Mrs. Macon had been in bad health for seven years, her condition was not considered critical and her death was unexpected." The official Tennessee death certificate contains one of the most unusual entries ever placed on such a document. Under the cause of death, the medical examiner simply wrote: "I do not know." In retrospect, modern medical opinion suggests that she died from a possible overdose of prescription medications. Given the fact that she experienced pain and tightness in her lower neck and shoulders—now widely recognized as classic symptoms of an impending coronary episode in women—the specific cause of death was likely a sudden heart attack.

In the aftermath of Tildy's death, the Dixie Dewdrop took a break from touring. Becoming steeped in nostalgia, he organized a return visit to the home of his youth. With his youngest son Paul at the wheel, Uncle Dave, Vesta, his sister Annie, and Annie's now middle-aged daughter, Ruth, piled into the family car and headed for Warren County. An hour or so later, they came upon Macon Manor, a place Dave and Annie had perhaps not visited since the Macons had departed from there for Nashville in 1883. The residents at the time welcomed the visitors, inviting them to tour the grounds. Dave saw a large, black haw tree, which had stood there when he was a boy, and its presence reminded him that the number of things in life that never change are indeed few. The footprint of a garden and grove of trees that Captain John had planted long ago was still visible; as a boy, Dave had equated that verdant plot with the Garden of Eden. Dave and Annie paused on Macon Manor's front steps to recall the terrible day their younger brother George had fallen there, resulting in his death. Dave departed Macon Manor for the last time convinced that the greatest memories and experiences of life are so strong and enduring that they certainly "accompany our souls into eternity."

Weeks later, family members gathered to help sort and divide Tildy's personal belongings. Ruth volunteered to go through Tildy's sewing and crafting materials, which were stored beneath her bed. She unexpectedly discovered an old suitcase bulging with contents buried among the materials.

Dragging the heavy piece of luggage out into the open, Ruth flipped open the latches and raised the top, expecting to find more cloth and materials. Instead, she gasped with surprise upon discovering the bag was crammed full with thick stacks of dollar bills. She had uncovered Tildy's private stash of cash, stored safe and secure from thieves and the uncertain clutches of Depression-era bankers. Even in death, Tildy Macon took care of her family; the money would serve her husband and sons well through the tough economic times still ahead.

CHAPTER 6

"Poor Sinners, Fare Thee Well"

WHILE UNCLE DAVE TOOK a brief respite from touring and performing following Tildy's passing, things continued to evolve at WSM and the Grand Ole Opry. During its first twelve years, the Opry had featured string bands augmented by an assortment of solo and duo musical and comedic acts, with Uncle Dave remaining its main star and premier vocalist. All the while, Judge Hay had served as a gatekeeper whose aim was to preserve the Opry's original tone and tenor in presenting old-time music. "Keep it down to earth!" was George Hay's constant mantra to aspiring performers and WSM management.

However, public music tastes and performance styles inevitably change over time. The Opry had begun to evolve as early as 1937 with the premier of Pee Wee King and the Golden West Cowboys. Reared within the popular music culture of Wisconsin, Pee Wee broke new ground by introducing waltzes, polkas, and cowboy songs to Nashville. He also debuted new instruments, including the trumpet, drums and eventually electric guitars. The band dressed in flashy western outfits, reflecting the rising popularity of the singing cowboy genre, first popularized a few years earlier by Gene Autry.

A second major development occurred when Roy Acuff came to Nashville. Born in East Tennessee in 1903, Roy displayed an early interest in music and sports. After an illness quashed his aspirations of becoming a professional baseball player, he turned exclusively to music. Starting in 1932, he began touring with his band in East Tennessee. About this same time, Roy had his first, brief encounter with Uncle Dave at a small hotel in Jonesboro, Tennessee. Roy's fiddling and singing talents finally gained a recording contract in

1936, but his first guest Opry appearance the following year fell flat. Uncle Dave had been standing offstage during that performance, and just as Roy closed his last number, an unidentified woman approached to ask what he thought of the new act. "He won't last too long on this show," the Dixie Dewdrop declared, not knowing that the woman to whom he spoke was Roy's wife, Mildred.

Roy Acuff's big break came at a second Opry appearance in February 1938 when a heartfelt rendering of "The Great Speckled Bird" endeared him to fans. In the following months, Opry broadcasts, touring, advertising, and the smash hit "Wabash Cannon Ball" gained Roy and his Smoky Mountain Boys national recognition. More than any other single event, Roy's ground-breaking 1938 performance marked the beginning of a transitional period for the Opry, from the era of amateur, hoedown string bands to a new epoch featuring polished singing stars backed by professional groups playing both acoustic and amplified instruments.

Bill Monroe and his Blue Grass Boys completed the triumvirate of new talent that would take the Opry in new directions. They first auditioned for the show in October 1939. Bill's forceful personality and complete dedication to his craft had already gained him considerable experience at WLS in Chicago and on WBT in Charlotte. His frenetic mandolin playing and high-pitched, lonesome singing made him stand out from the rest. During their Opry premier on October 28, 1939, Bill Monroe and his Blue Grass Boys won the house over with energetic renditions of "Foggy Mountain Top" and "Mule Skinner Blues." The complete elements of bluegrass music would not emerge for another fifteen years, but Bill Monroe was already making his mark as a professional band leader and trend-setting performer.

With new talent arriving and preliminary discussions of the Opry being broadcast over a national radio network, the Nashville Musicians Association became active in the form of the American Federation of Musicians (AFM) Local 257. The union's intent was to protect the interests of musicians in Nashville's increasingly tough business environment. To avoid the awkwardness of approaching the Opry's biggest star to ask if he would join, the leaders at AFM Local 257 took the calculated step of awarding Uncle Dave a lifetime, complimentary membership. More than any other single incident, the decision illustrates the Dixie Dewdrop's enduring stature and influence at the Opry, even at the close of the 1930s.

Not long afterward, Vito Pellettieri collared Dorris Macon to inquire if he had yet joined the union. When Dorris replied that he had not because he thought the annual $58 union dues seemed exorbitant, Pellettieri warned that if he failed to sign up, Dorris could no longer be booked onstage with his father. "They gave Pap a complimentary membership," Dorris retorted. "Why can't they give me one?" "Because you're not Uncle Dave," was Pellettieri's honest reply. Not long afterward, Dorris wrote the check and joined, maintaining an active union membership for the next thirty-six years.

In late 1938, the William Etsy Company, a New York advertising firm that had helped the Opry sign commercial sponsors for its separate show segments, became convinced that the program's popularity merited an even larger market. With its ties to NBC, the Etsy Company floated a proposal to broadcast an Opry segment over the network. Despite early skepticism, the idea caught on. The program's initial run would be limited until proving its own broad, popular appeal. The agreement called for twenty-six NBC affiliates—the full NBC network consisted of over 125 stations at the time—in a broad listening area stretching from the Appalachians to the Mexican border to carry the show. The interested sponsor for the thirty-minute segment was Prince Albert, the pipe tobacco branch of the R. J. Reynolds Tobacco Company. Acutely aware that WSM and the Opry would have more national exposure than ever before, management pulled out its biggest guns for the show's debut. The slate that first night included Uncle Dave and Dorris, Roy Acuff and his Smoky Mountain Boys, DeFord Bailey, and George Wilkerson and the Fruit Jar Drinkers.

At the precise appointed moment on Saturday evening, October 14, 1939, WSM transitioned from its direct signal to the NBC network, broadcasting the *Prince Albert Show* live from the War Memorial Auditorium, which had become the Opry's new home in downtown Nashville in July 1939. WSM's David Stone served as the lead announcer; Judge Hay was the master of ceremonies. Roy Acuff performed the opening number, a rendition of "Ida Red." For the next thirty minutes, music, public announcements, and advertising promos for Prince Albert streamed smoothly out over the airwaves. A number of personalities sent telegrams of congratulations, which David Stone and Judge Hay read on air, with advertising spots promoting Prince Albert as the "cool burning" tobacco with a "mild, grand taste" for the "smoking enjoyment" of men everywhere.

A highlight of that historic broadcast was the Dixie Dewdrop's rendition of three songs. During a profuse introduction, Judge Hay hyped Uncle Dave as the "senator from the Cannon County Hills" with his repertoire of "horse and buggy" hits. Uncle Dave then launched into "Cannon County Hills" and delighted in belting out the chorus:

Oh, bright lights on Broadway,
There's sunshine down in Dixie,
They'll have moonshine in the Cannon County hills.

Dorris accompanied his father on guitar, emphasizing certain words and notes with sharp shouts and gruff grunts. At the show's midpoint, the duo returned with the Jimmie Davis romance number "Nobody's Darling but Mine," which Uncle Dave delivered as more of a comedic piece using an exaggerated, operatic style, and loud, vibrating tongue rattles. Near the end of the program, they returned to perform "Way Out on the Mountain," but with a twist. Dorris sang lead while Uncle Dave chimed in with frenzied, full-throated yodeling. One of the true rarities of that first Prince Albert show came from Judge Hay. Caught up in the excitement of the moment, the Solemn Old Judge performed as an accompanist, tooting out a few notes on his steamboat whistle during several songs, including Uncle Dave's numbers.

The *Prince Albert Show* premier was an unqualified success. R. J. Reynolds was so excited that it invited Uncle Dave to become a national spokesman. The print campaign featured an advertisement with Uncle Dave smiling wide as he poured a portion of Prince Albert into the bowl of his pipe. In Kittrell, some were upset that Uncle Dave had agreed to the endorsement, knowing that he actually smoked a different brand. When a neighbor asked about the arrangement, Uncle Dave explained that Prince Albert paid him "just to play for them" and not to smoke their product. As a headliner for the *Prince Albert Show*, Uncle Dave had been at the center of efforts to offer country music to an even broader, national audience. Only one major entertainment medium had eluded him so far, but that was about to change; it was finally time for the Dixie Dewdrop to head to Hollywood.

Country music had first found its way to the silver screen in 1930 when Ken Maynard, a silent movie stunt rider and supporting actor, was the first to appear as a singing cowboy in a sound motion picture. In time, Maynard's debut performance created a demand for other country and western performers on film. Gene Autry had already established himself as a hugely successful recording artist and performer following a three-year stint on

WLS. In 1934, Autry ventured to Hollywood to cameo in two movies with Maynard, circumstances which soon opened an opportunity to star in his first feature film. His gentle and reassuring singing style, combined with a good-natured, appealing screen presence, propelled him to stardom, making Gene Autry the first nationally recognized country and western star. By 1940, Autry was a top Hollywood actor in his own right, who opened a path for others to follow, including Roy Rogers and Tex Ritter. As one form of entertainment increases, another inevitably collapses; the rising popularity of sound films and the economic stresses of the Great Depression finally brought the vaudeville stage era to a close.

Taken with Gene Autry's success, Republic Pictures sought new opportunities to feature country performers. As early as 1938, the studio had reached out to WSM and the Opry to open a dialogue about a possible movie. The first *Prince Albert Show* included on-air messages from Gene Autry who was "looking forward with much pleasure" to members of the Grand Ole Opry coming to Hollywood and another from Republic Pictures wishing the Opry great success on the NBC network. As 1939 progressed, Republic sent a producer to Nashville to explore the possibilities further. The representative met key managers and performers, but the trip's most significant moment occurred under a shade tree in Uncle Dave's front yard.

Wanting to roll out the red carpet of southern hospitality for the California visitor, Judge Hay came up with the idea of hosting an elaborate meal. When he heard the suggestion, Uncle Dave quickly volunteered to host the dinner in Kittrell. With Tildy no longer at the house, Dave was free to invite Opry stars and promoters there. A home meal in a relaxed atmosphere would allow the film producer to experience authentic southern ways and to become better acquainted with Judge Hay and Uncle Dave. In Kittrell, Aunt Myrt and Vesta went about planning and preparing a meal to remember.

On the set day, Judge Hay and the producer drove down from Nashville. When they arrived at the Macon homestead, a big Tennessee dinner with all the trimmings was spread on the main table. Judge Hay remembered the meal in fine detail:

> Friends, we hope someday that some of you will be fortunate enough to be
> Uncle Dave's guests at dinner. Until that day arrives, we fear that you will have
> missed a great deal in the realm of culinary art and true Southern hospitality.
> Uncle Dave asked the blessing and we were served a dinner which is not for
> sale anywhere in these United States, more is the pity. We were forced to be

satisfied with rich country ham, fried chicken, six or seven vegetables, done to a Tennessee turn, jelly preserves, pickles, hot corn bread and white bread. Then came the cake.

Afterward, the three men sat underneath a big shade tree in the front yard and together explored the real possibilities of making an Opry movie. Uncle Dave's hospitality and charisma made a big impression. During the return drive to Nashville, the Republic producer declared: "I have never met a more natural man in my life. He prays at the right time and he cusses at the right time and his jokes are as cute as the dickens."

By the spring of 1940, all the arrangements had been completed. A final cast slate was selected, which included Judge Hay, Uncle Dave and Dorris, and Roy Acuff and his Smoky Mountain Boys. The film's feature stars were the Weaver Brothers and Elviry, a vaudeville trio from the Ozarks whose comedy shows and musical talents had made them famous internationally. *Grand Ole Opry* was to be a lighthearted comedy, telling the story of shrewd, small-town hillbillies who employed common sense, fair play, and good morals to get the best of a corrupt, conniving cabal of newspaper bosses and politicians.

In early May 1940, the performers all headed west. Judge Hay and Uncle Dave had business in Chicago, so they traveled there first before continuing to California by train. Everyone else drove. Dorris rode with Roy and the band, cramming all their instruments and luggage into a tour bus. Apparently, Uncle Dave was concerned over the type of strange eats he might encounter in California, so he decided to take his own provisions. He carefully packed three salt-cured, country hams into a wooden crate, asking Roy to carry them to California. Before the days of the interstate highway system, it was not unusual for states to conduct agricultural inspections at their borders. In Arizona and California, state inspectors pulled Roy's vehicle aside, and their full attention soon focused on the packed meats. Following a long conversation explaining why they were carrying country hams all the way to California, the inspectors waved the Tennesseans through.

The hams and all the entertainers were soon assembled in Hollywood. By their own admission, the Opry stars were "as green as grass" when it came to moviemaking, and trouble started even before the cameras rolled. When Roy and his band went for their costumes, the wardrobe department presented them with cowboy outfits to make them appear as a Wild West group. Roy Acuff was livid; he embraced the term *hillbilly*, but loathed being portrayed as a *cowboy*. He ordered the band to remove the costumes and informed Republic that they would perform in the same clothes they wore at the Opry. If not, Roy and the others would pack up and head back to Tennessee, a credible threat that settled the matter.

The first week of filming soon commenced at Republic's North Hollywood studios. Uncle Dave found the whole moviemaking process frustrating and confusing. On set, he was baffled by false doors that didn't open, fake walls, and hallways that led to nowhere. He hated having makeup applied, fussing that it would stain his white shirt. The cold, impersonal stare of the camera lens was especially intimidating. Dorris found it unusually difficult to relax before the camera. During the first takes, he stood stiff as a board "plunking his guitar like a wooden Indian," but he finally loosened up. An impertinent line or two in the original script offended Uncle Dave's religious sensibilities, and he threatened to walk off the set. Necessary changes were made and production soon resumed. More than anything else, the Dixie Dewdrop chafed at the controls and instructions the director and film crew imposed. Apparently, no one explained to him what the command "Cut!" meant. On several occasions, while filming his musical numbers, the director cried "Cut!" but Uncle Dave just kept on playing until he finished the song. A frustrated Uncle Dave finally suggested that if he were allowed to take charge on the set, the result would be the most successful picture Republic had ever produced. Naturally, the idea fell on deaf ears. Nearly every day Uncle Dave pulled Roy Acuff aside to ask, "Roy Boy, who signed the papers for us to come out here?" His black grip was always handy, and Uncle Dave frequently slipped off set for a nip to steady his nerves.

When a change in the work schedule freed up a few hours, someone asked if there was anything in particular Uncle Dave wanted to visit while in southern California. He desired to see the Pacific Ocean, and before long, a driver took Uncle Dave and Judge Hay to the coast. When they arrived, the two friends strolled down the beach together, taking in the sun, wind, waves, and sand. Uncle Dave had become an avid souvenir collector through the years, with his fireplace mantle and house stuffed with trinkets and memorabilia from his extensive travels. That day he had an empty tobacco pouch on him, and he stooped down in the surf to scoop a handful of sand into the small bag which he carried back to Tennessee as a souvenir.

A second week of filming took place at Republic's remote lot in the San Bernardino Mountains east of Los Angeles where all the outdoor scenes were shot. Though he was cast as a town sheriff, Uncle Dave portrayed the roles of court bailiff, jailer, softball umpire, square-dance caller, and onstage performer. The studio had an editing shack where the director and crew could review their day's work, and at one point, they invited the Tennesseans inside to observe some unedited clips. Seeing yourself on film for the first time can be an unnerving experience, but not for the Dixie Dewdrop. When Uncle Dave first observed himself on film, he jumped from his seat, thrust his arms high overhead, and shouted, "Whee, that's me!"

One of the highlights of *Grand Ole Opry* is a performance of "Take Me Back to My Old Carolina Home" by Uncle Dave and Dorris. In addition to playing and singing, Uncle Dave is in constant motion the whole time, repeatedly doffing his hat to the audience, spinning and twirling his banjo, strumming the Gibson along the neck, fanning it with his hat, and even standing up at one point to perform jumping jacks while continuing to play. When the song refers to the "bang-a, bang-a, bang" of a Gatling gun, Uncle Dave lifts the banjo, pressing the pot to his cheek while pointing the long neck toward the audience, as if he were leveling a gun at them. The clip is the only known film segment of an Uncle Dave performance, and it demonstrates just how much of his showmanship was physical and visual as well as musical.

After two weeks of work, the film was in the can, and the Opry stars were ready to go home. Once again, Judge Hay and Uncle Dave would head back east by train, while the others drove. The salt-cured, country hams had been completely devoured during the outing, and Roy was looking forward to having more room on the bus during the return trip. Just as they were packing to depart, Uncle Dave came to him and said, "Roy Boy, would you mind taking that box back with you, I want to use it as a hen's nest." Roy dutifully packed the empty crate onto his bus and hauled it back to Tennessee. He did so without resentment or grumbling, true testimony to the respect and admiration the aspiring star had for the Grand Ole Man of the Grand Ole Opry.

While he held some reservations about moviemaking, Roy Acuff would eventually return to Hollywood during the 1940s to star in seven more films for Republic and Columbia. On the other hand, Uncle Dave was finished with the movies. *Grand Ole Opry* premiered at the Paramount Theater in downtown Nashville on Friday night, June 28, 1940. Uncle Dave was on hand for the premier and sat through the sixty-eight–minute film, but he did not like what he saw. Vesta stayed up late that night in Kittrell waiting for him to get home, curious as to what he thought of the film. When Uncle Dave finally arrived, he was unusually quiet and reserved as he stewed in his easy chair. Vesta finally had to ask how he liked the movie. Uncle Dave lowered his chin to his chest, shook his head back and forth in disgust, and grumbled, "That movie is an abomination before God!" Perhaps it was the uneven script or the film's unabashed stereotyping of southern hillbillies that disturbed him, but more than likely Uncle Dave was most disappointed because he had been denied any creative control over the moviemaking process or the final product.

Uncle Dave's dissatisfaction with *Grand Ole Opry* did not prevent him from exploiting the film's national exposure. Throughout the winter he worked hard to put together a nationwide tour. With Tildy no longer waiting at home for his return, Dave was willing to stay away longer than ever before. In the spring of 1941, Uncle Dave and Dorris departed Middle Tennessee by car on their most ambitious tour yet. Performing across Texas and Oklahoma, they continued with shows throughout the Southwest, finally arriving in southern California. Then it was up the West Coast. After playing at various venues, they looped back through the Great Plains, heading for Chicago. Following a number of appearances throughout the Midwest, the schedule carried them to the Mid-Atlantic region. Soon they returned to Dixie, completing the grand tour with a closeout performance on the Gulf Coast. In ninety days, the duo covered almost the entire United States by car, the most aggressive and extensive tour of the Dixie Dewdrop's entire career.

Esten Macon was worried. The sixth of Uncle Dave's seven sons and the only one to earn a college degree, he prided himself on staying abreast of current events. He had monitored the rise of the Nazis in Germany, even writing newspaper articles warning of the growing threat of totalitarianism. Esten had gone to Science Hill Church of Christ that morning for Sunday services, and when he returned home, WSM was broadcasting truly astounding news. The Imperial Japanese Navy had carried out a major, sneak attack on the American naval base at Pearl Harbor, Hawaii. None of the details were yet available, but Esten understood that the unprecedented disaster would thrust America headfirst into the Second World War.

More practical matters soon diverted his attention. Judge Hay was expected before long at the Macon home along with a young photographer named Ed Clark, who worked for the *Nashville Banner*. However, on the morning of December 7, 1941, Ed Clark was on assignment for *Life*, which was assembling a collection of new photos of major country music stars for a planned feature edition of the magazine. *Life* had already captured a remarkable set of photos of the Carter Family at their home in Maces Spring, Virginia. As usual, Uncle Dave was ready for action, having dressed that morning in an elaborate, three-piece suit and patterned shirt. When Judge Hay appeared to be running late, the Macons went ahead and ate lunch. A phone call soon came, informing them that the Solemn Old Judge was indeed far behind schedule, but that he would be there as soon as possible with the photographer in tow.

Judge Hay and Ed Clark arrived in midafternoon, sitting down for a quick meal before getting to work. Flashbulbs on Ed Clark's elaborate camera rig popped almost continuously throughout the two-hour session, producing dozens of remarkable photographs. The keen eye for lighting, composition, and setting that propelled Ed Clark to a renowned career as the photographer of U.S. presidents and Hollywood's biggest stars was clearly evident that day. Images captured Uncle Dave on his front porch, before his fireplace, and in his easy chair. He played a few tunes and even twirled his banjo as the photographer snapped away. Dorris had come to the house sporting a fancy dress shirt and tie and a plush leather jacket and sat with his father for several shots. Meanwhile, Judge Hay was busy working the phones, trying to book a Vanderbilt University historian and another military expert to discuss the Pearl Harbor attack during his live radio show the following morning on WSM. At one point, the Solemn Old Judge joined the Dixie Dewdrop at the fireplace for a relaxed photo. The sudden outbreak of war dashed plans for the *Life* special edition, but the Ed Clark photo session still produced some of the most iconic images of Uncle Dave Macon ever taken.

Like the Great Depression, World War II seriously challenged the entertainment industry. However, music played an essential role in fostering patriotism, maintaining morale on the homefront and entertaining the troops. WSM and the Grand Ole Opry took several measures to support the war effort. The Air Castle of the South greatly altered its programming to provide the public important news about the war and to allow contact over the airwaves between distant service members and families at home. The station frequently interviewed key leaders of mobilization programs and senior military commanders visiting Nashville and routinely sponsored clothing and scrap metal drives. The Opry sent its performers to stateside mobilization camps and, on rare occasions, even dispatched them overseas to entertain the troops. Southerners serving in the military were always proud and pleased when citizen-soldiers from other parts of the nation expressed their liking and fondness for WSM and the Opry. In its long history, the Opry has canceled its Saturday broadcast only twice, and one of those times was when President Roosevelt died in the spring of 1945 near the end of the war.

The rationing of gasoline and tires, along with a national speed limit of 30 mph to conserve fuel, tires and vehicles, impeded touring. In response to rationing, the Opry organized traveling tent shows to increase the ease and efficiency of touring, with large cargo trucks hauling tents big enough to seat 1,600 from one rural location to the next. Performers were once again assigned to "units" to appear at tent shows. Musicians themselves were not exempt from military service. For example, Alton Delmore was drafted into the navy for stateside duty, and Uncle Dave's own sideman, Smoky Glenn Stagner, was drafted into the army in 1943.

World War II changed most aspects of Uncle Dave's life and career. With individual travel by car restricted, he dropped the practice of booking single independent shows in favor of touring with other established acts. Roy Acuff specifically hired Uncle Dave as an opening act, knowing that he was still immensely popular and would help to draw large crowds. Throughout the war, Uncle Dave routinely toured with both Roy and Bill Monroe. Roy paid him a weekly salary of $75–150 depending on the number of shows performed, with Bill paying $20 for each individual appearance. After Glenn Stagner was drafted, Dorris or Kirk McGee accompanied Uncle Dave on the road. The Dixie Dewdrop did tour with Opry tent shows, but the extent of his involvement is uncertain. What is known is that during a tent show tour in Mississippi, a young Thomas A. "Colonel Tom" Parker approached Uncle Dave to suggest that he would benefit from professional management. Uncle Dave replied that he would have to think about it and never called Parker back. A steady work schedule allowed Uncle Dave to maintain his lifestyle and to continue support of his church. The roof he had put on Haynes Chapel in the early 1920s had badly deteriorated, and during the war, he again paid the full amount to have the church's roof replaced.

Uncle Dave and Roy Acuff developed an especially close relationship. The two had much in common and much to admire in one another. Both Tennesseans, they enjoyed and promoted the same brands of entertainment and music. Both were men of talent and action, onstage and off. Roy brought clarity, focus, and energy to his performances and business dealings, the same traits Uncle Dave had exercised to build and sustain his career. The Dixie Dewdrop saw that, compared with many other aspiring musicians, Roy needed little coaching regarding performing or show business. As a sign of affection, Uncle Dave always referred to Acuff as "Roy Boy." On the other hand, Roy clearly understood and respected what Uncle Dave had accomplished. The distinguishing characteristic he saw in the older musician was his uniqueness in appearance, performing style, and personal demeanor.

Touring with the bands brought Uncle Dave into contact with a new generation of young, aspiring musicians. Among those were Brother Oswald, Howdy Forrester, and Goober Buchanan, who all held Uncle Dave in the highest regard. With so many men serving in the military, performers' wives often became part of stage acts, and Uncle Dave enjoyed being around Howdy Forrester's wife, Billie, and Goober Buchanan's wife, Dixie Belle. In 1940, Uncle Dave met a new, female comedian backstage at the Opry. Minnie Pearl and Uncle Dave took to one another almost immediately, their shared love for jokes, wit, and laughter making them fast friends.

During this period, Uncle Dave became a mentor to David Akeman, a tall, lanky banjo player from eastern Kentucky who would become famous as "Stringbean." His first big break in music came when Bill Monroe hired him as a player on his barnstorming tent show baseball team, well before realizing that Akeman was a comedian and banjo player. The Dixie Dewdrop took Stringbean under his wing, teaching him a number of old-time banjo tunes. Like earlier performers, Stringbean admired Uncle Dave for his savvy in business matters. Over time, Stringbean's mix of wit, comedy, and music came to echo Uncle Dave's own performance style.

Traveling with Uncle Dave brought moments of true hilarity. Young band members would often ask how he was faring now that he was in his early seventies, and—with a big grin and a twinkle in his eye—Uncle Dave would reply: "Boys, I'm slowing down but still moving!" While touring with Bill Monroe, Uncle Dave continued his habit of peeking through the curtains before a show to measure the turnout. When the crowd was large, he would smile and proudly proclaim, "The old man can still bring 'em in!" When too many seats were empty, Uncle Dave would go to Monroe and rib him with, "Bill, you didn't advertise too well for this one!" While Bill Monroe could sometimes be aloof or dismissive toward others, he and Uncle Dave always got along well.

Goober Buchanan recalled one time crossing the Oklahoma state line while Uncle Dave dozed in the back seat of the car. When he suddenly stirred, someone asked him if he had just seen the sign that stated that it was illegal to transport whiskey into Oklahoma, even though no such sign had been posted. Uncle Dave thought for a moment, then opened his grip and pulled out his bottle. "We better drink this up, boys!" he declared as he passed the bottle among the younger performers, who always chuckled about the day they tricked Uncle Dave into sharing his whiskey with them.

Uncle Dave achieved a particular musical distinction in December 1942 when the Division of Music of the Library of Congress published its renowned "List of American Folk Songs on Commercial Records." Compiled by folklorist Alan Lomax, the list was a collection of the 350 best representative titles from a field of more than 3,000 recordings. The roster was an eclectic gathering of contemporary ballads and songs, traditional white and black sacred music, and even protest tunes. Three of Uncle Dave's recordings made the list, each annotated with cryptic notes: "Cumberland Mountain Deer Race" was an "excellent mountain ballad" with "traditional text and melody"; "Travelin' Down the Road" was noted for its spoken elements and labeled as a "genuine folk minstrel piece"; and "We're Up Against It Now" was a "Depression song" annotated for its "banjo minstrel style" and "fine instrumentation." The timing of the list's release demonstrates the role that music can play in the relations between nations and cultures. Historian Barry Mazor in his biography of Ralph Peer was no doubt correct that the Lomax list appeared "in part to buttress and further American culture" against the professed cultural superiority of fascist nations seeking global domination.

Like so many parents, Uncle Dave bore the burden of children serving in the military. Before World War II ended, three of his sons were overseas and serving in combat. His third oldest boy, Harry, who worked in Nashville as a truck driver, received his draft notice in March 1942. Unlike his father, Harry eschewed organized religion and was not a churchgoer. The news of Harry's impending induction hit his father hard, and Uncle Dave was concerned that his son might be killed in the war before developing a personal relationship with God. On March 31, 1942, Uncle Dave sat down in the Wadlington Hotel in Dothan, Alabama, and wrote a short letter to Harry, an earnest plea from an anguished father:

My Dear Beloved Son,

I saw a man last Saturday in Nashville and he said you told him you had, or rather thought you would be called, from the Draft Board for service in the war. So now I will be in Nashville this coming Saturday so you come to the Merchant's Hotel to see me about 5 or 6 o'clock p.m. Now I wish you would join some church, which ever one you prefer, and confess the Savior, as Jesus says whoever confesses me before man the same will I honor and glorify before the angels of God.

Well I was in hopes the war would be settled and everybody could be happy and could have our own way. But now we can only do the best we can and have to make the best of it. I am in hopes these few lines find you well and I and Dorris can see you Saturday at the Merchant's Hotel.

Your Loving Father,

Uncle Dave Macon

Whether the meeting ever occurred is unknown, but Harry went to war without joining a church. When the army discovered that he was a trained, experienced trucker, Harry was assigned to a transportation unit to haul petroleum, helping to refuel American bombers in North Africa and England. After the D-Day invasion, he hauled fuel and supplies in support of General Patton's Third Army offensives across France and into Germany.

Glen Macon was soon inducted, and the army cared not one whit for his proclivity for privacy and the familiarity of home. Glen completed his training, shipped overseas, and fought with the combat engineers in Europe. The youngest son, Paul Macon, was the last to serve. Perhaps feeling the effects of an absentee father and the loss of his mother early in life, Paul was already suffering from chronic alcoholism and reported drunk to basic training at Camp Blanding, Florida. He was already married with a small daughter, but the army desperately needed combat troops. Paul was sent to the infantry and served on the front lines in Europe with distinction, earning the coveted Combat Infantryman Badge.

On top of all these personal cares during the war, Uncle Dave suffered the loss of his mentally ill sister. Lou Macon passed away on July 8, 1942, at Central State Hospital at age eighty-three after a prolonged stay of thirty-five years. She had been bedridden for several years, and her death certificate identified "manic depressive insanity" as a condition of death. Uncle Dave claimed Lou's body and had it interred next to her deceased husband in the Macon family plot at Nashville's Mt. Olivet Cemetery. Afterward, he had an eight-foot-tall obelisk erected at the gravesite with the Macon name prominently displayed on the front as a permanent tribute to a woman who had suffered so much in life. Of the eleven original Macon siblings, only Annie, Dave, and Bob still remained.

It was about this time that Uncle Dave loved and lost. He joked to friends and family that he hoped to "talk some secondhand love to a rich widow I know for a housekeeper and hang my old banjo on the wall Saturday night." There was more truth to the statement than anyone knew. A wealthy widow woman in Woodbury had indeed caught his eye, and before long, he came calling. One Sunday afternoon, he arrived at the elderly widow's home for a visit, and sitting in the parlor beside her was a daughter, an only child who stood to inherit her mother's entire estate. Not long into the conversation, Uncle Dave explained that he wanted to advance the relationship to the courting stage in pursuit of marriage. The daughter suddenly rose to her feet, disappeared into a back bedroom, and returned moments later carrying a loaded revolver at her side. Without ever brandishing the pistol, she calmly but forcefully announced that her mother was not interested in getting married and that Uncle Dave should leave the house and never return. The southern gentleman kept his cool, rose to his feet, wished the ladies adieu, put on his hat, departed, and never went back.

Another personal crisis came in 1943 when all of the domestic help departed. Vesta had met and fallen in love with a young soldier during the army's 1941 Tennessee maneuvers. Elmer Kinney's halftrack had broken down in Kittrell, and it had taken the army nearly three weeks to get the armored vehicle repaired. In the interim, the residents of Kittrell adopted the young soldier from Maine as their own. He met Vesta in the front yard of the Macon home, and completely taken with her, he proposed marriage after only a few dates. Elmer's training prevented an immediate marriage, but once he settled at Fort Gordon near Augusta, Georgia, it was time to tie the knot. Vesta left Kittrell in the summer of 1943, after working and living with the Macons for just over seven years. Uncle Dave was away on tour the day she departed, and just as well, because that farewell would have been difficult for both.

Only a few months after getting married and settling in Augusta, Vesta saw a poster announcing that the Dixie Dewdrop was coming to town. Filled with excitement, she purchased a ticket and attended the performance. As the show ended, Vesta worked her way backstage and finally located Uncle Dave. He was surprised and overjoyed to see her, and with his most gracious words, thanked her for all she had done for his family and wished her all the happiness that marriage and a new life could bring. It was the last time the two ever met, even though Uncle Dave would reach out to her once more six years later.

The black married couple, Houston and Myrtle Jones, who had ably filled the roles of handyman and cook for over twenty years, left about the same time. With age setting in, Houston's health had given out, and he and his wife had fallen behind on their bills. Houston asked Uncle Dave for a loan of nearly $40. He confided to Uncle Dave that he was not feeling well, promising that if he lived, he would repay the loan in full. Houston passed away suddenly in April 1943 before he could repay the debt. With her husband's death, Aunt Myrt soon departed Kittrell to live with a sister in Murfreesboro. When one of Uncle Dave's sons suggested that they instruct the family lawyer to go after Houston's estate to recoup the money, Uncle Dave would hear nothing of it, explaining that the man had promised to pay only if he lived. A surviving business ledger from 1943 contains an entry for April 26, written in Uncle Dave's own hand, which closed the matter: "Bad debt. Loaned Houston $37.64. Poor man died. Unable to pay."

With his sons away in service and the domestic help departed, Uncle Dave attempted to remain living in Kittrell with the help of his son Esten and some of the Richardson relations. Following Tildy's death, Dave had the house wired for electricity, and the first major purchases included a refrigerator and a washing machine. However, the lure of modern conveniences was not enough to entice him to stay, and alternative arrangements were soon made. Uncle Dave had always used various hotels in Nashville as stopovers on tour or to rest after performing on the Opry. One of his favorites was the Merchant's Hotel on Broadway which featured a fireplace in every room. With its recent move to Ryman Auditorium, the Opry was now only a short walk from the hotel. Starting in 1943, he continuously maintained a private, reserved room at the Merchant's for nearly a decade. Extended stays allowed the Dixie Dewdrop to receive his mail, have his laundry done, and take meals in the hotel restaurant. While he did return to Kittrell on occasion, his main living arrangements for the next six years were at the Merchant's Hotel.

The move to Nashville reflected other developments in Dave's personal life. Esten Macon had followed in his mother's footsteps in becoming an ardent member of the Church of Christ and would eventually become a church preacher. As such, he developed an abhorrence for alcohol. Out of his own belief system, and perhaps in tribute to his departed mother, Esten launched a personal crusade to get his father off alcohol for good. Using a "cold turkey" strategy, Esten sought to keep the bottle away from his father, at least when Dave was at home. Even before Vesta left in 1943, Esten had come down hard on his father. At one point, they got in a physical altercation. Esten tried forcibly to take a bottle away from his father, and the two wound up wrestling on the floor until breaking things off. On another occasion, Dave was in bed resting and having a nip when he heard his son approaching. He rushed to screw the cap on the bottle and to hide it before

Esten came near, but happened to thrust the bottle beneath a pillow with the cap still loose. As the two spoke, the whiskey drained out, completely soaking the pillows, bedding, and mattress.

More and more, the delineations between Uncle Dave's private life and his public onstage persona became blurred. In so many ways, during the last years of life, he literally became Uncle Dave Macon, a change he welcomed and even promoted. In Kittrell most people still thought of him as "Mr. Dave," the freight company operator, farmer, and church member. His only moments of public recognition came when he played at local gatherings or when fans dropped by the house for a visit. At the same time, he had to deal too often with family members in trouble with the law. The move to Nashville brought him continuous adulation as a national star while distancing him from family problems. When walking down Broadway, drivers honked their horns while pedestrians greeted him with a smile and a wave or asked for an autograph. If Uncle Dave craved even more attention, he would play in the lobby of the Merchant's Hotel or at one of the nearby businesses and draw a crowd. Opry stars and WSM management often joined him at the hotel for meals, which drew other patrons and was good for business. He formed the habit of always signing personal letters "Uncle Dave Macon," even those addressed to friends, siblings, children, and grandchildren. No doubt all the attention was soothing to his ego.

With the end of World War II, all three of Uncle Dave's sons returned home safely, and everyone hoped that things would soon return to normal. The Dixie Dewdrop had grown used to touring with other stars as an opening act, and he was content to continue that practice after the war. Throughout 1946, he played several shows with Ernest Tubb and the Texas Troubadours, one of the Opry's top draws at the time. It was during one such trip that Uncle Dave experienced his only known vehicle accident. To accommodate the musicians, instruments, and equipment required on tour, Ernest Tubb had replaced a long, funeral home touring car with a used school bus, one of the first tour buses ever used by a country artist. Uncle Dave eyed the bus during a show in Florida, telling Ernest how much he admired it. Perhaps grown weary of long trips by car, Uncle Dave finally asked, "How about me riding in that bus to Boston with you?" Before long, the Dixie Dewdrop was on his way to Massachusetts, riding with the Texas Troubadours in the bus while Ernest Tubb convoyed along in his own car.

Trouble hit on the return trip. A winter storm blanketed the mountains of Virginia with snow and ice. While climbing a hill, the bus hit an icy spot, and with wheels spinning, the vehicle slid backward down the slope. It spun around and careened into a ditch, finally coming to rest while leaning to one side at a precarious angle. During the ordeal, Uncle Dave had grabbed hold of a vertical metal pole, hanging on for dear life. When the bus finally settled to a stop, he immediately headed for the door and got off. No one was hurt, but the other riders noticed that the pole the Dixie Dewdrop had hugged was severely bent, testimony to the man's physical strength, even at age seventy-five. When they finally got underway again, Uncle Dave respectfully declined to ride in the bus and accepted a ride with Ernest Tubb in his car back to Tennessee. Apparently, Uncle Dave never again rode on a tour bus.

Continued travels with Roy Acuff finally introduced Uncle Dave to a totally new experience: he went flying! Roy had chartered an airplane—a Douglas DC-3 christened *The Great Speckled Bird*—to ease his travel burdens. The reliable, twin-engine plane could get Roy and his band to a single engagement and back to Nashville in one day. Even more important, the plane could easily return the group from far destinations back to Nashville for their live Saturday night Opry appearance. Other performers accompanied Roy on the aircraft, but out of habit, Uncle Dave still insisted on driving to even the most distant shows, thereby complicating scheduling and travel arrangements.

One morning over breakfast at the Merchant's Hotel, Roy decided to invite Uncle Dave to start flying with him. When the topic came up, the older man lowered his fork and stared at Roy in disbelief. "Roy Boy," Uncle Dave declared, "I would rather get up a mule and plow and put in a crop before I'd go flying with you on that plane of yours." Roy soon departed, assuming he was completely defeated, but when he told Kirk McGee about the discussion, Kirk said that he would "work" on Uncle Dave. Work on him he did, and Kirk was successful in at least getting Uncle Dave to agree to inspect the airplane.

On a clear day, the pair drove to a local Nashville airport in Kirk's ragtop roadster. It was already hot when they arrived, and Kirk steered his auto onto the ramp, parking it in the shade beneath one of the plane's wide wings. Uncle Dave sat silent for a long time, looking up at *The Great Speckled Bird*'s sturdy engine cowlings, sheets of metal work, and riveting. "That ole thing is made pretty stout," he finally commented. Kirk then asked if he would like to see the interior, and they were soon inside. As Kirk showed Uncle Dave the passenger cabin, he mentioned that one of the advantages of air travel was that they could leave Nashville, put on a show, and fly back home without ever having to change clothes, a benefit which greatly appealed to Uncle Dave. The Dixie Dewdrop finally sat down on the front row of seats, pulled out his pipe and lit up. Uncle Dave was in deep thought, and Kirk left him alone.

"Kirk, can I ask you a question?" Uncle Dave finally said.

"Certainly, Uncle Dave," Kirk replied, convinced that he was about to hear the crux of the whole matter.

"When one of these things falls, does everybody get killed?"

"Oh, no, Uncle Dave, certainly not," Kirk replied, trying to calm the older man's fears. "Sometimes two or three of them live." Uncle Dave seemed satisfied with that less than accurate answer, no doubt believing that if anyone was likely to survive a plane crash it would be the Dixie Dewdrop.

Not long afterward, *The Great Speckled Bird* lifted off from Nashville, carrying Roy and his Smoky Mountain Boys, Uncle Dave, and Kirk McGee to a performance in Baltimore. The Dixie Dewdrop took to flying with ease. More than an hour into the trip, he left his seat at the front of the passenger cabin and entered the cockpit. When Uncle Dave asked about their location, the pilot replied, "10,000 feet over Roanoke." Uncle Dave chuckled and came back with, "Well, I guess I'll be going all the way to Baltimore with you then!" Afterward, he made his way to the rear of the aircraft where there was space for passengers to stand and stretch their legs. A group soon formed there, cutting up and telling jokes. Completely relaxed, Uncle Dave lit up his pipe. Sometime later, Roy came to the back of the airplane to ask everyone to return to their seats and buckle up as the aircraft began its descent into Baltimore. Uncle Dave looked at Roy in disbelief, convinced that he was playing a practical joke. "Roy Boy, I know nothing about flying," Uncle Dave replied, "but even I know there's no way that we are already at Baltimore." When Roy assured him they really were, Uncle Dave returned to his seat, completely taken aback by the speed of their two-hour passage. He was so impressed with the advantages of flying that Uncle Dave took a number of other flights while *The Great Speckled Bird* remained in service.

For a few years after the war, there was continued touring with Bill Monroe, where Uncle Dave first encountered Lester Flatt and Earl Scruggs. In the 1930s, the banjo had fallen from favor as a lead instrument, replaced by the guitar. Earl Scruggs's distinctive, three-finger picking style, which allowed him to play a variety of musical genres on the banjo with speed and clarity, would in time revive the instrument's popularity. Unlike most banjo pickers before him, Earl's focus was on the pureness and perfection of his music. During stage performances, Earl remained focused on his instrument and projected little toward the crowd.

What Earl Scruggs was attempting seemed totally lost on Uncle Dave. Even in the late 1940s, the Dixie Dewdrop was still immersed in the vaude-ville tradition, where entertainment never entailed the mastery of an instru-ment or the purity of the music. There may have been some professional jealousy as well. When asked about Earl's playing abilities, Uncle Dave ad-mitted that he was "pretty good on the banjo," but quickly added, "he ain't a damn bit funny." On another occasion, he said that Earl "can't sing a lick," even though Earl had a pleasant baritone voice. Still, in their direct personal relations, Uncle Dave, Lester Flatt, and Earl Scruggs not only got along well on the road but sought to spend much time together socially. Whenever hotels were short of rooms for the Monroe entourage, Uncle Dave, Lester, and Earl all piled into a single room together for a night's rest.

Mac Wiseman is one of the last surviving performers to have toured with Uncle Dave. By 1945 he was a rising vocalist and first encountered Uncle Dave professionally at a show in Harrisonburg, Virginia. Bill Monroe soon hired Mac as a vocalist, and they all toured together in the late 1940s. The young performer was in complete awe of Uncle Dave, considering him "music royalty" and "in a league all his own." Mac was impressed with Uncle Dave's conduct, especially toward other performers; he was never pretentious and always dignified and disciplined in his personal dealings.

One of Mac Wiseman's best recollections of the Dixie Dewdrop occurred during a show in Ohio, where he had the task of announcing a smooth tran-sition from Uncle Dave's opening act to the first appearance of Bill Monroe and his Blue Grass Boys. That night Mac waited expectantly for the right moment when Uncle Dave and Kirk McGee seemed to be nearing the end of their set. By the time the tune ended, Mac was already at center stage with microphone in hand, asking the audience to give Uncle Dave a big hand and announcing some preliminaries for Bill Monroe's entrance. However, there was no movement behind him to indicate that anyone was either leaving or entering the stage. Glancing over his shoulder, Mac was surprised to see Uncle Dave still seated in his chair and staring straight at him. "Son, I'm not done yet!" Uncle Dave suddenly exclaimed. Mac slowly slinked off stage as Uncle Dave and Kirk McGee launched into their closing number. Everyone took the incident in stride, and Mac came to cherish that moment as one of his most memorable interactions with the Dixie Dewdrop.

Roy Acuff's popularity had grown so great by late 1947 that he no longer needed an opening act to help draw a crowd. This left Uncle Dave free to tour with others, and he was soon on the road with Curly Fox and Texas Ruby. Curly Fox had a youthful band, and the Dixie Dewdrop had the experience of being around musicians experimenting with amplified, electric guitars. During one of these outings, Uncle Dave appeared on live television in the New York City area, but he didn't like it. Much like the film sets of Hollywood, television studios had too many restrictions that cramped his freewheeling style.

One of Uncle Dave's most memorable road incidents occurred while traveling with Curly Fox. The group had put on a show near Asheville, North Carolina, and they decided to head for Knoxville afterward. The steep, challenging descent from the Smoky Mountains occurred at night, and to complicate the hazard, a sudden, powerful storm hit. Lightning flashed, thunder boomed, and rain pounded down in sheets as the car careened through a continuous series of sharp, hairpin turns. Not far into the descent, all the car's occupants realized they were in a treacherous situation. Everyone fell quiet, lost in their own thoughts. Suddenly, Uncle Dave shouted from the back seat: "Lord, if you just get me off this mountain safe, I swear, I'll never touch another drop of whiskey!" The storm soon eased, and before long, the car made it to more level ground. A few minutes later, a calmer voice was heard from the back seat. "Boys, hand me my grip," Uncle Dave requested, "I've got to have a nip to calm my nerves."

A health crisis in 1949 changed Uncle Dave's life in nearly all respects. Prostate complications finally required an operation at Baptist Hospital in Nashville. Knowing that he would need quality care following surgery, he reached out to Vesta Blair Kinney. Vesta's husband had been wounded in the war, and to facilitate his healing, doctors recommended that the couple relocate to a hot, dry climate. They had settled in Yuma, Arizona, where Vesta's husband had acquired a good desk job with the railroad. Uncle Dave wrote Vesta an impassioned appeal, asking the couple to return to Tennessee to help care for him, volunteering to pay all the costs of their move and to help them find a good place to live. With a heavy heart, Vesta wrote back that she had started a new life in Arizona and that her husband could not leave his job there.

The health crisis brought him back to Kittrell to live. Uncle Dave's sons and the Richardson relatives rallied to get him through the surgery and recovery, with Glen serving as his father's primary caregiver. Uncle Dave had always been in excellent health, and the sickness revealed a difficult patient who was convinced that he was at death's door. During his recovery, Dave read the Bible extensively, telling his sons that he was looking forward to being reunited with his beloved Tildy. He sang and listened to sacred hymns, telling a reporter that he was "readying himself" for the end of life. A personal favorite was "Poor Sinners, Fare Thee Well," in which the saints anticipated the day they would wear "them-a golden slippers" while treading the byways of heaven. Melancholy hit at one point, and Uncle Dave wondered whether he had done wrong by "acting a fool" during his entertainment career and taking money from all who paid to see him. His sons assured Dave that everyone had freely paid to enjoy his performances and listen to his records, and he had done right by them all. His deep faith allowed him to see beyond death and to anticipate the Resurrection Day when he would arise from his grave at Coleman Cemetery. Dave told his oldest son Archie that when that glorious day came, he hoped the Lord would allow him the favor to pause briefly at Haynes Chapel and the Kittrell home one last time to give thanks for the blessings of his earthly life before his resurrected body and soul ascended into heaven to dwell there with God forever.

Other, more practical matters also occupied his thoughts. Looking back on his life, he was especially proud of three things: he had never been arrested, been sued, or had a serious fire on his farm. "Never get involved in a law suit," he counseled his sons. "Even if you win, you'll make enemies." Meanwhile, his gold-capped teeth were starting to bother him. Decades earlier, gold dental work had been a status symbol; the rich had the money to have their troubled teeth treated with gold, while the poor simply had their ailing teeth pulled. With his golden teeth deteriorating, Uncle Dave's sons encouraged him to have all his teeth pulled and replaced with dentures, a new treatment option at the time. Uncle Dave decided against it, afraid that he would not be able to sing very well with "a mouthful of false teeth."

Eventually, he recovered and took up the banjo once more. The days of touring were over, but he was determined to stay in the public eye. Whenever he traveled to Murfreesboro or Woodbury on business, he went in full suit and hat, often carrying his banjo. A favorite pastime was to go to Murfreesboro on Saturdays and spend most of the day playing and joking with friends and passersby on the courthouse lawn. Twenty years earlier, the Rutherford County sheriff had declared that if four separate venues were positioned at each corner of the Murfreesboro square and competing for listeners—a preacher proclaiming the gospel, an auctioneer conducting a sale, a medicine man peddling his elixirs, and Uncle Dave putting on a show—the Dixie Dewdrop was sure to draw the largest crowd. It was still true in the early 1950s. He always drew a large crowd on those occasions, and he was just as determined to put smiles on people's faces in his hometown in the twilight of his career as he had done during the largest shows of his peak performing years.

An absolutely essential task was to continue playing on the Opry. Dorris assumed the responsibility for getting his father to Ryman Auditorium every Saturday night and accompanying him onstage. When Dorris was unavailable, Uncle Dave would stand at roadside in front of his house and flag down the commercial Greyhound bus on its scheduled run from Chattanooga to Nashville. Once in Nashville, he would use his reserved room at the Merchant's Hotel as a haven for rest or an overnight stay.

A woman had gotten the best of Uncle Dave at a pedestrian crosswalk in downtown Chicago a decade or more earlier, and a second, similar incident occurred during one of those bus rides. The Greyhound was rather full that day, and when Uncle Dave took his place at a window seat, he placed his big black hat on the aisle seat next to him to maintain some modicum of personal space. Before long, almost every seat was taken. At the next stop, a pair of women got on, engaged in an intense, animated conversation. One of them, a rather large, buxom lady, plopped down next to Uncle Dave without first checking the seat. The Dixie Dewdrop sat silent and steaming for a while, knowing that the woman had completely flattened his hat without her even realizing it.

"Ma'am," Uncle Dave finally intoned, "do you happen to realize what you are sitting on?" She turned toward him, annoyed that the old man had been so impudent as to interrupt the important conversation with her friend.

"Sir, I certainly do know what I'm sitting on," she fired back. "I've had this thing for more than forty years, and I've sat on it every single day!" With that retort, she turned back to her friend, completely ignoring the Dixie Dewdrop. He finally reclaimed the crushed hat, but whether he was successful in salvaging it or had to buy an entirely new one is not known.

Throughout his life, Dave had believed in the philosophy that when life hands you lemons, you make lemonade out of it. One of the best demonstrations of his adherence to that philosophy occurred during another bus trip. One Saturday afternoon, the bus broke down halfway between Murfreesboro and Nashville. Realizing the problem was serious, the driver announced that he would have to call the bus company in Murfreesboro so a replacement vehicle could be dispatched. After the driver left to go find a phone, people exited the bus to stretch their legs and get some air. It wasn't long before Uncle Dave started to put on a show. In an open field adjacent to the highway he began performing, and all the other passengers were soon gathered about and enjoying the free entertainment. Passersby soon realized what was happening. Cars pulled off to the side of the road, with people rushing to join the excitement. Before long, the Nashville highway was completely snarled, with traffic backed up for a quarter of a mile in each direction, but neither the Dixie Dewdrop nor the growing crowd seemed to mind the pandemonium. Did Uncle Dave pass his hat for tips? Probably. When the relief bus finally arrived, the driver had to work his way slowly through the traffic jam, delaying the pickup of passengers, but they were all soon once again on their way to Nashville.

Uncle Dave maintained a steady presence backstage at the Ryman on Saturday nights. The Ryman staff had reserved for him a bentwood chair to sit in during performances, and he used the same chair backstage during the rest of the show. Often, he was still the center of attention, but more and more, visitors and other entertainers were drawn to the Opry's new, rising stars. Sometimes he stole off to the Merchant's Hotel to rest or enjoy a drink or two before returning to the Ryman for his closing set. One night, Roy Acuff noticed Uncle Dave sitting in his bentwood chair and brooding. When Roy asked what was wrong, Uncle Dave replied that he was growing tired of having to wait so long between performances and declared that he wished WSM would let him play the entire Opry show one night all by himself. At another time, Sid Harkreader found his old partner sitting backstage appearing distracted and troubled. When Sid asked what was wrong, Uncle Dave replied that there was "just too much meanness in the world." The Korean War had just broken out, and like many Americans, Uncle Dave could not believe that the nation was once again at war only five years after the close of World War II. Furthermore, Uncle Dave's youngest son Paul had rejoined the army in 1948 and was being rushed to Korea at that moment with other reinforcements to help reverse the tide of communist aggression.

Two special visitors to Kittrell in May 1950 resulted in the final music recordings. Charles Faulkner Bryant was a Tennessee composer and folklorist interested in researching the background to folk songs. Bryant had a new instrument in his toolkit to aid in data collection: an open reel tape recorder. The folklorist had asked a good friend, David Cobb, an announcer at WSM, if he could arrange a visit with the Dixie Dewdrop. Uncle Dave was glad to oblige, and when the pair arrived at his house, he had no difficulty in warming to the tape recorder.

With everyone in a relaxed mood, the talking, playing, and recording soon commenced. Uncle Dave performed a total of twenty-one songs, half of them having never been previously recorded. A mix of the performance elements of vaudeville, minstrelsy, and the medicine show was captured on tape as Uncle Dave tuned his banjo, told stories, laughed at his own jokes, and had a great time playing and singing in front of his fireplace. His voice was still strong and well-pitched only a few months short of his eightieth birthday. With a loss of dexterity and suppleness in his fingers due to aging, the banjo playing style was frailing and rapping rather than the elaborate, fingerpicking techniques of the past. In a few places, Uncle Dave momentarily got lost in the notes. A host of background noise—trucks passing by on the Woodbury Road, a rooster crowing, and family members talking—conveyed the intimacy and authenticity of the moment. The informal, impromptu session remains among the most unique recordings Uncle Dave ever made.

A capstone event in Uncle Dave's career came a few months later at Ryman Auditorium. In November 1950, the Grand Ole Opry dedicated one Saturday night show in honor of its silver anniversary. At the height of the program, two figures stood alone at center stage: George D. Hay and Uncle Dave Macon. The Dixie Dewdrop clutched his banjo in his right hand while balancing a large bouquet of flowers in the crook of his left arm and grinning for adulating fans. The crowd cheered for the two leading cast members who had been present at the Opry's creation twenty-five years earlier. Most others had already died or passed from the music scene, but the Solemn Old Judge and the Grand Ole Man of the Grand Ole Opry still endured.

The music died on Saturday night, March 1, 1952. Uncle Dave played on the Opry that night as always. His last set came late in the evening, and the final number—which was the last he ever performed—was "Eleven-cent Cotton, Forty-cent Meat," delivered from center stage at Ryman Auditorium. Upon finishing, he turned toward Dorris and declared in a hushed voice: "I can't get up! You boys are going to have to carry me off." Alarmed at his father's exhaustion, Dorris put down his guitar and quickly rallied a few other performers and stagehands to help. Gathering around Uncle Dave, the men gingerly lifted him, bentwood chair and all, and carried him backstage and close to an exit door.

Dorris scrambled to the musician's parking lot at the north end of the building and retrieved his car. He brought the sedan to a side door, and with the help of many others, eased his father down a short flight of stairs and into the car's front seat. Thinking on his feet, Dorris decided to return Uncle Dave to Kittrell and then assess the situation. Taking him to a local hospital in Nashville would have greatly complicated the situation for the family, especially if an extended stay became necessary. The two were soon on their way home. Leaving Ryman Auditorium, they passed near the intersection of Broadway and 8th Avenue in downtown Nashville. Nearly seventy years earlier, a young Dave Macon had passed that very same way to watch carnival performer Joel Davidson play and twirl his banjo, thus firing the youthful imagination of one of America's greatest entertainers.

Dorris made the drive to Kittrell without incident and put his father to bed. The whole event was perhaps not that unexpected to the family. In the last year, Uncle Dave had steadily lost strength and weight, coming to resemble one who was wasting away. A few surviving pictures from the period show a thin, frail man. Though his appetite remained good, he was experiencing choking incidents and difficulty in swallowing. He rested through the night, and the following morning, Glen cooked his father breakfast and fed him in bed. Dorris had called his oldest brother Archie, and he soon arrived at the house. When Uncle Dave was unable to keep his breakfast down, Archie made the decision to take his father to Rutherford Hospital in downtown Murfreesboro.

Uncle Dave was admitted, and the medical staff, under the direction of Dr. Carl E. Adams, a leading surgeon in the region, began a series of tests. It was soon determined that Uncle Dave had a possible obstruction near the juncture of the stomach and esophagus and that exploratory surgery was necessary. The procedure commenced on Thursday, March 6, and not long after it began, Surgeon Adams emerged from the operating room with dire news for the family. He talked primarily with Archie, informing him that an advanced, malignant tumor in the abdomen had been discovered. Knowing the family's wishes in the face of such a grim diagnosis, Archie instructed the surgeon to sew his father back up and to let nature take its course, rather than to continue with radical surgery.

Archie Macon stayed at his father's side near continuously following the surgery. Other family members were there too, insuring that Uncle Dave was as comfortable as possible and never alone. As the oldest son, it fell to Archie to make major decisions and to coordinate care with nurses, doctors, staff, and administrators. He was absolutely dedicated to his father's care, especially knowing that the end of life was near. After a sixteen-day marathon on death watch, Dorris encouraged his oldest brother to go home and get some rest, and at last, even Archie realized that he needed a break.

Before leaving the hospital, Archie asked if there was anything else he could do for his father. True to form, Uncle Dave made a distinctive request: would he read aloud from the Bible the entire Chapter 8 of the great Book of Romans? Archie found a Bible, pulled up a chair, and after both men were settled, he began reading: "There is therefore now no condemnation to them which are in Christ Jesus, who walk not after the flesh, but after the Spirit." For the next several minutes, Archie slowly and meticulously read the chapter, which contains some of the most potent peals of theological thunder ever issued forth from the pen of the Apostle Paul. Human flesh was weak, faulty, and mortal; God was omnipotent, perfect, and immortal. Despite the manifold challenges of life, "all things work together for good to them that love God, to them who are called according to his purpose." It was a moment for Uncle Dave to ponder the shortcomings of his own life while reaffirming the faith and trust in God he had openly expressed in his life and music since middle age. The chapter ends with some of the most powerful and lyrical verses in the New Testament, as Paul exhorts believers with the assurance that nothing "shall be able to separate us from the love of God, which is in Christ Jesus our Lord." When Archie finished reading, he studied his father. Uncle Dave lay still, staring up at the ceiling, and finally he murmured: "I'm ready now." Archie departed for home soon thereafter; it was the last time he saw his father alive.

Uncle Dave Macon died the next morning, Saturday, March 22, 1952. Dorris and his brother Harry were with their father when he exhaled his last and passed away peacefully. A short examination confirmed the final result, and a doctor called the time of death at 6:25 a.m. Over the next two days, the Macon family organized and participated in the memorials. On March 23, Murfreesboro hosted one of the largest and grandest funerals in the history of the state of Tennessee, and Uncle Dave was carried to his final resting place beside his beloved Tildy at Coleman Cemetery five miles east of town. The Grand Ole Man of the Grand Ole Opry had finally fallen silent, but his music and legacy would live on.

CHAPTER 7

The Macon Music Legacy

WITH THEIR FATHER DECEASED, the Macon brothers moved with due diligence to carry out his wishes regarding the disposition of his property. It all started with a jolt. Not long after the funeral, one of the sons walked into Murfreesboro's premier jewelry store and surrendered Uncle Dave's prized gold pocket watch for cash. Thinking the situation abnormal, the store's owner called Archie to inform him of the transaction and that the store would hold the precious watch for him. Archie drove to the jewelry store on the Murfreesboro town square, recovered the timepiece and then convened a meeting of all the brothers at the house in Kittrell where he laid the law down. None of their father's personal effects were to leave the house; whoever desired one of Uncle Dave's personal possessions for sentimental reasons would have to purchase it at a pending estate sale.

It was the second time since the funeral that Archie thought it necessary to exercise leadership as the eldest son. The day after Uncle Dave's burial he had gone to Kittrell to confront Glen, admonishing him for failing to attend his own father's funeral. Archie pointed out that while Glen had chosen not to attend the funeral of either his mother or his father, he would one day surely attend his own funeral. The confrontation had prophetic overtones. When Glen died suddenly in 1961, it was Archie who saw to the arrangements and burial.

The real battle royale among the sons over their father's worldly possessions had already occurred three years earlier. Uncle Dave's sickness and surgery in 1949 had compelled him to consider the final disposition of his key assets. The younger boys wanted to maintain the status quo, keeping the house and lands available as a safe haven and refuge whenever they were unable or unwilling to work. The older sons completely rejected any such notion, asking their father to have the house and farm sold and the resulting monies divided equally among the seven siblings. Uncle Dave's instructions for the settlement of his estate were recorded in his last will and testament of November 24, 1949. All of his earthly possessions were to be sold and the monies equally divided among his children. There was one exception. Glen had served as his father's primary caregiver in the final years, and in consideration of his efforts, Uncle Dave willed to him a small parcel of land at the corner of the farm where Glen built a small cabin for himself.

One of the most pressing items was the disposition of the Dixie Dewdrop's banjos. Archie was in overall charge of the pending estate sale, but admitting that he knew little about the instruments or his father's desires for them, he turned the whole matter over to Dorris. Fortunately, Dorris knew Uncle Dave's wishes for the gifting of his banjos, seven in all at the time of his death. Sadly, one of those was stolen from the Macon home not long after his passing. Five of the instruments went to Roy Acuff, Brother Oswald, Stringbean, Earl Scruggs, and June Carter; the disposition of the last one remains uncertain. The Gibson banjo bequeathed to Roy Acuff became part of the Acuff Collection and is today on display in a showcase on the rear wall of Ryman Auditorium. Uncle Dave had already given his big Slingerland banjo to a family in Rutherford County in 1940, where it remains today. The greatest mystery of all is the whereabouts of the Dixie Dewdrop's original Buckbee banjo purchased in Nashville when he was a teenager. The instrument remained at the Macon home until the mid-1920s, but its disposition afterward is unknown. The Buckbee remains the missing Holy Grail of all of Uncle Dave's instruments.

In the three months following Uncle Dave's passing, family and friends worked to prepare for the estate sale. The auctioneer's handbill listed the principle items for sale, including 140 acres of land, the main house and outbuildings, and a long listing of household goods, including a Victrola radio and "numerous souvenirs." The auction commenced on the morning of June 25, 1952. After more than fifty years, ownership of the Macon homestead passed to others. The house, outbuildings, and lands went for $9,800 with another $500 garnered for personal property. A number of family members acquired some furniture, clothing, records, and other personal items for sentimental reasons. After all fees and taxes were paid, the estate was settled, with each of Uncle Dave's seven sons receiving equal portions from the proceeds of the sale and their father's money holdings.

Even as Uncle Dave's worldly possessions were being sold, divided, and scattered, his music legacy was being preserved. In 1952, Folkway Records of New York issued its *Anthology of American Folk Music*, which was destined to become a recording classic. Compiled and edited by Harry E. Smith, an experimental filmmaker, record collector, and committed bohemian, the anthology was the first time commercial professional music was presented as a folk object. The collection included eighty-four choice folk songs presented on long-playing albums divided into three categories—ballads, social music, and songs—with extensive notes on each. Two of Uncle Dave's works made the cut: "Way Down the Old Plank Road" and "Buddy Won't You Roll Down the Line." Both were work songs, using music constructions that the Dixie Dewdrop had picked up from the singing and chanting traditions of plantation work groups and black stevedore crews on wharves and aboard steamships. The album notes stated that Uncle Dave employed wording and phrases from "widely known folk-lyric elements" and a regionalized "leader and chorus" singing pattern from the Upper South. The real significance of the *Anthology of American Folk Music* for Uncle Dave's legacy is that it set his work among the true classics of American traditional music.

About this time an unfortunate incident dealt a severe blow to the documented, historical record of Uncle Dave's legacy. Because of Tildy's indifferent attitude toward her husband's music, Annie Macon had taken the initiative to store much of the solid documentation of her brother's career at her home in Readyville, including copies of recording contracts, performance agreements, sheet music, personal correspondence, and other documents. The house caught fire in the middle of the night, with the family managing to escape unharmed, but with only the nightclothes on their backs. In that instant, much of the solid documentation of Uncle Dave's music career went up in smoke, never to be recovered.

A short time later, the Grand Ole Opry decided to erect a permanent monument to the Dixie Dewdrop's memory. Roy Acuff and Minnie Pearl took the lead in the development, placement and fund-raising for an appropriate historical marker. Because of Uncle Dave's close ties to the hills of Cannon County, the citizens of Woodbury took interest in the project. A local resident, James H. "Mister Jim" Cummings, who had served as Tennessee's secretary of state and a member of the Tennessee General Assembly for forty years, convinced the state to donate suitable acreage just east of Woodbury along U.S. Route 70S for a small park to locate the memorial. The tall, stone monument to Uncle Dave's memory was placed there and dedicated in April 1955. An attractive, artistic rendering on the monument's upper front facing features a head and shoulder profile of Uncle Dave and a banjo along with a single stanza of music containing the notes from the first line of the chorus of "How Beautiful Heaven Must Be." Engravings below give Uncle Dave's birth and death dates and the years he played on the Opry. The monument's main inscription identifies Uncle Dave as the one "who pioneered country music" while "entertaining on the Grand Ole Opry." The handsome, well-preserved monolith still stands today as a fitting tribute to the Grand Ole Man of the Grand Ole Opry.

Starting in the late 1950s and continuing unabated throughout the 1960s, the political and social strife resulting from the civil rights and antiwar movements prompted rebellious youth to seek new musical genres, and among those rediscovered was old-time music. Its simplicity and raw emotion was at the heart of the folk music revival, which became a widespread, popular movement. In 1958, The Kingston Trio recorded "Tom Dooley," and with six million copies sold, it became the most popular song of the era. Three years later, one of the top hit songs in America was the classic, nineteenth-century black spiritual, "Michael, Row the Boat Ashore," performed by The Highwaymen. But it wasn't all sentimentality and nostalgia. Inherent in the old music forms was a powerful tradition of social protest and commentary, and Uncle Dave's music once again commanded the attention of artists and listeners.

Perhaps the most widely recognized figure in the folk music revival was banjoist, performer, and activist Pete Seeger. He was only sixteen years old in 1935 when he first heard the banjo played at Bascom Lamar Lunsford's Asheville Folk Festival in North Carolina. Music fired his imagination more than academia, and after less than two years of studies at Harvard University, Pete moved to Washington, D.C., to work for Alan Lomax, the legendary folklorist at the Library of Congress. His first job there was to sort through high stacks of old 78 rpm records to identify those that might have the most interest to Lomax. It was during these long listening sessions that Pete Seeger first encountered Uncle Dave Macon and fell in love with his music. The Dixie Dewdrop's playing abilities further fired Seeger's interest in the banjo, and he went on to write and publish *How to Play the 5-String Banjo*, a brilliant treatise and analysis of the banjo and its unique instrumental style.

Pete Seeger promoted Uncle Dave and his music throughout the folk music revival and beyond. The 1962 edition of his banjo instruction book summarized the vast range of the Dixie Dewdrop's music:

His repertoire ranged from centuries-old ballads and country tunes, to comic ditties, work songs, topical songs about striking coalminers and sharecropping farmers, hymns and gospel songs. May he liven up the heavenly band!

Social commentary songs particularly appealed to the sensibilities of a new generation of activist musicians. Pete Seeger's most cherished protest song from Uncle Dave was "Buddy Won't You Roll Down the Line," a ballad based upon the forceful conflict between determined, striking coal miners and unyielding management during the violent Coal Creek War of 1891 in East Tennessee. In 1980, Pete Seeger declared that Uncle Dave was "one of the most important people in the history of American music" because of his ability to synthesize diverse genres of European and African music into new, coherent, and entertaining presentations. Pete Seeger's central role in the folk music revival made Uncle Dave and his music a considered influence in the movement, especially for those caught up in the banjo revival craze.

A second great advocate of Uncle Dave's legacy was music historian and entertainer Mike Seeger, Pete Seeger's younger half-brother. As a teenager, Mike Seeger had already fallen in love with the banjo and Uncle Dave's music. When he heard of the Dixie Dewdrop's death in 1952, Mike hosted a jam session in Uncle Dave's memory by inviting other teenage pickers to the Seeger home in Chevy Chase, Maryland. He wanted to entertain with the full richness and complexity of southern music while educating listeners as to its origins and meaning. A messenger needs a medium of communication, and Mike Seeger found it in his band, The New Lost City Ramblers. The group not only brought traditional southern music to the North but successfully transferred the sound from more rural locations to city centers and college campuses. Perhaps more than any other string band of the folk revival, The New Lost City Ramblers was the driving force in creating interest in southern music and reintroducing the public to the original performers from the 1920s and 1930s.

Mike Seeger held Uncle Dave in the highest regard and rightly credited the Dixie Dewdrop with introducing the vaudeville and minstrelsy traditions into the earliest country music venues. With his mix of straight frailing, "crazy double thumbing," and classic banjo playing styles, Mike considered Uncle Dave "one of the most natural performers of all time." Some folk revival musicians considered much of Uncle Dave's work too anachronistic, especially the romantic songs and ballads of the nineteenth century, but not Mike Seeger. If imitation is indeed the highest form of flattery, Mike

Seeger and The New Lost City Ramblers showed their regard for the Dixie Dewdrop with the release of the band's songbook in 1964. Of the 125 songs featured, nine of them were Uncle Dave tunes.

Reissues of Uncle Dave's recordings reestablished and sustained his musical presence. The first album of reissued songs resulted from a chance encounter in a hotel elevator. In 1961, Pete Seeger was in Montreal and stepping onto an elevator when he encountered Norman Tinsley, an avid record collector and Uncle Dave fan. During a brief conversation, both agreed that it was a shame that young musicians could not learn or enjoy the Dixie Dewdrop's music directly from his original recordings, which were either out of print or unavailable. Determined to repair the situation, Seeger worked with Tinsley and two other old-time music aficionados, Bob Hyland and Joe Hickerson. Between them all, they owned a copy of every one of Uncle Dave's originally issued 78 rpm records.

The effort resulted in the first reissue of Uncle Dave Macon recordings on the RBF Records label in 1963. The long-playing album, simply titled *Uncle Dave Macon*, featured an eclectic grouping of sixteen of the Dixie Dewdrop's best comedy, religious, romance, and work songs. A huge, added bonus was extensive album notes by Norman Tinsley, which included one of the first extended biographical sketches of the Dixie Dewdrop's life, though it contains numerous factual errors. The notes also contained perhaps the first printed discography of Uncle Dave's work, listing the original record label and issue number for each tune. For the first time since his passing, Uncle Dave's admirers could again enjoy his vocal and instrumental styles, revel in his roles as comedian, preacher, and social commentator, and appreciate his aptitude as a songwriter. More than any other print or recorded medium, *Uncle Dave Macon* reintroduced the Dixie Dewdrop to a new generation of young, adoring fans caught up in the folk revival.

One of the greatest accolades to Uncle Dave and his music came in 1966. Five years earlier, the Country Music Association had created the Country Music Hall of Fame to recognize and honor performers, songwriters, broadcasters, and industry executives for their significant contributions to the development of country music. In its first five years, only six personalities had been elected to the Hall of Fame: Jimmie Rodgers, Fred Rose, Hank Williams, Roy Acuff, Tex Ritter, and Ernest Tubb. It is believed that Roy Acuff played an influential role in having the Dixie Dewdrop nominated for membership and elected to the Hall of Fame in October 1966, in the same class with George D. Hay, Eddy Arnold, and talent agent and song publisher, James R. Denny. A Country Music Association bas-relief plaque cast in bronze included a nice portrait of Uncle Dave and a summary of his life and contributions to country music. The Hall of Fame recognized him as a man with a "delightful sense of humor and sterling character" who "loved humanity and enjoyed helping others." Uncle Dave's personality and music had "endeared him to millions," making him in his day "the most popular country music artist in America." His birth in 1870 makes Uncle Dave the earliest born member of the Hall of Fame, a unique, singular distinction he will always retain. It was no accident that George D. Hay and Uncle Dave entered the Hall of Fame in the same year. Already recognized as founding pillars of the Grand Ole Opry, their dual induction in 1966 further cemented that legacy. Today, Uncle Dave's plaque is on permanent display in the Hall of Fame Rotunda at the Country Music Hall of Fame and Museum in downtown Nashville.

Meanwhile, a number of entertainers kept Uncle Dave's music and performance style alive. Chief among those was Stringbean, whose banjo playing and comedic style retained the flavor of vaudeville. His dry wit and deadpan demeanor endeared Stringbean to legions of fans. Grandpa Jones had his own performance style much different from the vaudeville tradition, but still kept the image of the banjo-picking comedian before the public. Before Stringbean's awful murder in November 1973, he and Grandpa Jones brought the tradition of the banjo minstrel and jokester to a national audience with their memorable, comedic performances on the wildly popular television show *Hee Haw*. Brother Oswald too kept Uncle Dave's music alive by playing his songs, even as he picked the same banjo he had inherited from the Dixie Dewdrop.

A remarkable reissue of Uncle Dave's music came in 1979 with the album *Laugh Your Blues Away* from Rounder Records. The album is unique because of the rare sources of the recordings, including unissued test pressings, records from a rare private recording session by Uncle Dave and Dorris in 1945 and a mix of informal air checks and transcriptions. Remarkable liner notes by Charles Wolfe explained the album's origins and a recap of each song. A number of great Uncle Dave tunes appeared on the album, including "Go On, Nora Lee," "Don't You Look for Trouble," "How Beautiful Heaven Must Be," and the feature song, "Laugh Your Blues Away." The album caught the music world's attention, and twenty-seven years after Uncle Dave's passing, his music was nominated for a 1979 Grammy Award in the category "Best Ethnic or Traditional Recording."

Starting in the 1970s, a number of historical markers and public displays paid tribute to Uncle Dave's life and promoted his legacy. The Tennessee Historical Commission placed a roadside marker at Coleman Cemetery to identify Uncle Dave's burial site, and in 1974 his home in Kittrell was placed on the National Register of Historic Places. Warren County honored Uncle Dave as a native son with a historical marker on the south grounds of the Warren County Courthouse in downtown McMinnville, constructed in part with bricks from the original Macon Manor. Many of his personal effects, including furniture from the Kittrell home, were donated to the Museum of Appalachia in Clinton, Tennessee, and are on display there. In 1980, producers Blaine Dunlap and Sol Korine collaborated with historian Charles Wolfe to make *The Uncle Dave Macon Program*, an hour-long, award-winning documentary that aired on PBS and is still available on DVD.

The most significant and enduring tribute to Uncle Dave's music and legacy is the "Uncle Dave Macon Days" festival held every summer in Murfreesboro. The event began modestly in the summer of 1978 as the "Uncle Dave Macon Banjo Pickin' Contest," the brainchild of David Ramsey Macon, one of Uncle Dave's grandsons, and Jesse Messick, a local pharmacist and businessman. Six contestants entered and a single local band performed. One contest was intended to identify the musician who best reflected Uncle Dave's playing style. Cordell Kemp came all the way from Defeated, Tennessee, to enter and win the contest. Forty years earlier, Uncle Dave had stayed at the Kemp home while performing in the area, and over the course of several such stays, the Dixie Dewdrop had taught the young Cordell how to twirl the banjo. Cordell Kemp would go on to become an inspiration to a new generation of professional and amateur musicians. In the second year, organizers added a popular "Motorless Parade" to the festivities, a procession through downtown Murfreesboro of horse-and-mule–drawn conveyances meant to honor Uncle Dave's legacy as a local freight hauler.

In 1984, Gloria Christy became the festival's president and continues in that role today. Two years later, Congressman Bart Gordon of Tennessee's Sixth Congressional District inserted a proclamation into the Congressional Record designating Uncle Dave Macon Days as home to national championships in old-time banjo, clogging, and buck dancing. At present, the festival awards prize money in excess of $10,000. By 1989, the event had grown so much that it was moved from the Murfreesboro Square to its present location at nearby Cannonsburgh Village. Meanwhile, the festival's "Trailblazer Award" has become known for honoring those early musicians who helped to establish country music, including Sam and Kirk McGee, DeFord Bailey, the Delmore Brothers, and others. The festival's top honor, the "Heritage Award," has been presented to country music greats, including Roy Acuff, Bill Monroe, Dr. Ralph Stanley, Ricky Skaggs, Marty Stuart, and Mike Seeger. Uncle Dave Macon Days continues to thrive as a family-friendly environment and a gathering place each July for thousands of old-time music and dance contestants and enthusiasts. In 2014, the Southeast Tourism Society named Uncle Dave Macon Days as one of its "Top 20" entertainment venues in the Southeast.

Even in recent times, productions and markers still pay tribute to the Dixie Dewdrop. In 2004, Bear Family Records of Germany released *Uncle Dave Macon: Keep My Skillet Good and Greasy*, a comprehensive, boxed set of eight CDs containing all of Uncle Dave's known recorded music, a DVD of the movie *Grand Ole Opry*, and an illustrated book by Charles Wolfe containing a complete discography and a short biography. Uncle Dave's image has been enshrined at the Gennett Records Walk of Fame in Richmond, Indiana, and at the George D. Hay Foundation and Music Hall of Fame in Mammoth Spring, Arkansas. In 2014, the Dixie Dewdrop was elected to the Blue Ridge Music Hall of Fame in Wilkesboro, North Carolina, and Uncle Dave's life was celebrated with a historical storyboard at Cannonsburgh Village in Murfreesboro, which provides a brief sketch of his life in words and pictures. Most recently, Tennessee christened the structure spanning Cripple Creek on Route 70S not far from Uncle Dave's house as the "Uncle Dave Macon Bridge."

A new generation of music listeners has brought with it a popular resurgence in old-time music, and a number of acts have risen that perform traditional roots music with ties to Uncle Dave's legacy. The Grammy Award–winning band, Old Crow Medicine Show, has been prominent in the revival of old-time music with a contemporary twist. The Carolina Chocolate Drops pay homage to the black string and jug bands of the 1920s and 1930s. Leroy Troy and the Tennessee Mafia Jug Band play traditional songs with a performance style akin to the early Opry years. Two rising acts from Middle Tennessee openly promote their ties to Uncle Dave and his music: The Hogslop String Band and Uncle Shuffelo and His Haint Hollow Hootenanny. Individual acts also foster aspects of the Dixie Dewdrop's performance style. Opry member Mike Snider carries on the vaudeville tradition of the banjo-playing comedian. Norman Blake is highly renowned as an authentic and accomplished old-time songwriter, instrumentalist, and singer. Philip Steinmetz entertains in a genre rooted in Uncle Dave's style, even as he performs in period clothing and plays one of the Dixie Dewdrop's original Gibson banjos.

Because of so much interest regarding the fate of family members, a final word is in order about what became of those closest to Uncle Dave. Annie Macon survived her brother by several years. Even near the end of her life, Annie retained the wit, laughter, and deep faith that had sustained her for so long. "Hasn't the Lord been good to me?" she rhetorically asked a reporter in 1955. "Gave me good health, old age and good children. Who could ask for more?" Music remained a big part of her life, and she was a good piano player until her death in 1960, rendering most songs from memory. Bob Macon was the last surviving member of the original Macon family. He continued to prosper at his ranch near Vinita, Oklahoma, until his death in 1962.

While Archie Macon had always expressed an ardent love for his father, he did not come to appreciate fully Uncle Dave's music career until late in life. In the 1970s, he gave numerous interviews to historians and reporters about Uncle Dave's life and music career; Archie passed away from cancer in 1978. John Macon never got past the alcohol and died in the summer of 1970 from injuries suffered in an automobile accident. Harry Macon never married, completed a long career as a truck driver, and passed away in 1984. As previously mentioned, Glen Macon died in 1961. Dorris continued to play on the Opry with Sam and Kirk McGee and the Fruit Jar Drinkers until the show moved from Ryman Auditorium to the new Grand Ole Opry House in March 1974. His long run as an Opry performer for over forty-five years, during which he played at every location in Nashville that housed the Opry, is remarkable in its own right. His wife passed away in 1978, and Dorris suffered declining health in his last years. Alone and sick, he perished from a self-inflicted gunshot wound in February 1982. Esten Macon finally got over his father's alcoholism and became an ardent promoter of Uncle Dave's legacy. As a Church of Christ preacher, Esten came to realize that no matter where he preached or spoke, his father had performed there previously, leaving listeners with nothing but good memories. Esten wrote articles about Uncle Dave, spoke to reporters, and regularly attended Uncle Dave Macon Days before his passing in 1993. Paul Macon left the army and came home after the Korean War a broken man. Intense combat in Korea, during which Paul witnessed the gory spectacle of his best friend being blown to bloody bits by a Chinese artillery shell, imparted a severe case of posttraumatic stress. Whenever summer storms brewed up in Kittrell, the normal flash and bang of lightning and thunder prompted Paul to dive for cover behind furniture. Conflicts with an ex-wife and chronic alcoholism only added to his troubles. Six months following his father's death, Paul left Tennessee for good in September 1952. Despite efforts to locate his whereabouts, he was never found, and a Tennessee court finally declared him deceased in 1966.

In the end, what can we say about Uncle Dave Macon, the entertainer and musician? An original Grand Ole Opry cast member, Uncle Dave stands at the headwaters of the beginnings of the Opry and the entire country music industry. His presence on the Opry endured for twenty-six years, and during the first fifteen, Uncle Dave was the Opry's most prominent featured star. His longevity, performance style, and music made a distinct imprint, legitimately earning for him the title "The Grand Ole Man of the Grand Ole Opry." Ralph Peer, Jimmie Rodgers, and the original Carter Family had been at the center of the "big bang" of the 1927 Bristol recording sessions, which did so much to elevate country music as a recording interest. In the same way, Uncle Dave and George D. Hay were at center stage during the "big bang" of the country music broadcasting industry, which occurred in Nashville with the founding of the Grand Ole Opry and WSM's elevation to clear channel, 50,000-watt power status. By 1950, Dave had already acquired a legendary persona as an original cast member who had been present at the Opry's creation and on stage near continuously ever since. His final performance, done at center stage at Ryman Auditorium during his last Opry appearance, further cemented his everlasting ties to the institution. With his longevity, renowned performing style, and unique personality, Uncle Dave was a shaper of the developing, commercial country music tradition. If Jimmie Rodgers is the "Father of Country Music," Uncle Dave Macon should be considered the "Grandfather of Country Music."

The Dixie Dewdrop was the first Grand Ole Opry performer to accomplish a significant musical trifecta. He was the first to become a full-fledged Opry star, to gain a commercial recording contract, and to perform successfully on tour. Others in those early years managed to achieve one or two such distinctions, but Uncle Dave was the very first to attain all three. Furthermore, he continued to excel in all three endeavors for nearly twenty years. The standard he established for performers still endures. Aspiring new country music artists still seek to become Opry stars, recording artists, and successful, touring acts. Those select few who have risen to the very top of their profession can still look to Uncle Dave Macon as the pioneering country music entertainer who first achieved such renown.

Perhaps Uncle Dave's most defining characteristic as a performer was the uniqueness of his appearance and music. Roy Acuff best captured the individuality of the Dixie Dewdrop's appeal:

> There was never a person that I have come in contact with in the entertainment world that was more individual than Uncle Dave Macon. And a self-made entertainer. He seemed to copy nobody. He seemed to have a style of his own and everything that Uncle Dave did was Uncle Dave's style and nobody else's. . . . Uncle Dave was a great entertainer!

Few people saw Uncle Dave on stage more than DeFord Bailey, who held that no one else could even come close to matching Uncle Dave's unique personality, actions, and style. The harmonica wizard compared Uncle Dave to an extraordinary cook with the natural ability to take standard ingredients and transform them into an elaborate, delicious meal; the Dixie Dewdrop had the "sweets and stuff" to go with his music that other performers simply lacked. "Nobody else could catch Uncle Dave," DeFord proclaimed, "no matter which way they played. You wouldn't have nothing on him, no kind of way." Stringbean was a keen observer of Uncle Dave's mannerism and attributes and was the first to say famously of his mentor: "He's not the best player, and he's not the best singer, but he is the best something!" Mac Wiseman was even more pronounced in his estimate of the Dixie Dewdrop's distinctiveness:

> Uncle Dave Macon was country music royalty and definitely in a league all of his own. He was a complete natural, true to himself and the audience. You didn't copy Uncle Dave Macon: you might play his songs, but you can't do it the way he did it.

The few people yet living who witnessed a live show as children still testify to his uniqueness; to a person, they can clearly remember the Dixie Dewdrop's performance but can't recollect who else was with him on the ticket.

As a stage performer, Uncle Dave was second to none. Live appearances not only tickled the ears but gave the eyes much to relish. The Dixie Dewdrop hit the ground running when he first appeared on stage, grabbing the audience with an explosion of energy and talent. A booming voice, vigorous playing, and cackling laughter projected his personal zest for life onto the audience, who had to listen and watch closely just to keep track of what he was doing on stage and to anticipate what might happen next. The physical nature of stage shows was a key performance aspect that studio recordings could simply not capture. Wild facial expressions, exaggerated vocal imitations, sudden shouts, yodeling, tongue rattles, lip smacking, comical mispronunciations of certain words, the repeated doffing of his hat, and an endless offering of other physical antics all elicited a wide range of reactions. By debuting as a professional at age fifty, after three decades of performing as an amateur, Uncle Dave was at the top of his game from the very start in terms of picking and singing. An elaborate musical repertoire permitted him to shift continuously from the hilarious to the serious, and from the low to the lofty, as his songs formed strong emotional ties with listeners. The imposing hat, gold teeth, big Tennessee smile, elaborate suits, shirts and ties, and his shiny shoes, were a spectacle for the crowd to behold, even before he began twirling his banjo underneath and around his legs "like a monkey handles a peanut." If the crowd failed to respond, Uncle Dave had the experience and dexterity to shift on a dime and use different songs and material until he elicited a favorable response. He simply was not satisfied until all were enjoying themselves. In this regard, he possessed a deep, intuitive connection with his audiences that few other performers could match.

The spoken portions of live shows and recordings were just as important as songs in providing entertainment. Comedy was a central part of the spoken medium, with jokes, skits, one-liners, and stories connecting Uncle Dave to the everyday lives of his audience members. By listening to other comedians and entertainers and gathering jokes from books, newspapers, and the people he met, he amassed a nearly bottomless reservoir of comedic material. His humor contained a mix of wit and unusual perspectives on common themes, such as when he explained to a native pedestrian that New York City really was smaller than Tennessee's vast hills. Homespun, country philosophy and short sermons offered solace to listeners, especially those struggling with economic problems and lost love. Nothing was off limits. He went after crooked politicians and phony preachers unmercifully, even as he stood up to defend the underprivileged and the downtrodden. Furthermore, he voiced the common concerns of listeners who were enduring the upheavals of the Great Depression and World War II, adapting to societal change prompted by the automobile, the airplane, radio and rural electrification, and facing threats from the spread of the perceived, sinister theories of evolution, socialism, and fascism.

The Dixie Dewdrop is particularly remarkable for his prodigious and varied musical repertoire. Perhaps no other country music star has produced such a diverse body of work in terms of style and topic. In fourteen commercial recording sessions between July 1924 and January 1938, he cut 217 records, with 177 of those immediately released, an issue rate of 82 percent. Of those not released, most were preserved and eventually made available to the listening public. To put Uncle Dave's recording career in better historical perspective, one must realize that he commercially recorded 36 songs before first appearing on the Opry in April 1926, and by the time Ralph Peer conducted his famed field recording session in Bristol in 1927, the Dixie Dewdrop had already recorded 115 songs. The best estimate is that he composed approximately 100 original songs, and Sam McGee believed that he knew as many as 400 by heart. From his home in Springfield, Ohio, Bob Hyland regularly listened to Uncle Dave radio performances for nearly twenty-three years, always writing down the song titles. Bob eventually compiled a list of 218 tunes, which Uncle Dave used routinely but never recorded. After analyzing Uncle Dave's known discography and the Hyland list, the realization dawns that nearly half of Uncle Dave's total repertoire was simply never recorded.

Uncle Dave employed a wider variety of musical styles than most of his contemporaries, a distinguishing trait derived from his own personal experiences and background. Most of the aspiring, rural musicians from the 1920s had emerged from relatively isolated, rural locations, including the remote farms of the Piedmont, the high hills and deep hollows of Appalachia and the Ozarks, the dark recesses of the Mississippi Delta, and the scattered oasis towns of the Southwest. They were certainly aware of other musical genres due to radio and records, but had little direct exposure to them and even less personal contact with professional entertainers. For most aspiring performers, their direct exposure with other musicians was limited to local string bands, barn dances, church choirs, individual balladeers, and an occasional fiddle contest.

In contrast, Middle Tennessee had a much broader musical tradition, especially regarding black music. The years spent in Nashville as a young man gave Dave Macon direct exposure not only to different styles but to variable venues, including vaudeville shows, circuses, minstrel acts, medicine shows, and church music. Many of the musicians he encountered were hired theatrical professionals, who—by necessity—conveyed a higher performance standard in their playing and performing. After relocating to Rutherford County, he continued to soak up the music scene, especially black songs and sacred hymns. When he hit the big time, Uncle Dave easily drew from these experiences to make his stage shows and recording sessions richer and more varied than most of his younger contemporaries. The songs addressed nearly every aspect of the human experience, and the musical styles included ballads, romance, protest, comedy, work songs, and sacred hymns. Given the variety and complexity of musical styles that affected the Dixie Dewdrop, and the subsequent influence he had on the origins of early country music and the Grand Ole Opry, more historical research and writing needs to be done to capture and analyze this unique aspect of America's musical roots.

Of all the performing styles witnessed, nothing influenced him more than the professional entertainers of vaudeville. The purpose of a vaudeville show was to move and entertain an audience through a broad set of stage presentations, including comedy, physical acts, music, and commentary. In essence, his live shows and records were compact presentations of an entire vaudeville show. Supreme performing abilities allowed the Dixie Dewdrop to combine and project all the varied elements of vaudeville into a single smooth presentation—from an opening curtain call to a final musical crescendo. For nearly twenty years, until the advent of lead singers supported by professional bands, he grafted vaudeville performance methods onto the Grand Ole Opry.

For one who often eschewed new technology in his personal life, Uncle Dave readily adopted new entertainment mediums to advance his music career. In retrospect, the tremendous advances in entertainment technology Uncle Dave personally encountered during his long career are truly astounding. As an amateur entertainer, he had first ridden to local engagements in a horse and buggy, where he used the powerful projection of his own vocals to hold the crowd's attention. Similarly, his first recordings had been captured on the aged acoustic horn, soon replaced by the microphone. By the end of his career, he was flying to distant engagements by aircraft and transferred to large auditoriums by car, where thousands listened to him perform over elaborate electric sound systems. Uncle Dave's foray into radio illustrates one of his defining characteristics as an entertainment professional; he was always looking for new, more effective ways to keep in touch with his audience and to broaden his exposure to new listeners. His willingness to venture to Hollywood for moviemaking, to take flight on *The Great Speckled Bird*, and to dabble with television near the end of his career sprang from a willingness to exploit new technology to extend his entertainment reach. But try as he might, Uncle Dave never grew comfortable with the microphone, a perceived inhibitor to his freewheeling style.

Three important country music legacies are most closely associated with Uncle Dave's music and career. A product of the nineteenth century, Uncle Dave constituted a direct human link with America's musical past, even as he helped to preserve that tradition in a new era of radio and recordings. One of the most significant aspects of his discography is that it includes many nineteenth-century songs that would have otherwise been lost. Tunes from the Civil War and the Gilded Age remain alive today because of his recordings. Based on his extensive musicological research, Charles Wolfe concluded that the Dixie Dewdrop "preserved and transmitted more genuine folk songs than anyone in history." Certainly others did so as well, but Uncle Dave's perpetuation of traditional songs places him on par with folklorist Alan Lomax and the Carter Family. Second, even in the span of his own life, Uncle Dave came to represent the very beginnings of the Grand Ole Opry, with its emphasis on comedy, the barn dance, and old-time music. Today, the Dixie Dewdrop is best recognized as the ultimate personification of the traditional roots and earliest beginnings of the Grand Ole Opry and the entire country music genre.

What can we say about Dave Macon, the man? Even before the start of his professional career, he had a compulsion to please and entertain from the stage, a desire that grew commensurate with his increased fame. Whether performing for a few visitors on the front porch of his house or before large audiences in major city theaters, there was an obsessive need to please the audience and leave them wanting more. Uncle Dave was simply not satisfied until everyone in the crowd was either laughing at his jokes or deeply moved by his ballads, love songs, and sacred hymns. The strong irresistible impulse to entertain and please motivated him to stay on the road for nearly thirty years and well into advanced age. The fulfillment of his heart's desire to entertain on a grand scale definitely rolled back the black tide of depression that had clouded the first five decades of his life. Even during his peak performing years, occasional moods of melancholy hit but never enough to incapacitate and require hospitalization or to prevent him from making a scheduled appearance.

Dave Macon was a complex person who had the ability to adapt to variable roles and environments. In his personal life, he acted as brother, husband, father, farmer, business owner, church member, and part-time musician. His early stage acts and advertising often promoted the popular persona of the simple rube and hillbilly, but Dave Macon was neither. As his fame spread, he demonstrated the confidence to adapt to any situation, whether dealing with a hostile, small-town constable at an early show or projecting himself before millionaires at the famous Hotel Astor in New York City. A man of substance, he exhibited good judgment and considerable savvy in developing business arrangements but never sought to gain an unfair advantage. When completing business deals and at the close of performances, Dave would always ask promoters if they were satisfied, knowing that his personal reputation was his most valuable asset. Though he rarely harbored suspicions about others, Uncle Dave consistently turned to known, trusted friends and family members whenever challenges arose. A quick wit and the ability to think on his feet allowed him to avoid awkward situations or to turn them to his advantage. As he aged, Uncle Dave exhibited more guarded behavior by not exposing himself to possibly awkward or unpleasant situations and avoiding those he considered disagreeable.

Exceptional physical strength, nervous energy, and outstanding health were crucial personal attributes that fueled a long, public career. Even during the early freight-hauling years, others noted his exceptional physical strength and capacity for extended, hard work. That same physical strength and resilience allowed him to keep up with or outpace much younger musicians, to endure long repeated trips by car and train under harsh conditions, and to take the stage with the energy to perform a full active show. Nervous energy imparted the ability to manage his career and finances by himself, even while songwriting and gathering fresh material for jokes and skits. Uncle Dave's good health contributed to one of the most significant aspects of his career; he simply outlasted most of his peers. Between 1930 and 1945, several contemporaries who had started their music careers in the 1920s passed away, including Uncle Jimmy Thompson, Humphrey Bate, Jimmie Rodgers, and close friend Mazy Todd. Many more had their careers disrupted by sickness and divorce, or simply faded from the scene. The only personage who remained at Uncle Dave's side throughout most of his public career—with the possible exception of his son Dorris—was his good friend and confidant George D. Hay.

Despite coming from a large family and having seven children of his own, Dave Macon was in so many respects a man alone. The empty place created early in life by his father's murder seemed a harbinger of future isolation. His own siblings, with the exception of Annie and possibly Bob, thought that Dave's desire to launch a professional entertainment career was foolhardy. Dave's own wife and most of his children seemed incapable of appreciating his music career. Dorris was the exception; he witnessed on tour what his father was doing and what he had achieved. In spite of a gregarious personality and a love of humor, many professional activities were solo affairs, including initial song composition, banjo practice, long days traveling, and extended hours spent arranging touring schedules and corresponding with record companies, radio stations, and promoters. In all of these endeavors, he soldiered on alone, propelled by boundless energy and driven by the powerful motives to perform, entertain, and please.

Uncle Dave was often a man of eccentric behavior, which greatly added to his mystique and popularity. Even today, fans are enthralled and captivated by his habits of carrying his own meats into restaurants, stopping at railroad crossings, refusing to learn to drive a car, and always carrying a little black bag with his whiskey inside. How many performers would go so far as to emblazon their name across the front of their own house or put up theatrical posters in their front yard? Uncle Dave did, and such actions only further endeared him to his fans. In the end, the legacy of his peculiar, amusing behavior has helped to elevate him to near folklore status, especially in the South.

Another central aspect of Dave Macon's success in life was his faith in God. His religious belief system went far beyond the public projection of faith-based language and the playing of sacred hymns. Extensive Bible knowledge was the most overt manifestation of his faith. In the spoken introduction to the song "The Bible's True," he declared that "when it comes to the good ole Bible, from Genesis to Revelation, I'm right there." While many Christians might be knowledgeable regarding individual Bible stories, he was particularly well versed in the Bible's overall narrative, especially the salvation journey of mankind from its origins in the Garden of Eden to the final destination of the saints with God in the New Jerusalem. Uncle Dave manifested his religious faith in the daily reading of the Bible, regular attendance and tithing at Haynes Chapel Methodist Church, and generosity extended to family, friends, and strangers. He freely gave of his time and resources to others in need, from aspiring entertainers seeking better coaching to Depression-era drifters in need of food and money. Though his performances and recordings may have left the impression that he was a maverick and a rebel, Dave Macon at heart was a traditionalist through and through. His outrage against social injustices and poor government flowed from an understanding of the biblical teaching to love and care for others, rather than from a progressive political ideology. Some might view the inconsistencies between Dave Macon's own personal conduct and the profession of his religious beliefs as the height of hypocrisy, but in reality, he was trying to apply the latter to overcome the former, and he did so with demonstrated success.

Still, Uncle Dave was a man of some ego. He jealously protected his stage presence, insisting that he remain the central focus of the audience's attention. Though playing with many talented sidemen, he never let them get too much of the limelight. In many ways, Dorris was the perfect sideman; he was a good guitar player and singer who always had his father's best interests in mind and didn't care to promote his own music career. Though he was always kind and sociable to new, aspiring musicians in person, Uncle Dave habitually disparaged their music and predicted their hasty demise as performers. Whenever asked, the Dixie Dewdrop unabashedly declared that he possessed better clothes, banjos, and cars than other musicians. Uncle Dave's ego prevented him from throttling his freewheeling style in the recording studio, leading to awkward moments with sound engineers in New York City and confrontations with record company executives in Knoxville and New Orleans. Other than his single recording session with the so-called Fruit Jar Drinkers—the idea for the 1927 band recordings, as wonderful as they are, came from Brunswick and not Uncle Dave—he never again played professionally with a band. On tour with Opry tent shows or such acts as Roy Acuff, Bill Monroe, and Curly Fox, Uncle Dave performed as an opening act with a sideman but never played as part of the main band. When Uncle Dave informed a young Mac Wiseman that his portion of the program wasn't over yet, he was indicating that even in his later years, absolutely no one had the right to interrupt or curtail his stage act. After Tildy's death, Uncle Dave became even more absorbed in living out and projecting his onstage persona wherever he went. His willingness to do so was the natural extension of earlier efforts to develop himself as a unique, nationally recognized figure.

Alcoholism dogged Uncle Dave for much of his life, though his drinking habits changed considerably. Before the start of his music career, he had been a binge drinker, a condition that created considerable stress for his family. Once he was on the road and entertaining, Dave morphed into more of a maintenance drinker. During Vesta Blair's seven years in Kittrell, she remembered only one time when he was drunk in bed at home for an extended period. Dave always regretted his careless behavior in drinking in front of his young children. Determined not to repeat that failing, he never imbibed in front of Vesta. Drinking was a habit he desired to abandon completely but was hesitant to do so. "It's not the cost of the whiskey that bothers me," he told son Archie, "it's the cost of having to give it up." However, even the lure of the bottle was not strong enough to suppress his supreme motivation to entertain. Uncle Dave never allowed drunkenness to prevent him from performing on stage, a truth to which Roy Acuff and others readily attested. In the end, Uncle Dave's penchant for the bottle became yet another unique aspect of his life, which for many elevated his appeal as an entertainer and helped to propel him to folklore status.

The most telling assessments of Uncle Dave must come from those who knew him best. No country music personage was closer to him than George D. Hay. The Solemn Old Judge recognized from the beginning that in his personal appearance, musical abilities, and business acumen, Uncle Dave was simply a cut above the rest. In 1945, he wrote:

> We hope that the WSM Grand Ole Opry will last at least one hundred years. Regardless of how long a life it may have, the name of Uncle Dave Macon should always be remembered with gratitude by all the members of the cast and by the managers and officials of WSM. . . . Our hats are off to this grand Tennessee farmer who has done and is doing good wherever he goes with his three banjos, his plug hat, gates-ajar collar, gold teeth and his great big, Tennessee smile!

With the centennial anniversary of America's longest-lived radio show fast approaching, these prescient words will no doubt be proven true.

On the personal side, perhaps no one knew Dave Macon better than his oldest son. Archie Macon had ridden beside his father on freight wagons, accompanied Uncle Dave to his earliest shows, listened to his records, tuned in to hear him on WSM for a quarter-century, and helped to care for him in the last years. Prior to his own passing in 1978, Archie sat down for an interview with music historians and film producers to reflect on his father's legacy. "The body is gone; it went back to where God intended it," he observed at one point. "But Pap lives on . . . the sound of his voice, the words that he sang, the sounds of his music. Just think, they've got it all over the world!" The millions today who still cherish and revere his life and music worldwide would no doubt agree that the Dixie Dewdrop still lives.

The John and Martha Macon Family

John Macon	Married	Martha Ann Ramsey Macon
"Captain John"	December 9, 1855	1838–1906
1829–1886	Viola, Tenn.	
Burial Site		*Burial Site*
Evergreen Cemetery		Evergreen Cemetery
Murfreesboro, Tenn.		Murfreesboro, Tenn.

Name	Dates	Burial Site
1. Eugene LaVanderbilt Macon "Van"	1857–1938	Riverside Cemetery Woodbury, Tenn.
2. Eliza Lou Macon Edgecomb "Lou"	1859–1942	Mt. Olivet Cemetery Nashville, Tenn.
3. Bettie Macon Eddins	1861–1885	Mt. Olivet Cemetery Nashville, Tenn.
4. Emory John Macon "John"	1863–1908	Bentonville Cemetery Bentonville, Ark.
5. Samuel Ramsey Macon "Sam"	1865–1905	Evergreen Cemetery Murfreesboro, Tenn.
6. Sallie Macon Nichols	1867–1910	Nichols-Ford Cemetery Elmwood, Tenn.
7. Ann Macon-Walling Youree "Annie"	1868–1960	Evergreen Cemetery Murfreesboro, Tenn.
8. David Harrison Macon "Uncle Dave Macon"	1870–1952	Coleman Cemetery Murfreesboro, Tenn.
9. George M. Macon	1872–1874	Bonner Cemetery Viola, Tenn.

Name	Dates	Burial Site
10. Robert Macon "Bob"	1875–1962	Bentonville Cemetery Bentonville, Ark.
11. Pearl Macon Holden Harrison	1878–1916	Evergreen Cemetery Murfreesboro, Tenn.

(All children were born at "Macon Manor" at Smartt Station, Warren County, Tenn.)

The Dave and Tildy Macon Family

David Harrison Macon	Married	Mary Matilda Richardson Macon
"Uncle Dave Macon"	November 28, 1899	"Miss Tildy"
1870–1952	Kittrell, Tenn.	1877–1939
Burial Site		*Burial Site*
Coleman Cemetery		Coleman Cemetery
Murfreesboro, Tenn.		Murfreesboro, Tenn.

Name	*Dates*	*Burial Site*
1. Archie Emory Jesse Macon	1901–1978	Coleman Cemetery Murfreesboro, Tenn.
2. John Henry David Macon	1903–1970	Coleman Cemetery Murfreesboro, Tenn.
3. Harry Richardson Macon	1906–1984	Coleman Cemetery Murfreesboro, Tenn.
4. Glen Samuel Macon	1908–1961	Coleman Cemetery Murfreesboro, Tenn.
5. Dorris Vanderbilt Macon	1910–1982	Riverside Cemetery Woodbury, Tenn.
6. Esten Gray Macon	1913–1993	Coleman Cemetery Murfreesboro, Tenn.
7. Paul Franklin Macon	1919–1966*	Unknown

(All children were born at the Macon homestead at Kittrell, Rutherford County, Tenn.)

*Paul Macon was declared deceased by court order in 1966.

Notes

INTRODUCTION

Most of the details of Uncle Dave's sickness, death, and funeral are from a remarkable interview with Archie J. Macon conducted by Dr. Charles K. Wolfe and archived as part of the Dr. Charles K. Wolfe Collection at Middle Tennessee State University, Center for Popular Music, Murfreesboro, Tennessee. New interviews with Mary Macon Doubler, Uncle Dave's granddaughter; Vesta Blair Kinney, the Macon's housekeeper for several years; and Norma Delmore Weimer, Alton Delmore's daughter, provided additional details of the same events. Contemporary newspaper accounts from the *Tennessean*, the *Nashville Banner*, and the *Rutherford Courier* give good details of Uncle Dave's death and funeral. The guest sign-in book from Moore Funeral Home for Uncle Dave's visitation on March 22, 1952, is in the possession of the author.

INTERVIEWS

Mary Macon Doubler, interview by the author, Murfreesboro, Tennessee, September 9, 2014. Audio file is in the author's possession.

Archie J. Macon, interview by Dr. Charles K. Wolfe, Murfreesboro, Tennessee, June 4, 1977. Interview is audio file #00588 in the Charles K. Wolfe Collection.

Vesta Blair Kinney, interview by the author, McMinnville, Tennessee, August 29, 2013. Interview notes are in the author's possession.

Norma Delmore Weimer, interview by the author, Fayetteville, Tennessee, April 19, 2014. Interview notes are in the author's possession.

ALSO CITED

"Grand Ole Man: Uncle Dave Macon," *Cowboy Songs*.
Henson, "The Day I Met Hank Williams."

CHAPTER 1. "Rock About My Sara Jane"

Most of the information on the early Macon descendants in America is drawn from the private genealogy records of the National Gideon Macon Society, Inc., of Springdale, Arkansas. The records specific to Uncle Dave Macon's branch of the Gideon Macon descendants were compiled and organized by the late Edna Shewcraft Macon and Rusty Weber and are now in the author's possession. Detailed burial records at Mt. Olivet Cemetery in Nashville and Evergreen Cemetery in Murfreesboro were especially enlightening. The author's 2014 interview with recognized folklorist and musician Jim Costa of Talcott, West Virginia, was key to understanding Uncle Dave Macon's instruments and performing style. Two secondary sources by the late Dr. Charles K. Wolfe were helpful: *Uncle Dave Macon* (1995) and *Uncle Dave Macon: Keep My Skillet Good and Greasy* (2004). For an overview of American music at the end of the nineteenth century, see Ogasapian and Orr's *Music of the Gilded Age* (2007). The detailed history of the banjo is recounted in Dubois' *The Banjo* (2016).

INTERVIEWS

Jim Costa, interview by the author, Murfreesboro, Tennessee, July 14, 2014. Audio file is in the author's possession.

ALSO CITED

"Built in 1804, 'The Corners' Gave Gracious Shelter to Many Famed Men." No publication data available.
"Cutting Affray," *Daily American.*
Dillon, "Macon Family Has Deep Roots."
Dubois, *The Banjo.*
Eiland, *Nashville's Mother Church.*
Macon, C. R., "Gideon Macon Family Tree, 1670–2010."
Macon, Mrs. D. R., "Maj. John Macon."
Macon, Uncle Dave, Autobiographical Sketch to WSM Artists Service.
———, "My Life and Experience: Brunswick Topics."
Ogasapian and Orr, *Music of the Gilded Age.*
"Revenue Officer Charged with Murder," *Daily American.*
Wolfe, *Uncle Dave Macon.*
———, *Uncle Dave Macon: Keep My Skillet Good and Greasy.*

CHAPTER 2. "From Earth to Heaven"

The main sources for this chapter are six recorded interviews of members of the Macon family: Archie Macon, Uncle Dave's oldest son; Ruth Wood, a niece; Mary Macon Doubler, a granddaughter; and David Ramsey Macon, a grandson. The interviews were done at various times and places over a span of four decades. The Archie Macon and Ruth Wood interviews are part of the Dr. Charles K. Wolfe Collection at the Center for Popular Music, Middle Tennessee State University, Murfreesboro, Tennessee. The interviews of Mary Macon Doubler and David Ramsey Macon were conducted by the author and remain in his possession. Two previously cited publications by Dr. Charles K. Wolfe, *Uncle Dave Macon* (1995) and *Uncle Dave Macon: Keep My Skillet Good and Greasy* (2004), were again helpful in providing background information.

INTERVIEWS

Archie J. Macon, interview by Dr. Charles K. Wolfe, Murfreesboro, Tennessee, June 4, 1977. Interview is audio file #00588 in the Charles K. Wolfe Collection.

Archie J. Macon, interview by Dr. Charles K. Wolfe, Murfreesboro, Tennessee, December 5, 1974. Interview is audio file #00727 in the Charles K. Wolfe Collection.

Mary Macon Doubler, interview by Michael D. Doubler, Murfreesboro, Tennessee, September 9, 2014. In the author's possession.

David Ramsey Macon, interview by Michael D. Doubler, Owensboro, Kentucky, September 29, 2014. In the author's possession.

Ruth Wood, interview by Alvin F. and Mary Macon Doubler, Kittrell, Tennessee, July 1975. Interview is audio file #00532 in the Charles K. Wolfe Collection.

Ruth Wood and Miss Mary Hall, two-part interview by Dr. Charles K. Wolfe, Kittrell, Tennessee, March 15, 1979. Part One is audio file #00604, and Part Two is audio file #00605, both in the Charles K. Wolfe Collection.

ALSO CITED

Brownlow, *Why I Am a Member*.
"Evangelization of Rutherford County, Tennessee."
Haynes Chapel, "History of Haynes Chapel."
———, "Through the Years."
Macon, E., "Rambling Views."
State of Tennessee, Rutherford County, Certificate of Deed, "W. M. Freeman et al. To Dave Macon et al.," registered June 9, 1916. The Freeman & Coleman Graveyard was eventually reorganized as Coleman Cemetery, the designation it retains to the present.
State of Tennessee, Rutherford County, "Rutherford County Tax Books, 1877–2104."

CHAPTER 3. "Keep My Skillet Good and Greasy"

Two especially vital and informative sources helped in the reconstruction of Uncle Dave's early career. *Fiddlin' Sid's Memoirs: The Autobiography of Sidney J. Harkreader* (1976) provides key information not only on the early stages of Uncle Dave's career but on the origins of country music. A long interview of Fiddlin' Sid by Charles Wolfe from 1977 contains detailed material and unique insights regarding the artist's time with Uncle Dave. Similarly, two interviews of Sam McGee by Charles Wolfe contain essential information regarding Uncle Dave's earlier performances, especially the run of shows at the Loew's Bijou in Birmingham. The interviews are archived as part of the Dr. Charles K. Wolfe collection at the Center for Popular Music, Middle Tennessee State University, Murfreesboro, Tennessee. Tony Russell's magisterial reference work, *Country Music Records: A Discography, 1921–1942* (2004), provides detailed data on each of Uncle Dave's recording sessions. Charles K. Wolfe's *Uncle Dave Macon: Keep My Skillet Good* and *Greasy* (2004), gives an overview of each of Uncle Dave's recording sessions with emphasis on the background of each particular song. Barry Mazor's wonderful *Ralph Peer and the Making of Popular Roots Music* (2015) paints a vivid, detailed picture of the early days of the country music recording industry. John Doubler, a great-grandson of Uncle Dave and a very talented musician in his own right, provided an in-depth analysis of Uncle Dave's music and picking styles from the early New York City sessions. Eric Hermann, a PhD graduate from the University of Maryland at College Park, generously provided copies of articles from the Birmingham newspapers.

INTERVIEWS

Sidney J. Harkreader, interview by Dr. Charles K. Wolfe, Nashville, Tennessee, June 16, 1977. Interview is audio file #00373 in the Charles K. Wolfe Collection.

Esten Macon, interview by Dr. Charles K. Wolfe, Murfreesboro, Tennessee, July 8, 1982. Interview is audio file #02054 in the Charles K. Wolfe Collection.

Sam McGee, interview by Dr. Charles K. Wolfe, Franklin, Tennessee, October 1973. Interview is audio file #00484 in the Charles K. Wolfe Collection.

Sam McGee, interview by Dr. Charles K. Wolfe, Franklin, Tennessee, April 9, 1973. Interview is audio file #00485 in the Charles K. Wolfe Collection.

ALSO CITED

Fiddlin' Sid's Memoirs.

King, "Things Past and Present."

Macon, David Harrison, Executed contract and agreement between D. H. Macon and Sidney Harkreader. The original copy of this rare document is archived among the Uncle Dave Macon holdings in the Country Music Hall of Fame and Museum, Nashville, Tennessee.

Macon, Uncle Dave. Autobiographical Sketch to WSM Artists Service.

———, "My Life and Experience: Brunswick Topics."

Mazor, *Ralph Peer.*

"Mountain Farmer, with Banjo," *Birmingham News.*

Oliver, "Banjo Just like Life."

Russell, *Country Music Records.*

"'Uncle Dave' Again Features Loew's Bill," *Birmingham Post.*

Whittle, "Bessie, Dave Go Way Back."

CHAPTER 4. *"Take It Away, Uncle Dave!"*

A number of important works provide essential information on the formation of WSM and the Grand Ole Opry. Among these is George D. Hay's self-published memoir, *A Story of the Grand Ole Opry* (1945). Though inaccurate in much of its historical details, the narrative still provides Judge Hay's unique insights and opinions on the Opry's formative years, especially regarding the musicians and personalities involved. A number of publications and articles within the WSM and Grand Ole Opry Special Collections at the Jean and Alexander Heard Library at Vanderbilt University in Nashville provided contemporary views and detailed information on the music of the day and the earliest origins of WSM and the Grand Ole Opry. Other essential primary source materials include a number of interviews with Sid Harkreader, Dorris Macon, and Sam and Kirk McGee, all part of the Dr. Charles K. Wolfe Collection at the Center for Popular Music, Middle Tennessee State University, Murfreesboro, Tennessee. An award-winning documentary, *The Uncle Dave Macon Program* (1980), by Blaine Dunlap, Sol Korine, and Charles K. Wolfe, lends important primary source material about the Dixie Dewdrop's life and career on the early Opry. The most significant secondary works are Craig Havighurst's *Air Castle of the South* (2007) and Charles Wolfe's *A Good-Natured Riot* (1999). Once again, Tony Russell's *Country Music Records* (2004) and Wolfe's *Uncle Dave Macon: Keep My Skillet Good and Greasy* (2004) provide detailed information regarding Uncle Dave's many recording sessions throughout the Roaring Twenties.

INTERVIEWS

Sidney J. Harkreader, interview by Dr. Charles K. Wolfe, Nashville, Tennessee, June 16, 1977. Interview is audio file #00373 in the Charles K. Wolfe Collection.

Dorris Macon, interview by Dr. Charles K. Wolfe, Woodbury, Tennessee, n.d. Interview is audio file #00581 in the Charles K. Wolfe Collection.

Dorris Macon, interview by Dr. Charles K. Wolfe, Woodbury, Tennessee, March 11, 1979. Interview is audio file #00587 in the Charles K. Wolfe Collection.

Kirk McGee, interview by Dr. Charles K. Wolfe, location unknown, June 17, 1977. Interview is audio file #00567 in the Charles K. Wolfe Collection.

Kirk McGee, interview by Dr. Charles K. Wolfe, "Bluegrass Express" radio show, WMOT, Murfreesboro, Tennessee, March 14, 1981. Interview is audio file #00104 in the Charles K. Wolfe Collection.

Kirk and Sam McGee, interview by Mike Seeger and Ralph Rinzler, New York, New York, February 1965. Interview is audio file #01041 in the Charles K. Wolfe Collection.

Sam McGee, interview by Dr. Charles K. Wolfe, Franklin, Tennessee, April 9, 1973. Interview is audio file #00485 in the Charles K. Wolfe Collection.

Sam McGee, interview by Dr. Charles K. Wolfe, Franklin, Tennessee, October 1973. Interview is audio file #00484 in the Charles K. Wolfe Collection.

ALSO CITED

Burton, *Tom Ashley, Sam McGee, Bukka White*.
Havighurst, *Air Castle of the South*.
Hay, *Story of the Grand Ole Opry*.
"History of the Grand Ole Opry," WSM News Service.
Malone and Neal, *Country Music, U.S.A.*
Mason, *History of Cannon County, Tennessee*.
Uncle Dave Macon Program.
Wolfe, *Good-Natured Riot*.
WSM Official Grand Ole Opry History and Picture Book.
"WSM Radio and TV" and "Grand Ole Opry," Special Collections, Vanderbilt University.

The published and unpublished research materials supporting this chapter are especially rich and diverse. Alton Delmore's memoir, *The Delmore Brothers: Truth Is Stranger than Publicity* (1995) provides extremely unique information and insights on their years of touring with the Dixie Dewdrop. Two primary sources from Judge Hay proved valuable: an unpublished manuscript, "The Grand Ole Opry Hits the Road" (1949), and audio files in the Grand Ole Opry collection at Vanderbilt University. Two interviews with Dorris Macon provide choice accounts of Uncle Dave's activities throughout the 1930s. Similarly, the author's in-depth interview with Vesta Blair Kinney forms the core of the accounts of life at the Macon home during the 1930s and of Tildy Macon's sickness and death. Previously unexploited official records and local, published obituaries and news articles provide important details on the lives of Macon family members. In terms of secondary sources, a recent work, *The Knoxville Sessions, 1929–1930* (2016), by Ted Olson and Tony Russell, provides the latest scholarship on Uncle Dave's 1930 recording session. Chet Hagan's *Grand Ole Opry* (1989) offers a comprehensive overview of the Opry's transformation throughout the decades. Again, Charles Wolfe's *Uncle Dave Macon: Keep My Skillet Good and Greasy* (2004) provides good accounts of Uncle Dave's recording sessions.

INTERVIEWS

Everett Corbin and Charles Smith, interview by Martin Fisher, November 2, 2011. Interview is audio file #20111102 in the Everett Corbin Collection, Center for Popular Music, Middle Tennessee State University. Everett Corbin was the editor of *Music City News*, 1966–1967, and Charles Smith was the son of Ray Smith.

Vesta Blair Kinney, interview by the author, McMinnville, Tennessee, August 29, 2013. Interview notes are in the author's possession.

Archie J. Macon, interview by Dr. Charles K. Wolfe, Murfreesboro, Tennessee, June 4, 1977. Interview is audio file #00588 in the Charles K. Wolfe Collection.

Dorris Macon, interview by Dr. Charles K. Wolfe, Woodbury, Tennessee, March 11, 1979. Interview is audio file #00587 in the Charles K. Wolfe Collection.

Norma Delmore Weimer, interview by the author, Fayetteville, Tennessee, April 19, 2014. Interview notes are in the author's possession.

ALSO CITED

"Archie Glenn Stagner Dies," *Tennessean.*

Delmore, with Wolfe, ed. *Delmore Brothers.*

Dowland, Christmas Letter to Family and Friends. Dowland's informative missive on the Backusburg Musicale as well as festival posters are located in the John Doubler Collection, Clarksville, Tennessee.

Hagan, *Grand Ole Opry.*

Havighurst, *Air Castle of the South.*

Hay, "Grand Ole Opry Hits the Road."

"Last Rites Held Here Tuesday," *Cannon Courier.*

"Macey [*sic*] Todd, 53, Succumbs Friday," *Daily News Journal.*
Macon, Uncle Dave, "Songs and Stories."
Morton with Wolfe, *DeFord Bailey.*
"Mrs. Dave Macon Succumbs," *Cannon Courier.*
"Mrs. Mary Macon Rites to Be Today," *Daily News Journal.*
Olson and Russell, *Knoxville Sessions, 1929–1930.*
Rinzler and Cohen, *Uncle Dave Macon.*
Russell, *Country Music Records.*
State of Tennessee, Department of Health, Certificate of Death. "Mrs. Mary Matilda
    Macon, February 14, 1939," File #6173, filed March 18, 1939.
"True Story of the Famous WSM," *Rural Radio.*
"Uncle Dave Laments," *Knoxville News-Sentinel.*
Whittle, "Macon Was a Generous Man."
Wolfe, "Early Country Music in Knoxville."
———, *Uncle Dave Macon: Keep My Skillet Good and Greasy.*
"WSM Radio and TV" and "Grand Ole Opry," Special Collections, Vanderbilt University.

CHAPTER 6. "Poor Sinners, Fare Thee Well"

The narrative of this chapter relies heavily upon new primary source materials, including interviews and personal papers from the Macon family, allowing for many new accounts and perspectives of Uncle Dave's life and career. A number of interviews from the Charles K. Wolfe Collection, along with the memoirs of George D. Hay, further buttress the narrative. Two popular biographies, Elizabeth Schlappi's *Roy Acuff* (1997) and Richard D. Smith's depiction of Bill Monroe, *Can't You Hear Me Callin'* (2001) provide information on Uncle Dave's touring years with those two stars. The Mac Wiseman interview in particular provides unique, firsthand insights not only on Uncle Dave's music and personality but also on his interactions with other entertainers.

INTERVIEWS

Roy Acuff, interview by Dr. Charles K. Wolfe, Grand Ole Opry House, Nashville, Tennessee, September 19, 1977. Interview is audio file #00585 in the Charles K. Wolfe Collection.

Mary Macon Doubler, interview by the author, Murfreesboro, Tennessee, September 9, 2014. Audio file is in the author's possession.

Vesta Blair Kinney, interview by the author, McMinnville, Tennessee, August 29, 2013. Interview notes are in the author's possession.

Archie J. Macon, interview by Dr. Charles K. Wolfe, Murfreesboro, Tennessee, June 4, 1977. Interview is audio file #00588 in the Charles K. Wolfe Collection.

David Ramsey Macon, interview by the author, Owensboro, Kentucky, September 29 and 30, 2014. Audio file is in the author's possession.

Dorris Macon, interview by Dr. Charles K. Wolfe, Woodbury, Tennessee, n.d. Interview is audio file #00581 in the Charles K. Wolfe Collection.

Uncle Dave Macon, "Centennial of his Birth Tribute," Country Music Hall of Fame and Museum, Nashville, Tennessee, October 6, 1970. Recording is audio file #00467 in the Charles K. Wolfe Collection.

Kirk McGee, interview by Dr. Charles K. Wolfe, June 17, 1977. Interview is audio file #00567 in the Charles K. Wolfe Collection.

Mac Wiseman, telephonic interview with the author, August 17, 2016.

ALSO CITED

Buchanan, *Original Goober.*
Grand Ole Opry, directed by Frank McDonald. Republic Pictures, 1940.
"Grand Ole Opry," Special Collections, Vanderbilt University. A number of the audio
    files speak directly to the 1940 trip to California and the making of *Grand Ole Opry.*
"Grand Ole Opry–Prince Albert."
Hay, "Grand Ole Opry Hits the Road."
———, *Story of the Grand Ole Opry.*
Lomax, "List of American Folk Songs."
Macon, David Harrison, Personal business and financial records book.
———, Personal letter to his son.
Macon, E., "Rambling Views."
Pugh, *Ernest Tubb.*
Schlappi, *Roy Acuff.*
Smith, *Can't You Hear Me Callin'.*
State of Tennessee, Department of Health, Certificate of Death. "E. Lou Edgecomb, July
    8, 1942," File #469-41902, filed July 20, 1942.
Uncle Dave at Home, Spring Fed Records.

CHAPTER 7. **The Macon Music Legacy**

INTERVIEWS:

Roy Acuff, interview by Dr. Charles K. Wolfe, Grand Ole Opry House, Nashville, Tennessee, September 19, 1977. Interview is audio file #00585 in the Charles K. Wolfe Collection.

Archie Macon, interview by Dr. Charles K. Wolfe, Murfreesboro, Tennessee, June 4, 1977. Interview is audio file #00588 in the Charles K. Wolfe Collection.

Esten Macon, interview by Dr. Charles K. Wolfe, Murfreesboro, Tennessee, July 8, 1982. Interview is audio file #02054 in the Charles K. Wolfe Collection.

Uncle Dave Macon, public interviews by Dr. Charles K. Wolfe, Public Square, Murfreesboro, Tennessee, June 7, 1977. Interview is audio file #02084 in the Charles K. Wolfe Collection.

Mike Seeger, interview on National Public Radio, October 1975. Interview is audio file #01036 in the Charles K. Wolfe Collection.

Mac Wiseman, telephonic interview with the author, August 17, 2016. Interview notes are in the author's possession.

ALSO CITED

Chancery Court, *Betty Ann Singleton v. Paul F. Macon*. Murfreesboro, Tennessee, May 23, 1966.
"Dorris Macon, 71," *Cannon Courier*.
Hay, *Story of the Grand Ole Opry*.
Macon, David Harrison, "Last Will and Testament."
Malone, *Music from the True Vine*.
"Mrs. W. E. Youree," *Daily News Journal*.
New Lost City Ramblers Song Book.
Old-Time String Band Songbook.
Rutledge, J. R., "Auction Sale of Farm and Household Goods of Uncle Dave Macon (Deceased)." Auctioneers handbill, June 25, 1952.
Seeger, *How to Play the 5-String Banjo*.
"Uncle Dave Macon Auction," *Cannon Courier*.
United States Congress, "Uncle Dave Macon Days."
Welch, "CMA Names 4 to Hall of Fame."
Wilgus, "Current Hillbilly Recordings."
Wolfe, "Searchin' for Uncle Dave."
———, "Uncle Dave Macon Show."

RECORDINGS AND PRODUCTIONS

Anthology of American Folk Music.
Laugh Your Blues Away.
Uncle Dave Macon.
Uncle Dave Macon: Keep My Skillet Good and Greasy.
Uncle Dave Macon Program.

Bibliography

Archives, Collections, and Special Records

Charles K. Wolfe Collection, Center for Popular Music, Middle Tennessee State University (MTSU), Murfreesboro, Tennessee.

Coleman Cemetery. Records of deeds, burials and grave plots. Murfreesboro, Tennessee.

Country Music Foundation. Country Music Hall of Fame and Museum, Nashville.

Evergreen Cemetery. Records of deeds, burials and grave plots. Murfreesboro, Tennessee.

Grand Ole Opry Museum. Photographic and archival holdings. Opryland, Nashville.

Haynes Chapel United Methodist Church. "The History of Haynes Chapel United Methodist Church." Kittrell, Tennessee. The two Haynes Chapel collections comprise an organized and detailed account of the chapel's earliest history, including the participation of Uncle Dave Macon, the congregation's most acclaimed member.

———. "Through the Years: Haynes Chapel United Methodist Church." Kittrell, Tennessee.

John K. Doubler Collection. Clarksville, Tennessee.

Macon, Carrol R. "The Gideon Macon Family Tree, 1670–2010: The Uncle Dave Macon Branch." Rockwall, Texas: privately published, April 13, 2010.

Macon, David Harrison. Executed contract and agreement between D. H. Macon and Sidney Harkreader regarding the payment of record royalties and settlement of travel expenses, Knoxville, Tennessee, July 15, 1924. Witnessed by Charles C. Rutherford, Sterchi Brothers Furniture Company.

———. "Last Will and Testament." Woodbury, Tennessee: Hoyt Bryson Law Offices, November 24, 1949.

———. Personal business and financial records book, 1943. In the author's possession.

———. Personal letter to his son, Harry Macon, March 31, 1942. In the author's possession.

Moore Funeral Home. Guest Sign-In Book for the Funeral of David Harrison Macon. Murfreesboro, Tennessee. March 22, 1952. In the author's possession.

Mt. Olivet Cemetery. Records of deeds, burials and grave plots. Nashville.

National Gideon Macon Society, Inc. Springdale, Arkansas.

State of Tennessee. "Rutherford County Tax Books, 1877–2014." Rutherford County, Rutherford County Archives, Special Collection, Murfreesboro, Tennessee. This treasure trove of information and local history contains the personal tax records of David Harrison Macon, Mary Matilda Richardson Macon and family, Rutherford County, Tennessee, District 13, 1900–1952.

———. "W. M. Freeman et al. to Dave Macon et al." Rutherford County, County Court Clerk, Deeds Office, Certificate of Deed, Freeman & Coleman Graveyard, June 9, 1916.

United States Congress. U. S. House of Representatives. 99th Congress, 2nd Session, Vol. 32, No. 87. Proclamation by Congressman Bart Gordon, Sixth Congressional District of Tennessee. "Uncle Dave Macon Days," June 24, 1986.

"WSM Radio & TV" and "Grand Ole Opry" files. Special Collections Section. Jean and Alexander Heard Library. Vanderbilt University, Nashville.

Interviews

Acuff, Roy, interview by Dr. Charles K. Wolfe, Grand Ole Opry House, Nashville, Tennessee, September 19, 1977. Interview is audio file #00585 in the Charles K. Wolfe Collection.

Corbin, Everett, and Charles Smith, interview by Martin Fisher, November 2, 2011. Interview is audio file #20111102 in the Everett Corbin Collection, Center for Popular Music, Middle Tennessee State University. Everett Corbin was the editor of *Music City News*, 1966–1967, and Charles Smith was the son of Ray Smith.

Costa, Jim, interview by the author, Murfreesboro, Tennessee, July 14, 2014. Audio file is in the author's possession.

Doubler, Mary Macon, interview by the author, Murfreesboro, Tennessee, September 9, 2014. Audio file is in the author's possession.

Harkreader, Sidney J., interview by Dr. Charles K. Wolfe, Nashville, Tennessee, June 16, 1977. Interview is audio file #00373 in the Charles K. Wolfe Collection.

Harkreader, Sidney J., and Kirk McGee, interview by Dr. Charles K. Wolfe, Nashville, Tennessee, June 16, 1977. Interview is audio file #00922 in the Charles K. Wolfe Collection.

Kinney, Vesta Blair, interview by the author, McMinnville, Tennessee, August 29, 2013. Interview notes are in the author's possession.

Knowlton, Bill, "Bluegrass Ramble" radio program, WCNY-FM, Syracuse, New York. On-air tribute by Bill Knowlton to Archie J. Macon, June 1978. Recording is audio file #00887 in the Charles K. Wolfe Collection.

Macon, Archie J., interview by Dr. Charles K. Wolfe, Murfreesboro, Tennessee, December 5, 1974. Interview is audio file #00727 in the Charles K. Wolfe Collection.

———, interview by Dr. Charles K. Wolfe, Murfreesboro, Tennessee, November 6, 1975. Interview is audio file #00589 in the Charles K. Wolfe Collection.

———, interview by Dr. Charles K. Wolfe, Murfreesboro, Tennessee, June 4, 1977. Interview is audio file #00588 in the Charles K. Wolfe Collection.

Macon, David Ramsey, interview by Dr. Charles K. Wolfe, Greenbrier, Tennessee, January 28, 1979. Interview is audio file #00586 in the Charles K. Wolfe Collection.

———, interview by the author, Owensboro, Kentucky, September 29 and 30, 2014. Audio file is in the author's possession.

Macon, Dorris, interview by Dr. Charles K. Wolfe, Woodbury, Tennessee, June 6, 1977. Interview is audio file #00886 in the Charles K. Wolfe Collection.

———, interview by Dr. Charles K. Wolfe, Woodbury, Tennessee, March 11, 1979. Interview is audio file #00587 in the Charles K. Wolfe Collection.

———, interview by Dr. Charles K. Wolfe, Woodbury, Tennessee, n.d. Interview is audio file #00581 in the Charles K. Wolfe Collection.

Macon, Esten, interview by Dr. Charles K. Wolfe, Murfreesboro, Tennessee, July 8, 1982. Interview is audio file #02054 in the Charles K. Wolfe Collection.

Macon, Uncle Dave, "Centennial of his Birth Tribute," Country Music Hall of Fame and Museum, Nashville, Tennessee, October 6, 1970. Recording is audio file #00467 in the Charles K. Wolfe Collection.

———, public interviews by Dr. Charles K. Wolfe, Public Square, Murfreesboro, Tennessee, June 7, 1977. Interview is audio file #02084 in the Charles K. Wolfe Collection.

McGee, Kirk, interview by Dr. Charles K. Wolfe, location unknown, June 17, 1977. Interview is audio file #00567 in the Charles K. Wolfe Collection.

———, interview by Dr. Charles K. Wolfe, "Bluegrass Express" radio show, WMOT, Murfreesboro, Tennessee, March 14, 1981. Interview is audio file #00104 in the Charles K. Wolfe Collection.

McGee, Kirk, and Sam, interview by Mike Seeger and Ralph Rinzler, New York, New York, February 1965. Interview is audio file #01041 in the Charles K. Wolfe Collection.

McGee, Sam, interview by Dr. Charles K. Wolfe, Franklin, Tennessee, n.d. Interview is audio file #00487 in the Charles K. Wolfe Collection.

———, interview by Dr. Charles K. Wolfe, Franklin, Tennessee, April 9, 1973. Interview is audio file #00485 in the Charles K. Wolfe Collection.

———, interview by Dr. Charles K. Wolfe, Franklin, Tennessee, June 27, 1973. Interview is audio file #00488 in the Charles K. Wolfe Collection.

———, interview by Dr. Charles K. Wolfe, Franklin, Tennessee, October 1973. Interview is audio file #00484 in the Charles K. Wolfe Collection.

Seeger, Mike, interview on National Public Radio, October 1975. Interview is audio file #01036 in the Charles K. Wolfe Collection.

Weimer, Norma Delmore, interview by the author, Fayetteville, Tennessee, April 19, 2014. Interview notes are in the author's possession.

Wiseman, Mac, telephonic interview with the author, August 17, 2016. Interview notes are in the author's possession.

Wood, Ruth, interview by Alvin F. and Mary Macon Doubler, Kittrell, Tennessee, July 1975. Interview is audio file #00532 in the Charles K. Wolfe Collection.

Wood, Ruth, and Miss Mary Hall, two-part interview by Dr. Charles K. Wolfe, Kittrell, Tennessee, March 15, 1979. Part One is audio file #00604, and Part Two is audio file #00605, both in the Charles K. Wolfe Collection.

Books and Monographs

Brownlow, Leroy. *Why I Am a Member of the Church of Christ.* Fort Worth, Texas: The Brownlow Corporation, 2004.

Buchanan, James G., as told to Ruth White. *The Original Goober: The Life and Times of James G. Buchanan.* Nashville: Nova Books, 2004.

Burton, Thomas G., ed. *Tom Ashley, Sam McGee, Bukka White: Tennessee Traditional Singers.* "Chapter Two: Sam McGee" by Charles K. Wolfe. Knoxville: University of Tennessee Press, 1981.

Cohen, John, and Mike Seeger, eds. *Old-Time String Band Songbook.* New York: Oak Publications, 1976.

Delmore, Alton, with Charles K. Wolfe, ed. *The Delmore Brothers: Truth Is Stranger than Publicity.* Nashville: Country Music Foundation Press, 1995.

Doubler, Michael D. *Uncle Dave Macon: A Photo Tribute.* Murfreesboro, Tennessee: Macon-Doubler Fellowship, 2014.

Dubois, Laurent. *The Banjo: America's African Instrument.* Cambridge, Massachusetts: Harvard University Press, 2016.

Eiland, William U. *Nashville's Mother Church: The History of Ryman Auditorium.* Nashville: Grand Ole Opry, 2014.

Fiddlin' Sid's Memoirs: The Autobiography of Sidney J. Harkreader, edited by Walter D. Haden. University of California, Los Angeles: John Edwards Memorial Foundation, 1976.

Grand Ole Opry: WSM Picture-History Book, 50th Anniversary Issue. Nashville: WSM, Inc., 1975.

Hagan, Chet. *Grand Ole Opry.* New York: Henry Holt and Company, Inc., 1989.

Havighurst, Craig. *Air Castle of the South: WSM and the Making of Music City.* Urbana: University of Illinois Press, 2007.

Hay, George D. "The Grand Ole Opry Hits the Road." Unpublished manuscript, 1949.

———. *A Story of the Grand Ole Opry.* Nashville: privately published, 1945.

Hermann, Eric Neil. "'In the Good Old Days of Long Ago': Echoes of Vaudeville and Minstrelsy in the Music of Uncle Dave Macon." PhD diss., University of Maryland, College Park, 2016.

Lomax, Alan. "List of American Folk Songs on Commercial Records." Washington, D.C.: Library of Congress, Division of Music, December 4, 1942.

Macon, Uncle Dave. "Songs and Stories of Uncle Dave Macon." Self-published songbook, 1938.

Malone, Bill C. *Music from the True Vine: Mike Seeger's Life and Musical Journey.* Chapel Hill: University of North Carolina Press, 2011.

Malone, Bill C., and Jocelyn R. Neal. *Country Music, U.S.A.* 3rd Revised ed. Austin: University of Texas Press, 2013.

Mason, Robert L. *History of Cannon County, Tennessee.* Chapter XVI, "Uncle Dave Macon." Woodbury, Tennessee: Cannon County Historical Society, March 1984.

Mazor, Barry. *Ralph Peer and the Making of Popular Roots Music.* Chicago: Chicago Review Press, 2015.

Morton, David C., and Charles K. Wolfe. *DeFord Bailey: A Black Star in Early Country Music*. Knoxville: University of Tennessee Press, 1991.

The New Lost City Ramblers Song Book. New York: Oak Publications, 1964.

Ogasapian, John, and N. Lee Orr. *Music of the Gilded Age*. Westport, Connecticut: Greenwood Press, 2007.

Olson, Ted, and Tony Russell. *The Knoxville Sessions, 1929–1930*. Hambergen, Germany: Bear Family Records, 2016.

Pugh, Ronnie. *Ernest Tubb: The Texas Troubadour*. Durham, North Carolina: Duke University Press, 1996.

Rinzler, Ralph, and Norm Cohen. *Uncle Dave Macon: A Bio-Discography*. University of California, Los Angeles: John Edwards Memorial Foundation, 1970.

Russell, Tony. *Country Music Originals: The Legends and the Lost*. New York: Oxford University Press, 2010.

———. *Country Music Records: A Discography, 1921–1942*. New York: Oxford University Press, 2004.

Schlappi, Elizabeth. *Roy Acuff: The Smoky Mountain Boy*. Gretna, Louisiana: Pelican Publishing Co., 1997.

Seeger, Pete. *How to Play the 5-String Banjo*, 3rd ed. Beacon, New York: privately published, 1962.

Smith, Richard D. *Can't You Hear Me Callin': The Life of Bill Monroe, Father of Bluegrass*. Cambridge, Massachusetts: Da Capo Press, 2001.

Wolfe, Charles K. *A Good-Natured Riot: The Birth of the Grand Ole Opry*. Nashville: The Country Music Foundation Press and Vanderbilt University Press, 1999.

———. *Uncle Dave Macon*. Murfreesboro, Tennessee: Rutherford County Historical Society, Publication No. 35, 1995.

———. *Uncle Dave Macon: Keep My Skillet Good and Greasy*. Hambergen, Germany: Bear Family Records, 2004.

WSM Official Grand Ole Opry History and Picture Book. Nashville: WSM Radio, n.d.

Articles

"Archie Glenn Stagner Dies." *Tennessean*. February 9, 1987.

"Cutting Affray. S. G. Macon Seriously Wounded by J. C. Fowler. An Old Feud Results in a Street Fight and an Ugly Wound." *Daily American*. October 15, 1886.

Dillon, James A. "Macon Family Has Deep Roots." *Warren County News*. November 16, 1982.

"Dorris Macon, 71, Former Opry Star Dies, Rites Held." *Cannon Courier*. February 18, 1982.

Dowland, C. Reid. Christmas Letter to family and friends. John Doubler Collection, Clarksville, Tennessee. December 23, 1963.

"The Evangelization of Rutherford County, Tennessee." Kittrell, Tennessee: Science Hill Church of Christ, n.d.

"Grand Ole Man: Uncle Dave Macon." *Cowboy Songs*. September 1952.

Henson, Billy. "The Day I Met Hank Williams." Murfreesboro, Tennessee: n.d.

"History of the Grand Ole Opry." Nashville: WSM News Service, 1938.

Kimbrell, Dow. "Lizzie Saums Celebrates 100th Birthday at Home." *Daily News Journal.* July 9, 1993.

King, Adeline. "Things Past and Present: Uncle Dave Macon." *Rutherford Courier.* April 1, 1982.

"Last Rites Held Here Tuesday for E. L. Macon, 81." *Cannon Courier.* April 28, 1938.

"Macey [*sic*] Todd, 53, Succumbs Friday after Long Illness." *Daily News Journal.* January 13, 1935.

Macon, Esten. "Rambling Views." *Brundige Banner.* July 20, 1977.

———. "Rambling Views." *Southern Standard.* February 2, 1979.

Macon, Mrs. David Ramsey. "Maj. John Macon: A Revolutionary War Soldier & Great Grandson of Gideon Macon." *The National Gideon Macon Descendants News.* January 2005.

"Mountain Farmer, with Banjo, Plays Way into Ranks of Vaudeville Stars." *Birmingham News.* January 8, 1925.

"Mrs. Dave Macon Succumbs after Prolonged Illness." *Cannon Courier.* February 17, 1939.

"Mrs. Mary Macon Rites to Be Today: Wife of 'Uncle Dave' Died Tuesday Night at Home." *Daily News Journal.* February 15, 1939.

"Mrs. W. E. Youree, at 86, Looks after Details of Farm." *Daily News Journal.* March 31, 1955.

Oliver, Luke. "Banjo Just Like Life." *Birmingham Post.* January 10, 1925.

"Revenue Officer Charged with Murder." *Daily American.* May 27, 1887.

"True Story of the Famous WSM Grand Ole Opry." *Rural Radio.* November 1938.

"'Uncle Dave' Again Features Loew's Bill." *Birmingham Post.* January 20, 1925.

"Uncle Dave Laments State of Morals and Music." *Knoxville News-Sentinel.* April 13, 1930.

Uncle Dave Macon. Autobiographical Sketch to WSM Artists Service. May 23, 1933.

———. "My Life and Experience: Brunswick Topics." Brunswick Record Company. n.d.

"Uncle Dave Macon Auction." *Cannon Courier.* June 27, 1952.

Welch, Pat. "CMA Names 4 to Hall of Fame." *Nashville Tennessean.* October 22, 1966.

Whittle, Dan. "Bessie, Dave Go Way Back." *Rutherford Courier.* 1998.

———. "Macon Was a Generous Man." *Daily News Journal.* n.d.

Wilgus, D. K. "Current Hillbilly Recordings: A Review Article." *Journal of American Folklore.* Vol. 78, #309, July–September 1965.

Wolfe, Charles K. "Early Country Music in Knoxville: The Brunswick Sessions & the End of an Era." *Old Time Music.* Spring 1974.

———. "Searchin' for Uncle Dave." *Bluegrass Unlimited.* August 1979.

———. "The Uncle Dave Macon Show." Press release. January 3, 1980.

Recordings and Productions

Anthology of American Folk Music. Ed. by Harry E. Smith. 1952. Folkway Records, Folkway #FA 2951. 33 1/3 rpm.

Grand Ole Opry. Directed by Frank McDonald. Republic Pictures. 1940.

"Grand Ole Opry-Prince Albert-1939-10-14, Parts 1 and 2." Digital Archive, Country Music Hall of Fame and Museum. Nashville.

Laugh Your Blues Away. Notes by Charles Wolfe. 1979. Rounder Records. 33 1/3 rpm.

Uncle Dave at Home. Notes by Charles Wolfe. 2002. Spring Fed Records. Center for Popular Music, Middle Tennessee State University. Murfreesboro, Tennessee. CD.

Uncle Dave Macon. Conceived by Pete Seeger and selected and edited by Norman Tinsley, Bob Hyland, and Joe Hickerson. 1963. RBF Records, album #RF 51. 33 1/3 rpm.

Uncle Dave Macon: Keep My Skillet Good and Greasy. 2004. Bear Family Records. Boxed set.

The Uncle Dave Macon Program. Blaine Dunlap, Sol Korine, and Charles K. Wolfe. 1980. Public Broadcasting System. DVD.

General Index

son, 33; death, 209; death, memorial service, and burial, 1–11; death of grandchild, 115; debuts as Opry member, 129; declines to modernize freight company, 61; dinner for Republic Pictures, 186–87; discovered at Melton's Barbershop in Nashville, 96–97; dispute over dowry, 52; dispute with Judge Hay, 142–43; dissatisfaction with movie, 189–90; drunkenness on return trip, 111–12; dying request, 208; dynamite incident, 116; early bouts with depression, 52–53; eccentric behavior, 226; egoism, 227; embrace of entertainment technology, 223; episode on local buses, 204–5; exceptional health, 225; filming of *Grand Ole Opry*, 187–89; first records offered for sale, 112; flies on *The Great Speckled Bird*, 199–200; forgives debt, 197; fund-raiser in Morrison, 92; given name "Dixie Dewdrop," 120; guest on first Opry broadcasts, 128; horse-trading incident, 38; hospital admission and surgery, 207–8; hosts family Sunday dinners, 168–69; inducted into Country Music Hall of Fame, 214–15; interview with Birmingham reporter, 119–20; joins Haynes Chapel Methodist Church and baptism, 47; jumps from Ford Model T, 94–95; last will and testament, 209–10; learns to play banjo, 24; lends money to neighbor, 148–50; lives in Nashville, 197–98; living at The Corners, 30; Loew's offers nationwide contract, 120; meat preparation and "meat club," 42; meets Sam McGee, 117–18; membership in union, 183; money dealings, 38–39; monument erected, 211–12; national spokesman for Gibson instruments, 144; nostalgic trip to Macon Manor, 180; observing professional entertainers in Nashville, 21–22; observes new Ford Model T, 60; Opry's twenty-fifth anniversary, 206; organizes and operates freight hauling business, 35–38; origin of nickname "Uncle Dave Macon," 91; pays for roof replacement at Haynes Chapel, 113; performance legacy, 219–20; performance techniques, 50–51; personality traits, 40–41, 224–25; personal motivation, 224; plows straightest furrows, 43; poor disciplinarian as parent, 41; posts signage in front yard, 168; pricing and ticketing at shows, 95; on *Prince Albert Show*, 184 85; public reconciliation with brother, 170–71; purchases first automobile, 145; raises funds for church organ, 47–48; receives inheri-

tances, 45; reflections on life and career, 203; rejected marriage proposal, 195–96; relations with black neighbors, 44; religious faith, 226–27; remains in Nashville, 29; robbed at show, 101; sacred hymns on Opry, 155–56; shares whiskey, 193–94; son Dorris begins touring, 136–39; songwriting and practice sessions, 114; sons serve during World War II, 194–95; stage methods, 220–21; Tildy's sudden death, memorials, and burial, 176–79; tithing at Haynes Chapel, 167; trip to Oklahoma, 87–89; undergoes surgery, 202; upset over bank robbers, 167; varied repertoire, 221–23; witnesses father's slaying, 27; on WSM for the first time, 127;

Macon, David Harrison (performances and recordings): earliest organized performances, 49; early show in Cannon County, Tennessee, 93–94; early shows in Murfreesboro and Smyrna, 89–90; field recording at home, 205–6; first amateur performances, 31–32; first Birmingham show, 118–19; Charlotte recording sessions, 174, 176; Chicago recording sessions, 143–44, 145–46; first professional shows in Nashville and Middle Tennessee, and eccentric behavior on the road, 98–102; Jackson, Mississippi, recording session, 153–55; Knoxville recording session, 150–53; New Orleans recording session, 165–66; New York City recording sessions, 105–10, 120–21, 131–33; performance disaster in Birmingham, 130–31; performance disaster at Liberty, Tennessee, 57–59; playing in Murfreesboro, 203–4; plays for Sterchi Brothers and invited to record, 102–3; plays with Carter Family, 146–47; Richmond, Indiana, recording session, 164; string band recordings, 139–42

Macon, David Harrison (tours): Southern cities tour begins, 120; touring and personal relations with Acuff and Monroe, 192–93; touring during World War II, 192; touring with Curly Fox, 202; touring with DeFord Bailey, 158–59; touring with Delmore Brothers, 163–64; touring with Flatt and Scruggs, 200–201; touring with Sam McGee, 133–36; tours with Ernest Tubb, 198–99; tours with Glenn Stagner, 175–76

Macon, Annie Walling-Youree (Uncle Dave's sister): cares for sister Lou, 45; final years, 218; house fire, 211; piano lessons, 18; plays with Dave, 31; settles in Readyville, 29;

songwriting and practice sessions with Dave, 114; takes son to Oklahoma, 87–89; trip to Macon Manor, 180

Macon, David Ramsey, 216, 234n

Macon, Dorris Vanderbilt (Uncle Dave's son): birth, 46; Clark photo session, 191; distributes banjos, 210; drives father to Ryman Auditorium, 204; with father in hospital and at time of death, 208; father's death and memorials, 1–4; filming of *Grand Ole Opry*, 187–89; final performance with his father, 206–7; final years, 218; joins his father on tour, 136–39, 145; joins union, 184; Knoxville recording session, 151–53; marriage, 163; national tour, 190; outhouse anecdote, 169; on *Prince Albert Show*, 184–85; sells songbooks, 175

Macon, Emory John, 16, 19, 26–27, 29, 45

Macon, Esten Gray (Uncle Dave's son): birth and childhood disease, 46; cares for mother, 171; Clark photo session, 190; father's alcoholism, 197–98; final years, 218; mother's death, 177

Macon, Eugene LaVanderbilt (Van), 16; discourages Dave, 62; in Nashville, 19; public reconciliation and death, 170–71; purchases The Corners, 27–28

Macon, George M., 18

Macon, Gideon, 13–14, 234n

Macon, Glen (Uncle Dave's son): absent from father's funeral, 7; Archie admonishes him, 209; birth, 46; death, 218; father berates him, 179; inheritance, 210; refuses to tour with his father, 137–38; in World War II, 195, 207

Macon, Harrison, 13, 15–16

Macon, Harry Richardson (Uncle Dave's son): birth, 35; death, 218; love of transport, 44; with father at death, 3, 218; service in World War II, 194–95

Macon, John (Captain John; Uncle Dave's father), 13; confrontation, death, and burial, 26–27; at end of Civil War, 17; marriage and service in Civil War, 15–16; moves family to Nashville, 19; operates Broadway House, 21; during Reconstruction, 19; reinterred in Murfreesboro, 46

Macon, John (great-grandfather of Uncle Dave Macon), 14–15

Macon, John Henry (Uncle Dave's son), 7; birth, 35; death, 218; emotional breakdown at funeral, 10; failing marriage, 171; moves back home, 179–80; woodworking, 44

Macon, Lou, 16, 26; at Central State, 57; death and burial, 195; marriage, 30; nervous breakdown, 31; sent to mental hospital, 45

Macon, Martha Ann Ramsey (Uncle Dave's mother): Broadway House placed in her name, 19; death and burial, 45–46; hires legal team, 27; marries John Macon, 16, 17; moves to The Corners, 28; music lessons for children, 18; purchases banjo for son Dave, 24; working at The Corners, 29

Macon, Mary Matilda Richardson (Uncle Dave's wife), 4; advises on business matters, 113; against modern plumbing, 169; aversion for entertainers, 173; commits Dave to mental hospitals, 54–57; courtship and marriage, 33, 36; deals with Dave's depression, 136; death and burial, 176–80; death of grandchild, 115; declines to attend live shows, 173; dispute over dowry, 52; distrust of electricity, 44; failing health, 171–72; family cook and provider, 42–43; family disciplinarian, 41–41; feeds drifters, 168; meets Dave Macon at family dinner, appearance, disposition, 32; operates farm and home in Dave's absence, 112–13; personality traits, 40–41; secret money stash, 167, 181; struggles with Dave's alcoholism, 53

Macon, Melissa Weeks, 3, 7, 115

Macon, Nathaniel, 14

Macon, Paul (Uncle Dave's son), 7; birth, 56; final years, 218–19; in Korean War, 205; in World War II, 195

Macon, Pearl, 29–30, 45–46

Macon, Robert, 169

Macon, Romulus, 16

Macon, Sam, 19, 26, 27, 29, 44–45

Macon Manor (Smartt Station, Tennessee), 16–19, 43, 114, 180, 216

Macon Midway Mule & Mitchell Wagon Transportation Company, 35, 40, 61, 143

Malloy, Pat, 7

Mammoth Spring (Arkansas), 126, 217

McGee, Kirk: flies on *The Great Speckled Bird*, 199–200; Gennett recording session, 164; last years on Opry, 218; pallbearer at Uncle Dave's funeral, 7; sacred music, 156; string band recordings, 139–42; Trailblazer Award, 217

McGee, Sam Fleming, 5; auditions for Uncle Dave, 117–18; avoids deadly car crash, 100; first Chicago recording session, 143; first meets Uncle Dave, 116–17; first recording session in New York City, 131–33; first show

in Birmingham, 118–19; Gennett recording
session, 164; last years on Opry, 218; learns
guitar, 117; national endorser for Gibson
instruments, 144; pallbearer at Uncle Dave's
funeral, 7; string band recordings, 139–42;
touring with Uncle Dave, 133–36; Trailblazer Award, 217; Uncle Dave's repertoire,
222, 235n
McMinnville (Tennessee), 13, 15, 26
medicine shows, 21
Merchant's Hotel (Nashville), 197–98
Messick, Jesse, 216
minstrelsy, 21, 23
Mitchell Wagon, 35–36
Monroe, Bill: Heritage Award, 217; hires Uncle Dave, 192; joins the Opry, 183; pallbearer
at Uncle Dave's funeral, 7; relations with
Uncle Dave, 193
Moore, Bessie, 89–90
Moore Funeral Home (Murfreesboro), 3–5, 7
Morrison (Tennessee), 57, 92
Mt. Olivet Cemetery (Nashville), 26, 27, 31, 45,
195, 234n
Murfreesboro (Tennessee), 1, 3–5; active train
depot and post office, 36; early Dave Macon
performance, 49, 90; during the Great De-
pression, 148–50; horse-trading incident,
38; Macon transportation company, 35;
Sam Jones revival, 47; site of Uncle Dave's
funeral, 6–10, 17, 28, 32; town square, 40;
Uncle Dave plays in town, 203–4; Uncle
Dave records first go on sale, 112
Museum of Appalachia (Clinton, Tennessee),
216

Nashville (Tennessee), 4–6; downtown saloons, 24, 28–29; music scene in the 1880s,
20–21; new home for Macons, 19; railroad
to Chattanooga, 35; tent revivals, 46; Uncle
Dave's earliest shows there, 96–99
National Life and Accident Insurance Company, 125
The New Lost City Ramblers, 213–14

Oberstein, Eli, 165–66, 174
OKeh Records, 153
Old Crow Medicine Show, 217

Parker, Thomas A. (Colonel Tom), 192
Pearl, Minnie, 7, 193, 211
Peer, Ralph: "big bang" of country music,
156–57; discovery of Jimmie Rodgers and
Carter family, 219, 222; leaves RCA Victor,

165; Mazor biography, 194; 1927 and 1928
Bristol sessions, 151
Pelletieri, Vito, 158, 183–84
Pilot Knob, 37, 48
Prince Albert Show, 184–85

Ramsey, Polly Stroud, 16–17
RBF Records, 214
Readyville (Tennessee), 29–32; 34; black
neighbors to Macons, 44; local musicians,
39; near Pilot Knob, 37; post office, 36; post
office and Uncle Dave's business correspon-
dence, 92
Readyville grist mill, 31, 32
Republic Pictures, 186–87
Richardson, Jessie, 33, 34, 36
Richardson, Jim, 32
Richardson, Mary Bowling, 32, 37
Richardson, Patrick Henry, 32
R. J. Reynolds Tobacco Company, 184–85
RKO Theaters, 158
Rodgers, Jimmie, 6, 214, 219
Romans 8: 1–39, 208
Rounder Records, 215
Ryman Auditorium, 1; genesis of, 5–7; hosts
live WSM broadcast, 127; named after Tom
Ryman, 25; new home to Opry, 204; Uncle
Dave's banjo displayed, 210, 218; Uncle
Dave's final departure, 207
Ryman, Tom, 25
Rutherford County (Tennessee), 5, 28, 30;
Dave Macon's first public performances,
49; farming, 43; flooding, 39; during the
Great Depression, 148–49; Union encamp-
ments, 37
Rutherford Hospital, 1, 207

Sam McFlynn's Circus, 22, 25
Sanford, Hatton, 36, 39
Science Hill Church of Christ, 48–49, 179,
190
Scopes Monkey Trial, 132–33
Scruggs, Earl, 200–201, 210
Seeger, Mike, 213–14, 217
Seeger, Pete, 212–14
Skaggs, Ricky, 217
Slingerland banjo, 24, 91, 210
Smartt Station (Tennessee), 15–17
Smith, Ray, 148–50
Smyrna (Tennessee), 89, 92–93
Snider, Mike, 217
Stagner, Glenn (Smoky Mountain): Charlotte
recording session, 176; at church service,

Song Index

MICHAEL D. DOUBLER is a native of Murfreesboro, Tennessee, and the great-grandson of Uncle Dave Macon. He has enjoyed a long career as a soldier, scholar, and author. A graduate of the U.S. Military Academy at West Point, New York, he served for twenty-three years as an Army officer on active duty and as a full-time National Guardsman. He holds a doctorate degree in history from The Ohio State University and has authored several books as well as dozens of articles and special studies. His primary work, *Closing with the Enemy: How GIs Fought the War in Europe, 1944–1945*, received two national book awards. Mike serves as the director of the Macon-Doubler Fellowship, an organization dedicated to perpetuating old-time music and dance and the life and legacy of Uncle Dave Macon.

Woody Guthrie, American Radical   *Will Kaufman*

George Szell: A Life of Music   *Michael Charry*

Bean Blossom: The Brown County Jamboree and Bill Monroe's Bluegrass Festivals
   Thomas A. Adler

Crowe on the Banjo: The Music Life of J. D. Crowe   *Marty Godbey*

Twentieth Century Drifter: The Life of Marty Robbins   *Diane Diekman*

Henry Mancini: Reinventing Film Music   *John Caps*

The Beautiful Music All Around Us: Field Recordings and the American Experience
   Stephen Wade

Then Sings My Soul: The Culture of Southern Gospel Music   *Douglas Harrison*

The Accordion in the Americas: Klezmer, Polka, Tango, Zydeco, and More!
   Edited by Helena Simonett

Bluegrass Bluesman: A Memoir   *Josh Graves, edited by Fred Bartenstein*

One Woman in a Hundred: Edna Phillips and the Philadelphia Orchestra
   Mary Sue Welsh

The Great Orchestrator: Arthur Judson and American Arts Management
   James M. Doering

Charles Ives in the Mirror: American Histories of an Iconic Composer
   David C. Paul

Southern Soul-Blues   *David Whiteis*

Sweet Air: Modernism, Regionalism, and American Popular Song
   Edward P. Comentale

Pretty Good for a Girl: Women in Bluegrass   *Murphy Hicks Henry*

Sweet Dreams: The World of Patsy Cline   *Warren R. Hofstra*

William Sidney Mount and the Creolization of American Culture
   Christopher J. Smith

Bird: The Life and Music of Charlie Parker   *Chuck Haddix*

Making the March King: John Philip Sousa's Washington Years, 1854–1893
   Patrick Warfield

In It for the Long Run   *Jim Rooney*

Pioneers of the Blues Revival   *Steve Cushing*

Roots of the Revival: American and British Folk Music in the 1950s
   Ronald D. Cohen and Rachel Clare Donaldson

Blues All Day Long: The Jimmy Rogers Story   *Wayne Everett Goins*

Yankee Twang: Country and Western Music in New England   *Clifford R. Murphy*

The Music of the Stanley Brothers   *Gary B. Reid*

Hawaiian Music in Motion: Mariners, Missionaries, and Minstrels
   James Revell Carr

Sounds of the New Deal: The Federal Music Project in the West   *Peter Gough*

The Mormon Tabernacle Choir: A Biography   *Michael Hicks*

The Man That Got Away: The Life and Songs of Harold Arlen   *Walter Rimler*

A City Called Heaven: Chicago and the Birth of Gospel Music   *Robert M. Marovich*

Blues Unlimited: Essential Interviews from the Original Blues Magazine   *Edited by
   Bill Greensmith, Mike Rowe, and Mark Camarigg*

The University of Illinois Press
is a founding member of the
Association of American University Presses.

———————————————————————

Text designed by Jim Proefrock
Composed in 11/14 Minion Pro
with Western Bang Bang display
at the University of Illinois Press
Cover designed by Dustin J. Hubbart
Cover illustration: Uncle Dave Macon,
Collier's, vol. 128, no. 4 (July 28, 1951).
Used with permission of JTE Multimedia.
Manufactured by Sheridan Books, Inc.

University of Illinois Press
1325 South Oak Street
Champaign, IL 61820-6903
www.press.uillinois.edu